Applications of Family and Group Theraplay

Applications of Family and Group Theraplay

Edited by
Evangeline Munns

Jason Aronson

Lanham • Boulder • New York • Toronto • Plymouth, UK

Published in the United States of America
by Jason Aronson
An imprint of Rowman & Littlefield Publishers, Inc.

A wholly owned subsidiary of
The Rowman & Littlefield Publishing Group, Inc.
4501 Forbes Boulevard, Suite 200, Lanham, Maryland 20706
www.rowmanlittlefield.com

Estover Road
Plymouth PL6 7PY
United Kingdom

British Library Cataloguing in Publication Information Available

Library of Congress Cataloging-in-Publication Data

Applications of family and group theraplay / edited by Evangeline Munns.
p. ; cm.
Includes bibliographical references and index.
ISBN 978-0-7657-0594-5 (cloth : alk. paper)
eISBN 978-0-7657-0645-4
1. Group play therapy. 2. Group psychotherapy for children. 3. Family psychotherapy. I. Munns, Evangeline.
[DNLM: 1. Play Therapy. 2. Child. 3. Family Therapy—methods. WS 350.2 A652 2009]
ISBN 978-1-4422-5090-1 (pbk : alk. paper)

RJ505.P6A67 2009
618.92′891653—dc22 2008047584

Printed in the United States of America

∞™ The paper used in this publication meets the minimum requirements of American National Standard for Information Sciences—Permanence of Paper for Printed Library Materials, ANSI/NISO Z39.48-1992.

With gratitude and love to my parents, Nick and Vera Scraba, for their caring and dedication to the welfare of all of their children,

to my siblings, Jean, Mary, Lois, Ernie, Diana, and Gail for strong family ties that will always last,

and to my present family, my husband Tom, and daughter Catherine, for their patience, love and support.

Contents

Preface

This book was inspired by the often amazing results I saw in the work of Theraplay® therapists across North America during my travels teaching workshops in Theraplay. This was particularly true when I was teaching the more advanced workshops and was able to view tapes of Theraplay sessions offered by professionals from varying backgrounds: psychologists, social workers, child care workers, nurses, teachers, early childhood specialists, speech therapists, physiotherapists, occupational therapists, the occasional psychiatrist, and other workers in the mental health field. Troubled children and their parents were being helped in a comparatively short time, even though their problems were often severe in nature and chronicity. Therapists often commented that previous treatments had not worked, but Theraplay was moving their clients in a positive direction. Sometimes Theraplay had to be modified (particularly with traumatized clients) and this led to some very creative approaches or led to combining Theraplay with other treatment methods. This book reflects some of those modifications and integrations with other treatment methods—a growing trend in the play therapy field. As well, I was impressed with the variety of populations that Theraplay seems to help—in terms of types of problems and in cultural diversity. I felt that workers in the mental health field needed to know about the significant results that were obtained by the authors in this book, whether they were working with families or groups.

This book begins with an overview of the fundamentals of Theraplay including its theory, main dimensions, and research to give a grounding for readers who may not be that familiar with Theraplay.

Part two focuses on the use of Theraplay with a wide range of populations especially those who have relationship and/or attachment difficulties such as the dysregulated child, the resistant child, those who have been adopted, autistic children, and those who have been placed in residential care.

Part three looks at the adaptability of Theraplay to a diversity of cultures around the world—from the aboriginal peoples in Canada living with a traumatic past, to the Asian and German families coping with a strong cultural pressure for achievement, and to those in a multi-cultural environment in the United States, where a variety of cultural traditions need to be respected and incorporated into treatment.

Part four looks at how Theraplay has been integrated with other treatment methods. Theraplay, by itself, has been successful with many clients, but sometimes other treatment methods are needed when problems are very severe or complex or unique. The chapter "In Sync" describes integrating Theraplay with the Circle of Security program with 0 to 6 year olds, while the next chapter deals with using Dan Hughe's Dyadic Developmental Psychotherapy and Theraplay with traumatized children. Including the parent is extremely important. Often their own history interferes with treatment progress. This is addressed in the chapter on forming a therapeutic alliance with the parent. Theraplay often uses sensory motor activities to engage the child and fits in well with sensory motor approaches as described in chapter 15. Using Theraplay to help children say goodbye to their birth parents created a unique program for grieving children about to be adopted (Relinquishment Visits chapter). Children often relate easier to animals than to humans. Using horses to promote caring and nurturance and building relationships with the help of Theraplay is described in the chapter on equine assisted therapy.

Part five focuses on group Theraplay such as father/son Theraplay groups that often have profound effects on the parent/child relationship. In the mental health field the emphasis is most often placed on mother/child relationships, but fathers have a very important role to play too. The need to be included was reflected in almost perfect attendance in these groups and comments from fathers that the Theraplay hour was the most precious time of the week for themselves and their sons. The chapter on adolescents describes how Theraplay was used with a reactive and difficult to engage age group—troubled adolescents and juvenile offenders.

This book covers the very wide range of social, emotional, and behavioral problems and ages where Theraplay has been used to help children and parents grow within themselves and in their relationships with each other. An attempt has been made to give this book a practical emphasis so that the reader can translate theory into how Theraplay sessions actually are carried out. The majority of authors have included agendas from their Theraplay sessions, and activities are described in full detail in many of the chapters and in the appendix at the end of the book. It is hoped that this book will stimulate readers to stretching their thinking on how Theraplay can be used successfully in their own work.

Acknowledgments

First of all I would like to acknowledge the often heroic efforts of the therapists I have encountered in my field. One has to believe in the resiliency of the clients we work with, no matter how troubled, to put out so much effort in our attempts to help the families with whom we work. We also need to have a belief and a passion for what we do, and I want to thank Ann Jernberg and her right-hand person, Phyllis Booth, for giving us Theraplay, a treatment method that we can believe in and one that frequently is so effective in a short period of time.

I also want to thank Peter Rossborough, the former executive director of Blue Hills Child and Family Centre in Aurora, Ontario, who entrusted me to form and direct the play therapy services department where I first started using Theraplay and became so motivated from the results we were getting.

I also want to thank the authors of this book, who put so much time and energy into their chapters and reacted with such grace when they were asked to do further drafts. Their creativity and courage in attempting to find new ways of adapting Theraplay to such a wide range of clients is admirable.

Thanks as well to my daughter, Catherine, for her encouragement and excitement with the clinical results using Theraplay with her own clients.

My husband, Tom, was invaluable in helping me with computer challenges and without his support and help this book would not have been completed in any timely fashion.

Finally, I want to thank the staff at Jason Aronson for their help and flexibility.

Introduction

In the early 1980s I attended a workshop on Theraplay® that was given by Dr. Ann Jernberg, the founder of Theraplay. I was so impressed with this comparatively new therapy. I felt that children would love it. The emphasis was on building the positive strengths of the child, resulting in a boost of self-esteem, which all children need, but particularly those who walk into the doors of our clinics. Those children know that something is wrong and somehow they are to blame; "He's nothing but trouble!" This has often been drummed into them by parents, teachers, siblings, and peers. They come reluctantly with head hung low or with open defiance ready to resist whatever. Instead, the Theraplay therapist greets him or her with a cheerful hello and starts noticing something positive—"Hi Johnny, I've been looking forward all morning to meeting you. I notice that you have shiny dark brown hair and your eyes match the color of your hair. And wait a minute—do you know that there's a sparkle in your eyes when the light shines on them—wow!" The therapist then engages the child in something playful and fun or if he feels the child is receptive, may nurture the child by noticing his bruises or "boo-boos" and putting soothing lotion or powder on them. The child has already learned three things. "This adult thinks there is something positive about me (she is not going to start talking about my difficulties), she is taking care of me, and I don't have to perform or achieve something to get her approval." This is a healthy start to changing the negative self-concept (or inner working model) that children usually have when they are brought into treatment.

Theraplay's main goals are to enhance the positive relationship and/or attachment between child and parent and to increase self-esteem and trust, all often needing attention in troubled children. These goals can be applied to parents as well. I felt that it was crucial to involve parents if one hoped to achieve good generalization of treatment effects. This was another facet of Theraplay that appealed to me. Parents first observe the therapist with their child for a few sessions (modeling sessions) and then directly participate with their child under the guidance of the therapist. As well, I always included a parent counseling session immediately after the Theraplay session where debriefing could take place, as well as a discussion of child management issues at home or at school. Sometimes this discussion would lead to examining the parents' own family histories whose issues were sometimes repeated with their own children (intergenerational transmission of attachment patterns) (Zeanah and Zeanah, 1989).

Living under restrictive budget and time constraints (common problems in the mental health field) made Theraplay even more appealing as it uses no toys and treatment is usually short-term (from 8 to 16 sessions—possibly longer for more severe cases). As well, Theraplay can be applied across the age span from infants to the elderly and is applicable to a wide range of emotional, social, and behavioral difficulties.

I started experimenting using Theraplay soon after Dr. Jernberg's workshop and decided this was a treatment method in which I wanted to be fully trained. With the support of Peter Rossborough, then the executive director of Blue Hills Child and Family Services, I arranged for a series of Theraplay workshops at our agency, led by Dr. Jernberg and Phyllis Booth (then the training director of the Theraplay Institute in Chicago). In 1991 Mr. Rossborough asked me to start and direct a new department, Play Therapy Services, in our agency which led to forming a training school where professionals came to be trained not only in Theraplay, but in non-directive play therapy and filial play therapy. However, Theraplay was the main thrust of our dept. Our efforts soon become recognized in the community and at one time we had a 5-year waiting list. This motivated us to adapt Theraplay where more clients could be seen through parent/child groups and multi-family groups. The father/son groups for example, were exceptionally powerful where fathers and their sons became closer, enjoyed each other, and children were more cooperative. Usually, the participants did not want the groups to end. We learned that some families with particularly complicated problems could not be adequately treated through groups and those were given more individually focused treatment. Meanwhile, our training school grew to be the largest training school in Canada. I became a certified Theraplay therapist, supervisor, and trainer and gave workshops across North America, which I do to this day. Professionals have been trained from every province in Canada, and there are centers that practice theraplay in most of the provinces. With the leadership of the Theraplay Institute in Chicago, which serves as an international training center and sends trainers worldwide, Theraplay has become an important therapeutic model and is currently practiced all over the world.

The therapeutic atmosphere that we work in today is changing and is being influenced by the latest research from psychobiologists and neuroscientists in their studies on the effect of the environment on the developing brain. The emphasis on verbal therapies with their dependence on higher cortical functioning is being questioned when working with traumatized clients or young children, whose emotional responses may be governed by the mid-brain and lower brain centers. Non-verbal therapies are being increasingly recognized such as sandplay, EMDR (eye movement desensitization remediation), art and play therapies, movement and dance, meditation, sensory-motor training, etc., as well as Theraplay.

There are well-controlled research studies (Field, 2001) that are being recognized in the field of touch and pointing to the importance of touch for all human beings. Not only are we a herd animal, but our early beginnings are dependent on warm nurturing, responsive touch. When we are born, the most advanced sensory system is the sense of touch. But in North America, we live in a touch phobic society that is reflected in the fear that both parents and teachers have in touching even young children. We have laws now that prohibit not only teachers from touching their children in any way, but in some parts of the country, peers are not allowed to touch each other—not even positive touch such as hugging. It has been suggested that not touching might be another form of abuse and that children may be reaching out for touch through aggressive acts and learning that aggressive touch such as pushing, shoving, pinching, and hitting are more acceptable in our society. There is a growing concern over the rise of violence in our country. Research (Thayer, 1998) has shown that violence rates within countries are correlated with the amount of positive touch among family units.

Theraplay is a non-verbal therapy that replicates normal parent-child interactions emphasizing the importance of touch, of consistent, attuned responsiveness to the child's needs and co-regulation of the child. There is also the belief that if the child has missed out on this early caring, that giving the child these missing elements when he/she is older will help to fill in these gaps. It is not known conclusively whether the gaps get filled, but what is known at least clinically and now to a certain extent research-wise, is that families receiving Theraplay function in a more positive way with closer family relationships, higher self-esteem, greater cooperation, and less anger and defiance among its members. The families become more functional.

REFERENCES

Field, T. (2001). *Touch*. Cambridge, MA: MIT Press.

Thayer, T. (1998). March Encounters. *Psychology Today*, 31–36.

Zeanah, C. and P. Zeanah. (1989). "Intergenerational Transmission of Maltreatment. Insights from Attachment Theory and Research." *Psychiatry*, 52, 171–196.

I

BACKGROUND AND FUNDAMENTALS OF THERAPLAY

1

Family and Group Theraplay

Evangeline Munns

Theraplay® is a structured form of play therapy that children often view as "fun! I could come here forever!" (This statement came from an aggressive adolescent.) They frequently do not want therapy to end and often try to prolong sessions. Attendance is usually very high. Why does this happen? The answer is multi-faceted, but a key factor may be Theraplay's emphasis on noticing the positive strengths in a child and trying to strengthen them. So a child comes into the clinic expecting a reiteration of all the problems he has and instead he is treated as someone who is special, valuable, has many interesting qualities, and is a delight to be with. This is a new beginning for him or her. Parents' perceptions of their child during the first few sessions, where they are observing through a one-way mirror or sitting quietly in a corner of the room, start to change. Just maybe there is hope for their child—just maybe he is not really the little "monster" they have come to label in their minds "or that troubling child." Positive changes often occur within a short period of time—sometimes therapy lasts for as few as 8 sessions, but if difficulties are very severe or complex, then 16 or more sessions may be required. Sometimes Theraplay is used as a starting point with other treatments recommended later or integrated right within the Theraplay sessions (see chapters in part four of this book).

Sessions are based on therapist/parent/child interactions. No toys are used so therapy is cost effective. The sessions are structured, and led first by the therapist, while parents observe for 3 or 4 sessions (ideally behind a one-way mirror with an interpreting therapist to explain the activities, but this may not always be possible). Parents are then brought into direct participation with their child. In later sessions parents are encouraged to lead the activities. Four checkup sessions are held during the year following the end of treatment.

Essentially, Theraplay is non-verbal, although reflections are given, "that made you uncomfortable, we'll try another way," but no interpretations are given to the child and no probing questions are asked. Theraplay is not a cognitive or insight-based therapy with its involvement of the cortex or higher brain (although sometimes Theraplay has been integrated with such therapies—see chapters13 and 19). It is involved more with reaching the emotional or lower part of the brain (brainstem and diencephlon) (Gaskill, 2008).

Clients suitable for Theraplay come from a wide age range. Children from infancy, preschoolers, latency-age, adolescents, adults, and the elderly have been treated successfully by theraplay. As well, Theraplay has been used for a variety of emotional, social, and behavioral problems ranging from the acting out aggressive child; the impulsive, dysregulated child; the timid, fearful child (including mutism); the neurotic or character-disordered child; and those who are depressed and even suicidal. Theraplay is most suited to children who are poorly attached or have difficulty in forming relationships such as autistic children, those who have been adopted or fostered, and step-children who have to form new relationships (see chapters in part two). Theraplay would not be recommended for children who have been very recently traumatized such as children who are grieving from a death in the family, those recovering from recent surgery or abuse or those who panic at the approach of an adult. More traditional therapies would be used first with possibly Theraplay used later.

THEORY

Theraplay tries to replicate the normal interactions that occur between parent and a young child (Jernberg and Booth, 1999). It is based on attachment theory that proposes that the first relationship a child has, forms the template for all other relationships and if that first attachment is not a healthy, strong one, then the child will have difficulty in forming connections with others and will have emotional and social difficulties later in life. Attachment research from around the world has supported this premise (Rutter, 1994)

After taking a thorough developmental and family history and obtaining assessments such as the Marschak Interaction Method (DiPasquale, 2000), the theraplay treatment plan goes back to the developmental stages where the child's emotional growth stopped and the attachment process was disrupted. The histories of troubled children often reveal that there were early periods where conditions were not optimal for the child for creating a secure attachment base with a chief caregiver. Theraplay tries to meet the child at his/her emotional level, (which is often much younger than the chronological age of the child) and to give to the child the positive, attuned attention, warm nurturing, the feeling that he/she is valued and important and will receive consistent responsive caring, and help in regulating his/her feelings, that were missing in his/her early childhood. This approach is substantiated by some of the latest findings from neuroscientists such as Dr. Bruce Perry, who starts interventions at the developmental stage where there was neglect or trauma and then progresses to the child's biological age (neurosequential programming) (Perry and Szalavitz, 2006). (This will be discussed in greater detail later.)

In theraplay, sometimes nurturing may take the form of cradling and rocking the child and singing a special song using the child's name while feeding him/her a lollipop. Lotioning or powdering of "hurts" or "booboos" on the child's hands or feet is included in every session. Nurturing is emphasized with all children, but particularly with those who have been abused, neglected, deprived, or traumatized. Care is taken to modify activities so they are acceptable to the child. Nothing is forced. (These children need to be empowered, not disempowered.) In later sessions, more activities are geared to the child's chronological age.

There is a lot of positive, physical contact in Theraplay sessions, partly because this replicates what normal parents do with their young children and we know that the tactile sensory system is the first and most highly developed sensory system in the newborn. Children need affectionate touch to thrive (Gerhardt, 2004) (Sunderland, 2006). How a child is touched, held, rocked, picked up or put down, gives the child his/her first images of self, and the feeling as to whether he is valued and wanted (Ford, 1993). Most babies are soothed when they are picked up. Close bodily contact activates the release of calming hormones such as opioids and oxytocin, thus regulating the baby's arousal system while promoting bonding between parent and child. "There is a mass of scientific evidence to demonstrate that the more touch a child gets in childhood, the calmer and less fearful he is likely to be in adulthood. This is because physical contact helps regulate the stress response system in the brain—which, without this regulation, can become hard wired for oversensitivity. When this is the case, it can be very difficult for the child, as he grows up, to calm himself down when stressed" (Sunderland, 2006, p. 171). As well, there are many well-controlled studies showing that positive touch (such as massage) helps the baby to thrive physically, emotionally, and socially (Field, 2001) (Field and Reite, 1985). Additionally, a lack of touch has been significantly correlated with rates of violence (Thayer, 1998). The less touch in a society, the more aggression. There is a growing concern that children in our touch phobic society may be using aggressive touch such as pushing, hitting, shoving, pinching as attempts to obtain physical contact. They have learned that aggressive touch may be more acceptable in our society, than affectionate touch. This needs to be explored further, considering that the rates of violent acts within our society appear to be rising.

Touch and rhythm are necessary for organizing the first areas of the brain to be developed (lowest and most central brain regions). Since neural systems are organized and become functional in a sequential manner, it is important that each system gets adequate stimulation at each developmental stage. Dr. Bruce Perry has incorporated this knowledge into treating neglected and traumatized children using a neurosequential approach (as has been mentioned before). "These children need patterned, repetitive experiences appropriate to their developmental needs, needs that reflect the age at which they'd missed important stimuli or had been traumatized, not their current chronological age" (Perry and Szalavitz, 2006, p. 138). Dr. Perry targets his interventions to the areas of the brain that were damaged, or underdeveloped in the order in which they were affected by neglect or trauma. In describing his neurosequential programming with an adolescent boy who had suffered early neglect from infancy, Perry first used massage (with the mother's aid) in a gradual, repetitive, systemic way to give the child the affectionate touch he had missed early on. Later, a music and movement class helped him to develop a sense of rhythm which was a factor in regulating his stress response system. In a later phase of treatment, socialization skills were taught on a one to one basis and finally, much further along in treatment, a more cognitive, verbal approach was taken where problems were discussed. Theraplay uses an approach that has similarities to Dr. Perry's program in that activities are first geared to the emotional level of the child (sometimes this is at an infant or toddler level, where appropriate touch and nursery rhymes are included) and then progresses to the child's chronological age as treatment moves forward.

It has already been mentioned that a baby needs an adult to help regulate his/her feelings. If a parent responds to the baby's signals then they are "helping the baby's nervous system to mature in such a way so that it does not get overstressed" (Gerhardt, 2004, p. 210). Parental responsiveness not only helps the baby develop a healthy immune system and stress response system, but helps the baby's brain to develop such as the prefrontal cortex, which is associated with the "child's capacity to hold information in mind, to reflect on feelings, to restrain impulses, that will be a vital part of his or her future capacity to behave socially" (Gerhardt, 2004, p. 210). However, a parent not only has to help soothe a baby, so that stress hormones like cortisol are not produced in such quantity that damage occurs in its vulnerable, developing brain (van der Kolk, 2003), but a parent also needs to stimulate the baby, and in so doing, the child learns how to manage more exciting events. New experiences can sometimes be frightening to a little one, but with the parent's reassurance the child is not overwhelmed. The baby has to learn that taking some risks can bring mastery, wonder, and excitement. Children need exhilaration and a sense of joy (Schore, 1994). Sunderland (2006) writes about "joy juice." Optimal levels of dopamine and opioids in the brain, with surges of adrenaline throughout our body, can produce excitement and joy. These peak experiences can help a child to develop spontaneity, to be hopeful and optimistic, to be motivated, and to feel awe, wonder, and delight. This is what makes us alive! This also promotes resilience—a feeling of being able to handle minor stresses. Futhermore, physical play, where there is lots of body contact, where there is laughter and delight, can produce powerful emotional states that activate emotion-regulating regions in the frontal lobes of the brain (Panksepp, 1993). Lots of physical play can help children to manage their emotions and stress (Sunderland, 2006).

The theraplay therapist helps the child to regulate his/her feelings. This is done by interspersing soothing, calming activities with more stimulating ones. If a child is dysregulated (such as the ADHD child) then more calming activities are introduced and structure is increased, until the child relaxes and slows down. With the easily excited child, some stimulating interactions take place, but gradually, so the child learns how to respond, without losing control of his feelings or impulses. If the child is withdrawn and depressed, more stimulating activities are carried out. All children need to learn how to be quiet and relaxed, but also how to let go and experience "joy juice" in their lives.

RESEARCH

The research using Theraplay is discussed in the next chapter. Although Theraplay's main goal is to enhance parent/child relationships and attachments, there is a dearth of Theraplay studies that use attachment measures. Part of the difficulty lies in the fact that there are few attachment measures that are valid and cost effective with children across the age span. Nevertheless, studies that obtain significant results improving parent/child and peer relationships using Theraplay have been obtained. As well, several studies indicate that Theraplay does have a significant impact in reducing aggression in behavior disordered children and self-esteem is raised (see the next chapter for details and for more research results).

There has been a welcome increase in research with Theraplay using randomized control groups. More are needed. What still needs to happen is to have control groups with some face to face interaction so subjects in the control group believe that they will be helped, thus controlling for the "placebo effect." Finally, research is needed that compares theraplay with other treatment methods that have been well validated. There are a number of research projects in progress (in the United States, Finland, Germany, and South Korea), so hopefully this will happen in the near future.

THERAPLAY DIMENSIONS

When Dr. Jernberg was given a federal grant to increase the attachments between headstart mothers and their children in 1967, in Chicago, she made hundreds of observations of normal parent/child interactions. She categorized these observations under 4 main dimensions which underlie all Theraplay activities. Certain dimensions are emphasized depending on the child's needs. They are: Structure, Challenge, Engagement, and Nurture. All activities are done in a playful atmosphere.

Structure

The structure in a child's life brings a sense of orderliness, predictability, and security. The regularity of feeding, sleeping, bath and play times helps to create a rhythm in the child's daily routine promoting his own self-regulation. As the child gets older, more rules for behavior are put into place so the child learns to control his impulses and distinguishes what is acceptable socially. The parent ordinarily is in charge, which gives the child a sense of safety.

In Theraplay, structure is evident in the format of the session with a clear beginning and end and usually limited to approximately a half-hour time wise. It is usually started with a fun entrance, a welcome song or special handshake, an inventory or checkup (where positive physical features of the child are noticed—i.e., "I see you have brought your rosy cheeks, bright blue eyes and that dimple in your chin! Let me see that strong arm. I'm going to measure those big arm muscles with this fruit loop and then feed it to you!"). This is followed by activities representing all of the dimensions and the session ends with a goodbye song or handshake.

Structure is also maintained with the therapist preplanning and leading the activities and making certain rules such as "no hurts," are followed.

This dimension is particularly needed with children who have come from chaotic backgrounds or are impulsive, having little self control or have become tyrants in their homes or are parentified.

Challenge

All children meet and need challenges in their life gaining a sense of mastery and self-confidence on the way. The child learns to communicate his or her needs, to sit, walk, and run, all the while learning that taking risks can bring its rewards. Hopefully the challenges he meets are within his capability of achieving so that he ends up feeling competent and strong. He may fail, but he must learn how to cope with that too.

In Theraplay challenges are geared to the developmental abilities of the child, so the child can succeed and feel confident. Some risks are built in so the child has to stretch himself a little, but still within the range of his capabilities. The child might be asked to remember a progressively more complicated sequence of clap patterns, or walk a straight line while balancing a bean bag on his head, or blow cotton balls away from his area and into his opponent's, or arm/thumb wrestle, etc. Challenge is needed by timid, fearful children who have been overprotected and not allowed to take risks. Challenging activities usually require some cooperation with another person and are also a safe way to release inner tensions within aggressive children.

Engagement

Parents learn to engage their children often in delightful ways such as playing peek-a-boo with their baby, lifting them up in the air, giving them a horsey ride, reciting nursery rhymes, etc., playfully intruding in their child's space, but in a way that brings pleasure and joy to both. The child learns about his body image and boundaries, that surprises can be fun and that he can be a source of delight to others. Engagement creates connection with others. He is not alone.

In Theraplay the therapist must engage the child right from the beginning. This is done with a cheerful greeting and an involvement of the child in an appealing way (entrance) into the room, such as walking on "stepping stones" (small sheets of paper) that have an M&M hidden under some of the stones leading to a cushion or bean bag chair in the room where other activities will continue.

The therapist soon learns to make transition periods short, so that the child's attention is not lost in between activities, especially when working with a hyperactive child. The therapist strives to be attuned to the child's cues so that interactions are mutually enjoyable, but also geared to the child's needs.

Engagement is particularly needed with withdrawn children, those who are depressed or fearful, or have protective, rigid barriers such as autistic children.

Nurture

This is the most important dimension of all and needed by all children. Every child needs nurturing to thrive. Parents show their love through fulfilling their child's needs through tender caring of their child such as feeding, bathing, cradling, rocking, caressing, hugging, kissing, singing, praising, and expressing their affection in many ways. If this is done in sensitive responsiveness to their baby's signals consistently, the child will most likely develop a positive inner image (inner working model) and a secure base, a secure attachment to those parents (Bowlby, 1988).

In Theraplay, every child receives some nurturing in every session. This is done through activities such as feeding of snacks (occasionally through feeding a juice box or bottle while cradling and singing to the child), lotioning or powdering of "hurts" on hands or feet, rocking the child in a blanket while singing a special song about him, cotton ball soothe (moving a cotton ball on the child's face and/or hands while noticing positive facial features), powder hand prints, etc. These activities are low key and often soothing and calming for the child.

Children who have come from deprived, neglectful, or abusive environments are in need of a lot of nurturing. Acting out, aggressive children who are constantly in trouble also need much nurturing, as do those who are pseudomature or overachieving.

(For more Theraplay activities please see the appendix.)

Sessions typically take about a half-hour followed by a parent counseling session (the latter was introduced by the present author and is not always included in other clinical settings) where debriefing and discussion of home and school issues takes place.

Parents are encouraged to practice Theraplay activities at home. If siblings want to be included as well, then that may be allowed depending on the progress of the referred child. Sometimes siblings are brought into the Theraplay sessions right from the beginning of treatment under the guidance of the therapist. This may happen if there is a lot of sibling rivalry.

SESSION (4TH) EXAMPLE

Entrance: (child follows the leader into the room imitating animal motions and sounds)

Welcome Song (sitting while holding hands) or *special handshake*: "Hello, Johnny, hello Sally hello everyone—we're glad you came to play"

Inventory or Checkup: therapist comments on positive physical features of the child ("you have shiny, curly hair") and may make a few measurements such as height, length of arms compared to legs, size of arm muscles, number of freckles, etc.

Lotioning or powdering of hurts: therapist notices and lotions any bruises, scratches, "boo-boos" on child's hands or feet.

Mirroring: therapist and child stand facing each other. Therapist moves his arms and body slowly and child imitates movements exactly at the same time, acting as a mirror.

Parents enter room.

Balloon toss: A balloon is tossed from one person to another and then everyone tries to keep the balloon in the air. Several more balloons may be added.

Simon Says: Everyone stands in a row facing the leader who says: "When I say Simon says, you do it, but if I don't say Simon says first, you don't do it. Okay, Simon says to raise up your arms," etc. The theraplay twist to this activity is to add commands like: "Simon says to give your neighbor a hug (or a handshake)" or "Simon says to say one thing you like about your neighbor."

Pass a funny face: With everyone sitting in a circle, the leader makes a funny face that the next person imitates and passes around or makes up a new funny face.

Peanut-butter jelly: the leader calls out "peanut-butter" and the group answers "jelly." The leader changes the loudness and pace and tone of the words and the group imitates.

Tracing shapes and back rubs: Parent traces, with her finger, a simple shape, or letter or number on the back of child who guesses what has been traced. The parent then rubs off the shape by moving her hand across the child's back (like a back rub or massage) and then traces another shape for the child to guess.

Feeding: Therapist feeds the child several potato chips and then feeds everyone (use whatever snack is appealing to the child). Parents take a turn feeding child and others.

Goodbye Song: "Goodbye Johnny, Goodbye mom, Goodbye dad and Sally. We're glad you came today."

(Mom and dad might then enter a playful race to see who can get Johnny's shoes on the fastest.)

PHASES OF TREATMENT

Introduction: The therapist introduces himself/herself in a cheerful manner and conveys the idea by her attitude that she will be in charge, that the session will be fun and active, that the sessions will be regularly held in a certain time and place and parents will at first be observing and later will be participating.

Exploration: Child and therapist get to know each other in ways that emphasize positive features, i.e., "Did you know that you have a dimple in your left cheek when you smile and you have another cute dimple in your chin and gee I have a dimple in mine too! They may compare handprints or footprints, or see who has the greatest amounts of freckles. The aim is for the child (and parents) to see himself in a new distinctive way that is clear and positive and that he views the therapist that way too.

Tentative Acceptance or Honeymoon: There is usually a honeymoon period where the child is cooperative and easily engaged. The child seems interested and may even be enthusiastic.

Negative Reaction or Resistance: A resistive phase may occur where the child turns away, pouts, whines, or cries or may refuse to do a number of activities. The therapist reflects the child's feelings, tries to find a way that is more comfortable for the child, but ultimately tries to cheerfully and calmly carry on, often using humor or surprises or the use of paradox (joining the child in its resistance—i.e., "you turn around so well, can you turn around even more?" (changing this resistance into a game). It is important to meet this resistance in an upbeat, but firm manner. The child may be testing boundaries or testing if the therapist will still accept him if he shows his negative side. This is especially true of children who have been rejected in the past. Fear of further intimacy may also be a factor. If the child is genuinely fearful, then the therapist should stop and find an activity that still has the same goal, but approach it in a way that will make the child less anxious. For example a child may not want his "hurts" to be lotioned. The therapist may use a bandaid or colorful sticker instead, or simply may blow on the scratch or make powder handprints. Parents may have to be helped to know a resistant phase is to be expected, but will pass.

Growing and Trusting: This is a phase where the therapist and child really get to know each other in a more intimate and enjoyable way. The child is more cooperative and trusting, is more confident in taking appropriate risks, has greater self-esteem, and feels valued and cared for. Parents are brought in at this stage and gradually start leading the activities. The therapist emphasizes the interactions between their child and themselves, promoting ways to increase their attachment to each other.

Termination: When it is felt that the referring problems have disappeared or been greatly reduced, it is time to end therapy. (Treatment of course can be extended if needed and all parties are agreeable). This is the end phase where strengths are emphasized and termination is put in a positive light—"Johnny, you are doing so well at home and with your friends you won't need so see me anymore. We have 3 more sessions and then we will be stopping Theraplay. We are going to celebrate with a party during our last session. What are your favorite activities? We'll be sure to include them." In the remaining sessions the therapist reminds the child that there will be only 2 and then 1 session left. A party is planned where not only favorite activities of both child and parents are included, but also parents are asked to bring favorite food and drinks. Party hats are supplied and exchanged at the party, photos taken and theraplay souvenirs such as hand or body outlines are given to the child, along with a small present which acts as a souvenir of the therapist and theraplay. Activities are included that focus on the positive attributes of the child such as making a necklace made from short strips of colored paper on which everyone has printed what they like about the child. The child wears this necklace as he walks out the door.

Four followup sessions take place within the year after treatment is terminated. An appointment should be made for the first checkup, before everyone leaves. The therapist can give the child a warm goodbye hug saying something like, "Johnny, I enjoyed being with you and I will miss you, but I will be seeing you again in 4 week's time and I look forward to that!"

GROUP THERAPLAY

Dr. Phyllis Rubin and Janine Tregay in the 1980s started using Theraplay groups in the classroom hoping to create a family atmosphere and sense of cohesion in Janine's special education class (Rubin and Tregay, 1989). Soon after that, the present author started her first experiences using Theraplay through groups with troubled preschoolers (including some autistic children) in a special class. The teachers noticed benefits such as reduced aggression, more spontaneous caring among peers, more cooperation, and the teachers themselves felt closer to the children. Other Theraplay groups with older residential children including adolescents, groups with mothers/sons, mothers/daughters, fathers/sons, high-risk pregnant teenage mothers, and multiple dysfunctional families, were also successful. The attendance was always very high with these groups, particularly with the father/son groups no matter what the weather and even when a child might be sick, but still insisting on coming. Plans for having a Theraplay group with mothers having deprived, neglected, or abusive histories is still something the present author hopes to fulfill.

The four dimensions of Theraplay: structure, challenge, engagement, and nurture are basic to all activities. A balance of active, stimulating activities with calming, soothing ones, so the group does not escalate out of control, is very important. This is preplanned by the leader and co-leader. If there are a number of acting out, impulsive children, then structure is emphasized along with calming activities which are often nurturing as well. Preschoolers often need structure along with rhythmic, singing activities where there is lots of physical contact and nurturing. Adolescent groups need more structure and challenge. The elderly need much nurturing, affectionate physical contact, and stimulation, but not much physical movement as their mobility is often limited.

Groups start and end with a definite beginning and end—songs, special handshakes, or "high fives" can be used. They usually last about 45 minutes, but with preschoolers, 20 minutes may be enough. If the group consists of emotionally disturbed children, then 4 to 8 children is recommended. However, groups of up to 30 children in a normal kindergarten class, have been conducted successfully. Groups are held regularly at least once a week lasting about 3 months when an evaluation can take place (ideal is to have some pre and post measures contrasted with a control group). Another 3 month contract may be made. It is very important that written permission is obtained from the parents and approval from supervisors, principals, and directors, before groups are started.

Discipline Problems

The main leader leads the activities, while the co-leader keeps an eye out for trouble spots and moves quickly to support a child that is having difficulty managing. If a child is hurt, the leader immediately stops the activity and gives attention to the injured child. If it is an accident, the child's sore spot is gently rubbed or maybe lotion, powder or a Band-aid is applied. If an aggressor has injured the child, then the leader tries to find out what has happened and instructs the victim to say clearly "don't hurt me" to the aggressor. The leader then guides the aggressor to help make some form of restitution by gently rubbing the sore spot, or blowing on it, or helping to put powder or a Band-aid on it. This may require hand over hand help on the part of the leader. Restitution is a powerful technique for helping to reduce aggression. The aggressor becomes very aware of the consequences of his actions, but also is a part of making things better for the victim. (The aggressor is not shamed or made to say "sorry"—often a useless exercise.) The victim feels cared for. This is an important lesson for the whole group and helps to create a sense of safety.

Goals for Group Theraplay

- To enhance the ability to relate to others and to become more aware of others and their needs.
- To promote feelings of acceptance, a sense of belonging, and increased trust.
- To enhance self-esteem and self-confidence.
- To promote feelings of care and concern for others and for themselves.
- To promote a feeling of safety with others.
- To increase inner controls for those who are impulsive or act out.
- To increase the ability to wait and take turns and to tolerate attention going to others.
- To experience joy, laughter, and having fun with others.

EXAMPLE OF A GROUP THERAPLAY SESSION AGENDA

At the beginning of group sessions the leader reminds the children of 3 rules:

1. no hurts (physical or verbal)
2. we stick together (we all follow the leaders directions)
3. we have fun!

Agenda:

Entrance: Choo-choo train (children marching one behind the other with their hands on the waist of the child in front of them all chanting "choo-choo, toot, toot" until desired spot is reached in the room)

Welcome Song: each child's name is included in the song

Inventory or special welcome of each child: "Debbie you have brought your beautiful smile!" "Tommy, you have brought your strong muscles."

Three Rules: No hurts, Stick together, Have fun

Lotioning or powdering of hurts (by leaders or by peers)

Motor Boat: All join hands and walk in a circle chanting "Motor boat, motor boat go so slow, motor boat, motor boat go so fast, motor boat, motor boat step on the gas, motor boat, motor boat go so slow, motor boat, motor boat go so fast, motor boat, motor boat, out of gas! Everyone falls down and ends in a sitting position.

Duck, Duck Goose: Everyone sitting in a circle while "it" walks behind tapping heads as he says "Duck," "Duck," but when he says "Goose" that person jumps up and races in the opposite direction around the circle. When "it" meets this person they give each other a hug or a handshake and continue running to see who first gets to the empty spot left by the person that had been tapped as the goose. Whoever gets there last is the next "it."

Mother May I: Everyone stands in a row facing the leader on the opposite side of the room. Object is to see who will get to touch the leader first. Each person in the row gets a turn to advance, but must first say "Mother may I" If they don't, then they will miss their turn. Example: "Mother may I take 3 giant steps forward?" Leader says "yes you may or no you can't—you may take 2 giant steps."(This is a great activity for defiant children when their parents are the leaders.)

Pass a Gentle Touch: everyone sits in a circle. Leader starts by touching a neighbor in some gentle way. This is passed on to the next person, and so on. A variation is for each person to imitate what others have done and then to add on his/her unique (but gentle) touch.

Feeding: the leader feeds a potato chip to each child and makes several rounds of doing this. The co-leader takes a turn feeding others as well. Sometimes children can feed each other.

Goodbye Song: A simple song is sung with a goodbye associated to each name of the people in the group. The leader gives a direct gaze and smile to each person as their name comes up

See appendix for more activities.

If one is conducting a parent/child group then the Theraplay session is followed by a parent counseling session, while one of the leaders takes the children to a separate room for quiet puzzles, reading, crafts, or play outside. Extra juice and cookies are given to the children and a beverage and cookies for the adults too.

The parental discussion sessions create a sense of companionship, that others have similar problems, new solutions are reached, parents support each other, and often new friendships are formed with invitations for each others' children to birthday parties, play times, overnights, etc.

REFERENCES

Bowlby, J. (1988). *A Secure Base, Parent–Child Attachment and Healthy Human Development*. New York: Basic Books.

DiPasquale, L. (2000). "The Marschak Interaction Method." In *Theraplay: Innovations in Attachment Enhancing Play Theraplay*, edited by Evangeline Munns. New Jersey: Rowman & Littlefield Pub., 27–51.

Gerhardt, S. (2004). *Why Love Matters: How Affection Shapes a Baby's Brain*. New York: Brunner-Rutledge.

Field, T. (2001). *Touch*. Cambridge, MA: MIT Press.

Field, T. and M. Reite. (1985). *The Psychobiology of Attachment and Separation*. New York: Academic Press.

Ford, C. W. (1993). *Compassionate Touch: The Role of Human Touch in Healing and Recovery*. New York: Simon and Schuster.

Jernberg, A. and P. Booth. (1999). *Theraplay: Helping Parents and Children Build Better Relationships Through Attachment-Based Play*. San Francisco: Jossey Bass Pub.

Panksepp, J. (1993). "Rough and tumble play. A fundamental brain process." In *Parents and Children Playing*, edited by K. B. MacDonald. Albany, New York: SUNY Press, 147–84.

Perry, B. and M. Szalavitz. (2006). *The Boy Who Was Raised as a Dog*. New York: Basic Books.

Rubin, P. and J. Tregay. (1989). *Play With Them: Theraplay Groups in the Classroom*. Springfield, Illinois: Charles C. Thomas.

Rutter, M. (1994). "Clinical Implications of Attachment Concepts: Retrospect and Prospect." Paper presented at the International Conference on Attachment and Psychpathology, Toronto, Ontario, October.

Schore, A. (1994). *Affect Regulation and the Origins of Self: The Neurobiology of Emotional Development*. New Jersey: Lawrence Erlbaum Associates.

Sunderland, M. (2006). *The Science of Parenting*. New York: DK Publishing Inc.

Thayer, T. (1998). March Encounters. *Psychology Today*, 31–36.

van der Kolk, B. A. (2003). The Neurobiology of Childhood Trauma and Abuse. *Child Adolesce. Psychiatr. Clin. N. Am.* 12(2), 293–317, ix.

Zeanah, C. and P. Zeanah. (1989). "Intergenerational Transmission of Maltreatment. Insights from Attachment Theory and Research." *Psychiatry*, 52, 171–196.

2

Research on Theraplay Effectiveness

James L. Wardrop and Linda A. Meyer

INTRODUCTION

In this chapter, we reprise our attempts to identify or create a research base for assessing Theraplay®'s effectiveness as an intervention method, identify some current trends and developments, and speculate about future directions Theraplay research might take. Our interest in doing research on the effectiveness of Theraplay began several years ago. We believed that data would support Theraplay's long-standing reputation for effectiveness, as claimed by virtually every Theraplay therapist that we had come into contact with for over five years, and we thought there would have been some advances since Munns (2000) wrote, "The research pertaining to the direct use of Theraplay is not extensive and clearly needs attention" (p. 14). Accordingly, we decided to conduct a meta-analysis of research on Theraplay covering its thirty-five year history. Toward this end, in 2003–2004 we did the following:

1. Obtained copies of all research documents that had been collected at the Theraplay office.
2. Requested copies of all research projects from individuals on the Theraplay listserve.
3. Harvested leads from bibliographies of published works about Theraplay.
4. Combed through Sally Popper's (Popper, Miesse, and Stephenson 2002, Popper and Miesse 2003) research reviews prepared for ATTACh.
5. Conducted an online search using PsychINFO, covering journals, books, and dissertations from 1967 to 2004.

For a study to be included in the meta-analysis, a study had to be published in a refereed professional journal (including *Dissertation Abstracts*), and it had to incorporate each of the following:

1. Present comparison data, either from a group that did not receive Theraplay utilizing a treatment-control experimental design, or from a pretest of Theraplay clients before treatment began (a pretest-posttest design). We would prefer studies that did both, using a pretest-posttest control-group design.
2. Include a sufficient number of participants to permit detecting treatment effects of a size that might reasonably be expected. (Typically, we would expect this to require a minimum of 8–10 participants per group.)
3. Use one or more outcome measures providing objective assessments of treatment effects, and provide evidence supporting the quality of the measures used.

We anticipated that after thirty-five years of Theraplay's existence, we would find well over the minimal number of studies (twelve) we felt we needed to carry out a meaningful meta-analysis. Much to our surprise, at that time we located a very small number of studies investigating the effectiveness of Theraplay, even without applying the criteria specified above. (Fortunately, as is shown in sequel, the current status of research in Theraplay has been much improved.) Our standards for including a study in a meta-analysis are rather rigorous, because we are convinced of the need to base findings on research that will stand up to close scrutiny of the internal and external validity of the results. We recognize the difficulty of conducting such research in a clinical setting, but we will continue to advocate for it as the surest way to determine just how effective Theraplay is, with whom and under what conditions.

LITERATURE REVIEW: UPDATE

In the years since our initial survey, more research has been done, but little of it yet appears in refereed journals. Taking a look at the broader array of studies dealing with the effectiveness of Theraplay, and relaxing our demand for peer review as an indicator of quality, we have identified a substantial number that provide grounds for optimism that in the next couple of years we will see a meaningful accumulation of research addressing Theraplay effectiveness.[1] Our primary criterion for this broader survey was that the study must report either pre-post data or comparison group data. In addition, we looked more broadly at studies that combined Theraplay with other kinds of intervention, such as Ammen's (2000) use of Theraplay with massage. We also considered studies that used Theraplay with special populations, such as Bernt's (1992) study with failure-to-thrive children and mothers, and the studies conducted in Germany by Franke and Wettig (2006) (Franke, 2007). Finally, we considered the recent reports from the Third International Conference on Theraplay held in 2007, including the research summary prepared for that conference by Lender and Lindaman (2007).

In a very early study, Ritterfeld (1989; cited in Munns, 2000) used three matched groups of language-disabled children, The group receiving Theraplay scored significantly higher on measures of socio-emotional constructs (and also language expression) than did groups receiving speech and language therapy or arts and crafts activities.

Much more recently, in her doctoral dissertation focused on validating the Marschak Interaction Method Rating System (O'Connor, Ammen, Backman, and Hitchchock, 2004), Bojanowski (2005) used the Rating System (MIMRS) and the Achenbach Child Behavior Checklist (Achenbach and Rescorla, 2000) as pre-Theraplay and post-Theraplay measures with 11 parent-child dyads. Using a significance level of .05, she found significantly positive treatment effects on two of the five dimensions of the MIMRS: Nurture and Challenge. Additionally, changes on the Engagement and Separation-Reunion dimensions were in the expected direction, but not significant, and there was only a slight difference between pretest and posttest scores on the Structure dimension. Curiously, Bojanowski did not report sufficient data for the CBCL to determine whether it also demonstrated significant pre- to post-treatment changes.

Because of the lack of peer-reviewed studies located in our attempt to do a meta-analysis of Theraplay research, we (Meyer and Wardrop, 2005) conducted a pilot study in which one Certified Theraplay Therapist administered the *Kinship Questionnaire* (Kappenberg and Halpern, 2004) before and after Theraplay treatment to all families (n=10) that were referred to her during the 2004–2005 academic year and who met the age criteria. Even with this small sample, the statistical evidence for Theraplay's effectiveness was impressively strong, and the results support the clinical experiences that many Theraplay therapists report: that Theraplay was effective with a wide variety of children, many of whom had been adopted. In addition, these results document that changes occurred in most of these children rapidly, despite the fact that many of them had been substance exposed *in utero* and/or had multiple placements.

Siu (2007) carried out a controlled study of Theraplay among Chinese children. The primary objective of this study was to evaluate the effectiveness of Theraplay on reducing internalizing problems among young children in Hong Kong. Forty-six children, who were described as at-risk for developing internalizing disorders (based on a standardized questionnaire on children's behavior), were randomly allocated to either the Theraplay condition or the waitlist control condition. There were 14 children from grade 2, 16 from grade 3 and 16 from grade 4. The mean age for children in the Theraplay condition was 7.84 (SD = 1.36), and the percentage of girls equaled 56. In the waitlist control condition, the mean age was 7.89 (SD = 1.32) and the percentage of girls was 54. All children completed the standardized measures on internalizing symptoms and self-esteem both before and after an eight-week period. Change scores on the measures were calculated, using pre-intervention scores as covariates. Results showed that children from the Theraplay condition showed significantly higher self-esteem and fewer internalizing symptoms when compared to the waitlist group.

Cross and Howard (2007) found that Theraplay was effective with children diagnosed with PDD or mild-to-moderate autism. A number of studies, some employing appropriate controls and focusing on effectiveness have been conducted at Sookmyung Women's University in Seoul, Korea. Lacking access to English-language versions of these reports, we have chosen not to comment on them here, but simply note that the interested reader may track down the following unpublished reports: Hong, 2007; Kim, 2007; H. Lee, 2007; J. Lee, 2007; Shin, 2007; and Yoon, 2007. These are all referenced without description in the Lender and Lindaman (2007) summary from the Theraplay Third International Conference. Elsewhere, Franklin (2007) reported significant Theraplay effects for a very small sample (n=8) of children diagnosed with Pervasive Developmental Disorder or mild to moderate autism. (This report is a product of a collaborative effort between the Theraplay Institute and the Institute of Child Development at Texas Christian University to study the effectiveness of Theraplay intervention with autistic children.)

In Sweden, research by Makela and his colleagues has provided some results supporting Theraplay's effectiveness. The Makela and Vierikko (2004) study, for example, involved 20 foster children living with long-term foster parents. Using the Child Behavior Checklist to assess outcomes, they found significant positive change following a series of Theraplay sessions using a two-therapist model. More recently, Lassenius-Panula and Mäkelä (2007) have reported positive results when examining the effects of Theraplay on changes in symptoms, parent-child relationships, and stress hormone levels of children referred for psychiatric care at three locations in Finland.

Wettig and Franke have collaborated on a number of important studies of the effectiveness of Theraplay. The results of a controlled longitudinal study carried out in Germany from 1998 to 2005 are summarized in Wettig, Franke, and Fjordback (2006; see also Franke and Wettig, 2003). They reported on research in Germany using Theraplay with children referred because of delayed language development and behavior disorders. This study involved 60 children aged 2.6–7.11. The children with learning disabilities participated in an average of 15 to 16 Theraplay sessions, while those diagnosed with Pervasive Development Disorders required an average of 29 sessions. These children receiving Theraplay were compared with a similar sample of nonsympotmatic children, matched by age and sex. An important set of outcome measures was scales on the German version of the Clinical Assessment Scale for Child and Adolescent Psychopathology (CASCAP-D: Doepfner et al., 1999). Theraplay was "highly effective" both clinically and statistically in reducing symptoms of attention, activity, social behavior, affective, and anxiety disorders. As impressive as they are, these results are of limited generalizability because of the use of a homogeneous treatment population and reliance on a single, highly skilled Theraplay therapist.

These deficits were overcome in another study also reported in Wettig et al. (2006; see also Franke, 2007), a multi-center study conducted in Germany and Austria. Two hundred ninety-one children received Theraplay treatment from 14 different therapists in 9 different treatment settings. These children were diagnosed with behavior disorders and speech language deficits. Outcomes—specifically, reduction in symptom severity of behavior disorders—were again assessed using scales from the CASCAP-D. Once again, significant positive changes were reported on scales of internalizing and externalizing behavior disorders as well as neuropsychological disorder symptoms. Importantly, this study used multiple therapists (often using a two-therapist model), and it obtained participants from multiple and diverse settings. It stands at this time as the strongest evidence that Theraplay is a highly effective intervention for large numbers of children.[2]

STATUS AND PROGNOSIS

Based on our pilot study (Meyer and Wardrop, 2005), we concluded that additional research is needed with a much larger group of therapists and children, preferably using different assessment instruments from those we employed. This broader and updated review of research on Theraplay's effectiveness serves to reinforce that recommendation. There are any numbers of anecdotal reports and case studies in which therapists conclude that Theraplay is effective, alone or in combination with other approaches, with a variety of clinical populations, and across several countries. Happily, there are an increasing number of controlled experiments and quasi-experiments demonstrating Theraplay's effectiveness in several settings, with diverse nationalities, age groups, and clinical diagnoses. What is not yet available is an adequate set of refereed, peer reviewed publications (including dissertations among this group) that report statistically sound, comparative studies utilizing objective assessments of outcomes (the sorts of studies that include several of those reviewed here) that place Theraplay in the mainstream of validated intervention approaches. The increase in research-oriented presentations across the years of the International Conferences on Theraplay (2003-05-07) and the apparent enthusiasm with which the most recent presentations have been received, give us grounds for optimism that such studies will be appearing with increasing frequency in major social-science publications.

NOTES

1. We acknowledge with gratitude several suggestions from the editor concerning candidate studies for consideration.

2. For other reports from this pair of scholars, access the German website www.theraplay-research.de/ (especially the sections dealing with research results and publications).

REFERENCES

Achenbach, T. M., and Rescorla, L. A. (2000) *Manual for the ASEBA Preschool Forms & Profiles*. Burlington, Vt.: University Department of Psychiatry.

Ammen, S. (2000) "A play-based parenting program to facilitate parent-child attachment." In *Short-Term Play Therapy Approaches with Children*, ed. H. Kaduson and C. Schaefer. New York: Guilford Press, 345–369.

Bernt, C. (1992). Theraplay with Failure-to-Thrive Children and Their Mothers. In *The Theraplay Institute Newsletter*, Fall 1992, 1–3.

Bojanowski, J. J. (2005) "Discriminating Between Pre- Versus Post-Theraplay Treatment Marschak Interaction Methods Using the Marschak Interaction Method Rating System." Psy. D. diss., Alliant International University, Fresno, Cal.

Cross, D., and Howard, A. (2007) "An evaluation of Theraplay with children diagnosed with PDD or mild to moderate autism." (Paper presented at The Third International Theraplay Conference, Chicago, Ill.)

Doepfner, M., Berner, W., Flechtner, H., Lehmkuhl, G., and Steinhausen, H. C. (1999) *Psychopathologisches Befund-System für Kinder und Jugendliche (CASCAP-D)*. (English: *Clinical Assessment Scale for Child and Adolescent Psychopathology.*) Goettingen: Hogrefe Verlag für Psychologie.

Franke, U. (2007) "An analysis of the therapeutic treatment process using Theraplay with oppositional, defiant children and shy, withdrawn children." (Paper presented at The Third International Theraplay Conference, Chicago, Ill.)

Franke, U., and Wettig, H. (2003) "Evaluation of the effectiveness of Theraplay: Changes in children with communication and behavior disorders and in parent's attitudes after Theraplay." (Paper presented at The First International Theraplay Conference, Chicago, Ill.)

Franklin, J. (2007) An Evaluation of Theraplay Using a Sample of Children Diagnosed with Pervasive Developmental Disorder (PDD) or Mild to Moderate Autism. (Paper presented at the 21st National Conference on Undergraduate Research, San Rafael, Cal.)

Goodman, R. (1997) "The strengths and difficulties questionnaire: A research note." *Journal of Child Psychology and Psychiatry 38*: 581–586.

Hong, J. (2004) "The effects of a family resilience promotion program applying family Theraplay." Sookmyung Women's University, Seoul, Korea.

Howard, A., Purvis, K., Cross, D., and Lindaman, S. (2007) "An evaluation of Theraplay® using a sample of children diagnosed with a pervasive developmental disorder (PDD) or mild to moderate autism." (Paper presented at the Third International Theraplay Conference, Chicago, Ill.)

Hughes, D. A. (Undated) *Parents Questionnaire* and *Parenting Profile for Developing Attachment.* (Author, 571 Vassalboro Rd., China, Me 04358)

Kappenberg, E. S., and Halpern, D. F. (2004) *Kinship Center Attachment Questionnaire.* Claremont, Cal.: Berger Institute for Work, Family, and Children, Claremont McKenna College.

Kim, Y. (2007) "Development and evaluation of a group Theraplay program to enhance attachment of infants." (Unpublished manuscript, cited in Lender and Lindaman)

Kwon, E. (2004) "The effect of group Theraplay on the development of preschoolers' emotional Intelligence Quotient." (Unpublished manuscript, cited in Lender and Lindaman)

Lassenius-Panula, L., and Mäkelä, J. (2007) "Effectiveness of Theraplay with symptomatic children ages 2–6: Changes in symptoms, parent-child relationships and stress hormone levels of children referred for psychiatric care in three university hospital districts in Finland." (Paper presented at the Third International Theraplay Conference, Chicago, Ill.)

Lee, H. (2007) "The effect of group Theraplay applied to Montessori kindergarten on children's behavior problems, self-concept and social competence." (Unpublished manuscript, cited in Lender and Lindaman)

Lee, J. (2007) "The effect of group Theraplay program for improving social competence of children in group homes." (Unpublished manuscript, cited in Lender and Lindaman)

Lender, C., and Lindaman, S. (2007) "Research supporting the effectiveness of Theraplay and Marschak Interaction Method." (Paper presented at the Third International Theraplay Conference, Chicago, Ill.)

Marschak, M. (1960) "A method for evaluating child-parent interaction under controlled conditions." *Journal of Genetic Psychology* 97, 3–22.

Meyer, L. A., and Wardrop, J. L. (2005) "Research on Theraplay." (Paper presented at the Second International Theraplay Conference, Chicago, Ill.)

Munns, E. (2000) *Theraplay: Innovations in Attachment-Enhancing Play Therapy.* Northvale, N.J.: Jason Aronson.

O'Connor, K., Ammen, S., Hitchcock, D. and Backman, T. (2001). *Marschak Interaction Method Rating System.* Unpublished manual. Alliant International University, Fresno, Cal.

Popper, S. D., Miesse, K., and Stephenson, M. (2002) *Recent Research on Adoption, Attachment, and Related Fields.* Association for Treatment and Training in the Attachment of Children. www.attach.org/researchnotes.htm (March 19, 2005).

Popper, S. D., and Miesse, K. (2003) *Recent Research on Adoption, Attachment, and Related Fields.* Association for Treatment and Training in the Attachment of Children. www.attach.org/researchnotes.htm (March 19, 2005).

Randolph, E. (2000) *Randolph Attachment Disorder Questionnaire* (3rd Ed.). Evergreen, Colo.: The Attachment Center Press.

Randolph, E. (2002) *Manual for the Childhood-Onset Bipolar Disorder (COBD) Screening Test.* Evergreen, Colo: RFR Publications.

Ritterfeld, U. (1989) "Theraplay: Evaluation einer Psychotherapeutischen Interventionsmethode bei Sprachgestörten Vorschulkindern" [Evaluation of a psychotherapeutic intervention method, theraplay, with language disordered preschool children]. Unpublished study for the Diploma in Psychology. Heidelberg: Psychologisches Institut der Ruprecht-Karls-Universität.

Shin, H. (2007) "A Qualitative Study of Theraplay Interaction." (Unpublished manuscript, cited in Lender and Lindaman)

Siu, Angela (2007) "Theraplay in the Chinese world: An intervention program for Hong Kong children with internalizing problems." (Unpublished manuscript, cited in Lender and Lindaman)

Wettig, H., Franke, U., and Fjordback, B. (2006) "Evaluating the effectiveness of Theraplay." In *Contemporary Play Therapy*, ed. C. Shaefer and H. Kaduson. New York: Guilford Press, 103–235.

Yoon, J (2007) "Effects of family group Theraplay to enhance interaction between child and mother in low-income families." (Unpublished manuscript, cited in Lender and Lindaman)

II

THERAPLAY WITH SPECIAL POPULATIONS

3

The Dysregulated Child in Theraplay

Lisbeth DiPasquale

WHAT IS DYSREGULATION?

There are many different reasons an individual child may be referred for therapy. For a therapist, some of the more challenging cases involve children who encounter extreme difficulty regulating the way they respond to many normal everyday situations. Problems occur when they experience strong negative emotions like anger, worry, or fear, but may also occur in response to positive feelings like excitement, anticipation, or joy. They often overreact to sensory input (e.g., loud or unexpected sounds, certain textures, or light touch), and have difficulty controlling their attention, normalizing their activity level, or regulating their mood. Because their reactions are well beyond what is considered to be adaptive, these children are said to exhibit "emotional dysregulation."

For some of these children, the problems involve externalizing or acting out behaviors. They tend to be irritable or easily angered and have difficulty tolerating frustration, stimulation, lack of structure, changes in routine, or new situations. They may respond explosively, have a tantrum, race around wildly, or possibly lash out physically by hitting, kicking, biting, or throwing objects. These episodes are often unpredictable and challenging to bring back under control. In the throes of a "meltdown" the child loses control and is unable to respond to orders to stop, attempts to negotiate or reason, or even attempts to soothe or calm him. The safety of the child and anyone around him may become an issue. Although it often appears that the child is being deliberately defiant and oppositional, his emotions are so strong that he cannot think and problem solve in the moment. After some time has passed and he is able to calm down, he will be better able to process what has happened and may regret his actions.

Many different diagnoses are associated with a child with externalizing behavior problems, such as, Attention Deficit Hyperactivity Disorder (ADHD), Oppositional Defiant Disorder (ODD), Anxiety Disorder, Depression, Bipolar Disorder, or Autism Spectrum Disorders. If a child has severe mood dysregulation and exhibits sudden rages or explosive episodes, the diagnosis is most likely to be either a combination of ADHD and ODD or "narrow phenotype bipolar disorder" (Carlson, 2007).

In contrast to the children with externalizing behavior problems, there are many others who internalize their problems and respond to strong emotions by pulling back, becoming overly shy and withdrawn, or exhibiting a high level of anxiety. These children retreat inward and try to avoid any situation that causes heightened arousal or strong emotions. Negative feelings like fear, anger, anxiety, or humiliation are the most obvious emotional triggers, but for many of these children situations that should be positive, such as receiving individual attention or being praised or encouraged, might cause them to freeze and become unresponsive, or to try to escape by running away. Diagnoses that are frequently associated with the anxious, withdrawn child are Anxiety Disorder (Generalized Anxiety, School Phobia, Separation Anxiety), Posttraumatic Stress Disorder, Selective Mutism, or Depression.

THE EFFECT ON THE FAMILY

Having an emotionally dysregulated child in a family can be very stressful. When a preschool child is prone to hyper-vigilance, high agitation, anxiety, and/or meltdowns, the unpredictable nature of the episodes can result in the family becoming increasingly isolated from the outside world. A fear of being helpless or humiliated in public during a child's outburst, or concern about being judged as incompetent, will often lead parents to reduce or even eliminate outings into the community. Opportunities for time together as a couple can also be difficult since it may be very hard to find someone who is willing or able to care for the child in the parents' absence. Worries compound if the child becomes physically aggressive toward his siblings or peers.

At school, outbursts are most often triggered by frustration, overstimulation, annoyance, or anger. For example, if the child is asked to do something he finds challenging, if he experiences disappointment or humiliation by losing at a game or doing something wrong in class, or if the situation lacks structure, such as recess or gym, his emotions may accelerate quickly and suddenly. By identifying and anticipating situations that tend to trigger an outburst, the teacher can be pro-active and intervene before the child loses control to help ease the situation and problem solve with the child so he will develop better coping strategies. For many of these children, however, the responses can be so sudden and unpredictable that it is difficult to take action in time to prevent the outburst. Safety is often a major concern. As a result, parents may be called to come take the child home, resulting in missed time at work.

A child who internalizes his worry or fear, on the other hand, may cling to his parents when faced with a new or stressful situation and find it very hard to separate. It can become a problem just to get the child to school or to have him stay there for a full day. When he becomes anxious or upset, he may react by crying uncontrollably, trying to escape by running away or hiding, or simply staring blankly, becoming non-responsive and dissociating from what is going on around him. Parents of a withdrawn, anxious child often become overly protective and try to shield him from any stressful situation, which may unwittingly exacerbate the situation.

The cause of emotional dysregulation is not always easy to pinpoint. Some children seem to be born with a heightened arousal system. Even as babies, they are easily upset, fretful, and difficult to calm, perhaps due to a genetic family pattern. Children may also learn to respond in an anxious, frightened manner or in an angry, aggressive way by watching and modeling the response style of a parent. In other cases, as recent research on the brain has revealed, regulatory problems can be triggered when a young child is exposed to a high level of stress or trauma. Experiences such as physical, sexual, or emotional abuse; loss of a parent figure; hospitalization or severe injury; or even witnessing the abuse of a parent or sibling, can be very traumatizing to a young child. Neglect and abandonment have also been implicated in children with significant emotional regulation problems. It should be noted that if a child is very young at the time the trauma occurs, he is more likely to develop the dissociative response, which is a primitive reaction to fear when an individual is incapable of fighting or fleeing the situation (Perry and Szalavitz, 2006).

THE DYSREGULATED ACTING OUT CHILD IN THERAPLAY®

When a dysregulated child with externalizing behaviors begins Theraplay it is essential for the therapist to be vigilant and attuned to the child so that problems can be anticipated and responded to quickly. Foreknowledge of the child's unique difficulties, issues, and triggers will help with the planning of the sessions to reduce unnecessary stress for the child. Does he have problems with flexibility and transitions? Are there certain textures, smells, tastes, or sounds that are likely to set upset him? The better a therapist understands the child before Theraplay begins, the better prepared he will be to provide the kind of support required. The activities need to be carefully selected so that the therapist maintains a physical connection to the child at all times, such as holding hands or keeping a hand on his shoulder. "Row, Row, Row Your Boat" (see appendix) is a good example of a game that is contained, but playful. It is imperative to be vigilant and prepared for sudden moves, attempts to bolt or possible aggressive acts. Because a dysregulated child is easily over-stimulated and has difficulty modulating his reactions, the first sessions should be low-key, highly structured, and contained. A calm, supportive environment is key to helping him feel safe so that he can begin to develop the adaptive skills to better handle his emotions (Greene, 1998). The child may have great difficulty accepting limits or following directions and will easily become over-excited or "wound up." He is likely to feel much safer when he is in control so he is likely to try to change the rules or modify a game in some way. Resistance to doing an activity at all is not unusual, and he may even try to run away if given the opportunity. Some of the typical Theraplay activities that are designed to be engaging and stimulating may be too much for the child to handle successfully at this point, but they may lend themselves to being modified or adapted to a more structured format. An activity like "Cross the room in funny ways" (see appendix) that is usually done independently by therapist and child can be performed in a structured way by having the therapist and child hold hands making the activity into a team effort rather than a race. Even "Pop bubbles" (see appendix) can be played in a more structured way by instructing the child to pop only one bubble the first time, then two, or by having him use a body part other than his finger to pop them. While the game is still fun, the child is less likely to get carried away and the instructions are easily adjusted to allow for more or less stimulation. It is important to remind the child of the instructions and repeat a step if he changes the rules or doesn't follow the guidelines. The therapist must be mindful that the activities still need to be playful and enticing so the child will want to join in. As Theraplay progresses and the child is better able to exert self-control, the sessions can be loosened up and more stimulation gradually introduced at a pace that is manageable for the child.

Some children have sensory issues and become upset or agitated by certain smells or sensations, such as the smell or feel of the lotion or baby powder used in some Theraplay activities. It is important to respect this, but since nurturing touch is so integral to Theraplay, it is important to try to find alternatives, such as using scent free products or simply substituting gentle touch for the lotion or powder. Sometimes the child may be able to accept these products more easily during the fun activities, e.g., "Ghost prints" (see appendix). This might actually de-sensitize the product altogether. If the child overreacts to gentle touch, saying it tickles when it is supposed to be calming and nurturing, he may find it soothing if more pressure is used, e.g., using a firm stroke during "Cotton ball soothe" (see appendix). Alternatively, a different kind of nurturing touch can be substituted, such as giving a back massage. The touch sensation must be pleasant for the child or it does not serve the purpose of the activity.

For children who are upset by noise or loud voices it is important to avoid the louder games or modify them. Sound level should be increased slowly in a controlled way. Many Theraplay activities that might encourage a child to "let it all out" can be done just as easily with a moderate voice level, e.g., "Hum garden" (see appendix) could be modified to go from a whisper to a normal voice instead of to a shout. "Silent scream" (see appendix) might be substituted since only a muffled sound is audible.

Each Theraplay session has an agenda carefully planned ahead of time to focus on the goals established for each child and family. Every agenda includes activities designed to tap into the four main areas of focus: Nurture, Structure, Engagement, and Challenge. The nurturing activities use gentle touch, soothing voice, positive comments, and appreciation for the child's unique and special qualities, making him feel valued and cared for. The structured tasks help him learn to listen to instructions, wait his turn, follow directions, and control his impulses. Engaging activities help the child and parent have fun together, enjoy each other's company, and connect with each other. Challenging tasks help build the child's self-esteem, as well as help encourage him to strive to improve and reach his potential.

For an acting out child, the sequence of activities during a session should be planned so that an active, stimulating activity is followed by one that is quiet and calming to bring his arousal level back down. His ability to cope must be constantly monitored to ensure that he is not over-excited. The goal is to help him be successful, so by introducing the stimulation in this managed way, he will learn how to modulate his emotions and develop his self-control. Because transitions are often a problem, it is important to make sure there is a clear start and a clear stop to each activity, with warnings as a game is coming to an end, A cue word signals the start or end of a game or even when to stand up from a sitting position. It may be as simple as saying "One, Two, Three, Go" or more playful by using a "Magic Word." With the "Magic Word" technique, the therapist will tell the child, "When I say 'Apples,' I want you to. . . ." The therapist then lists random fruit ending with "Apples," at which point the child and therapist act together, hand in hand. The child has to listen, contain his impulse to act too soon, and follow the directions given. If he responds before the cue, he must try again. Without realizing it, he is beginning to learn impulse control. It is often very hard for a child with regulation problems to change his mindset and stop doing something he is enjoying, but he needs to learn that the therapist means what he says and that extending the game is not negotiable.

Counting down the number of repetitions will help him get his mind ready for a change, saying for example, "We're going to do two more" and then, "This will be the last one." As the child becomes familiar with how Theraplay works, becomes less resistant and more compliant, the tight control can begin to ease, but the therapist must remain watchful. It is not unusual for a child's behavior to regress after the first few sessions and he may begin to test the limits again, requiring tighter control.

Every Theraplay session is followed by a debriefing session with the parents. This is an opportunity for the therapist to explain the purpose of each of the activities, discuss the methods used to help the child be successful, point out how the therapist dealt with any resistance, and encourage the parents to transfer these same strategies into their everyday life at home. Homework is also assigned where the parents choose a few of the Theraplay activities to do between sessions. The goal is to help them incorporate these kinds of fun or nurturing parent/child activities into their everyday life.

After a few sessions observing from behind the mirror and learning the techniques, the parents join the therapist and child in Theraplay. Regression in the child's behavior is not unusual when the parents first join in, so tighter control may be necessary. At first the parents are participants following the therapist's lead, but they gradually begin to take on more of the leadership role. When the parents first start to lead activities, the child may ignore the instructions and fall into old habits. He will need to be guided by the therapist to listen and follow what his parents say just as he needed to learn to follow the therapist's instructions. Also, even though the parents have been observing and learning about the techniques from behind the mirror, it is quite different when they are actually expected to take the lead and give directions and cues to start and stop the activities. Practice and direct support from the therapist improves their skills. Any kind of aggressive act by the child toward a parent, even if the child does not appreciate his strength and squeezes too hard in a hug or the act appears to be accidental, needs to be addressed. The parents need to understand the importance of not ignoring this kind of action, because the child needs to learn the limits of his strength and when he is going too far.

Over time, the parents learn how to give clear, explicit instructions, to provide warnings before transitions and to follow through when the child does not comply. They learn how to be playful, to acknowledge the child's specialness, to praise and encourage his skills, to use nurturing gentle touch to help calm elevated emotions, to give focused attention, and to listen to what he is saying, all in a positive, loving way. They become increasingly attuned to his moods, his feelings, and his reactions. As these skills are transferred to the home environment, the relationship between parent and child is strengthened, the parents take back control, the child feels safe in letting them do this and his responses become increasingly adaptive and manageable.

The effectiveness of Theraplay in helping children with behavior problems has been researched. A recent longitudinal study was conducted by Ulrike Franke and Herbert H. G. Wettig at the Theraplay Institute in Oftersheim, Germany, running from April 1998 to January 2006. The purpose was to measure the effectiveness of Theraplay in the treatment of oppositional defiant children and shy withdrawn children when compared to a control group of non-symptomatic peers matched for sex and age. The results were quite dramatic. With the oppositional defiant children, over the course of treatment there was a significant decrease in oppositional defiance to the same level as the children in the control group. At the same time there was a measurable increase in frustration tolerance, attention, self-confidence, empathy, trust in others, and sociability. While all these positive behaviors did not fully reach the levels of the control group, the improvement was considerable and the effectiveness of the Theraplay treatment was clearly demonstrated. Results from the study also revealed that the oppositional defiant children who improved as a result of the Theraplay treatment, maintained this level of improvement in a follow-up two years later (Franke and Wettig, 2007).

A CASE STUDY OF A DYSREGULATED ACTING OUT CHILD IN THERAPLAY

Jeffrey (not his real name) was almost seven when he began Theraplay. He was a stocky boy with a sturdy build and quite strong. His parents described him as an angry boy who challenged authority. He had problems listening and following instructions at school and at home, would test the limits to the extreme with any new adult, was verbally and physically aggressive toward peers and sometimes adults, had very poor social skills, would often isolate himself from others, and had no friends. When he got angry or upset he would become extremely active, run around wildly, yell, hit, kick, and throw things. It was very difficult to calm him down. Jeffrey was brought into treatment because of strong recommendations from his school. The staff felt that his behaviors were beyond what could be handled with normal behavior management techniques at school. His parents were also becoming increasingly concerned about Jeffrey's aggression toward his two-year-old brother.

When he began treatment, Jeffrey had great difficulty following the therapist's instructions and would begin running around the room or hiding in the cupboard at every opportunity. At one point he even ran out of the room and had to be enticed back. If he did not like a task, if he became frustrated, or if there was a delay between activities, his behavior would quickly escalate. Because it was difficult to bring things back under control or encourage him to participate when this happened, the therapist needed to be creative and flexible to ensure that the session plan was followed, even if this meant doing a nurturing activity, like caring for hurts, while Jeffrey was inside the cupboard. From this, Jeffrey learned that the therapist was in control and would follow through with the activities and the expectations in spite of any attempts to sabotage.

Over the course of seven sessions, gains were made in Jeffrey's cooperation, and his tendency to run away decreased. His parents were sensitive and caring to him when they joined in the sessions and were learning to be more consistent and to follow through at home. His father, however, continued to have difficulty giving clear instructions for activities or warnings for transitions to prepare Jeffrey. As a result, he struggled more than his wife to get Jeffrey to comply. Although there were some improvements at home, the messages to Jeffrey were inconsistent from one parent to the other and they did not always support each other in their parenting decisions.

Unfortunately, summer intervened and there was an unavoidable break in treatment, but the family planned to return in the fall to continue Theraplay. Because of a lack of routine over the summer and the fact that no Theraplay was done at home, Jeffrey's behavior regressed to the pre-treatment level. When the family returned in the fall, they decided to include the younger brother Corey (not his real name) who had not yet turned three, since Corey was beginning to mimic his big brother's maladaptive behavior. Because Jeffrey's previous therapist no longer worked for the agency, Jeffrey had been assigned a new therapist and a second therapist joined the group to work with Corey. Another change in Jeffrey's life was that he was now attending a community classroom for children with behavior problems, which was in a new school.

Children with regulation problems do not handle change easily and Jeffrey had a very hard time adjusting to the new dynamics in Theraplay. He seemed to resent his brother's intrusion into his realm, but at the same time could become very protective if Corey showed any kind of distress. Jeffrey required extensive structure, very firm control, and much encouragement to join in the activities. He would often sabotage a session from the outset by entering the room running wildly, which would set off his little brother as well. He would also refuse to listen and would challenge every instruction, often becoming physically aggressive toward the two therapists.

It was decided to have the parents join the sessions earlier than planned, because Corey had great difficulty separating from his mother. Jeffrey's behavior improved with his parents present, although he resisted following instructions when his mother or father were "in charge." He began to make better eye contact, but was unaccepting of many kinds of touch. The sessions needed to be highly structured and tightly controlled to help contain his actions, with clear expectations for his participation and plenty of praise and encouragement for anything positive that he did. The turning point seemed to come when he totally lost control during a session and had an explosive outburst or meltdown. Jeffrey's therapist and one parent gave him focused, caring support to help him through his outburst while the other participants continued with the session. The fact that he had been given such understanding and positive support when he was unable to control himself may have been what helped turn things around, or maybe it was the fact that the session continued without him. Perhaps he was reassured by the fact that the adults in his life were there for him, to help him cope when he needed it. Whatever triggered the change, Jeffrey became a very different boy after this crisis. He was no longer wild, but became more relaxed and involved. He would listen and follow directions and was able to participate in and enjoy the remaining sessions. The change in his behavior was quite dramatic.

Initially, Jeffrey's parents had shown a high tolerance for his negative behaviors, both at home and during the sessions. However, over the course of Theraplay they became more confident in the parenting role, began to work more as a team, learned to take charge in a fun manner and provided clear guidelines and expectations for his behavior. They also incorporated Theraplay activities into their everyday lives. In a follow-up session several months after treatment ended, it was encouraging to learn that the progress Jeffrey made during treatment had been maintained, consistent with the findings of Franke and Wettig, as referenced above.

SAMPLE THERAPLAY AGENDAS FOR THE DYSREGULATED ACTING OUT CHILD

(See appendix for description of activities.)

Agenda 1:

1. Entrance: Choo-choo Train
2. Welcome Song
3. Inventory - Playdough Prints
   - Caring for Hurts
4. Feather Blow
5. Hide Under the Blanket
6. Hello Ball
7. Red Light-Green Light
8. Handstack
9. Row, Row, Row Your Boat
10. Crisscross, Applesauce
11. Feeding
12. Goodbye Song

Agenda 2:

1. Entrance - Follow the Footprints
2. Welcome Song
3. Inventory - Measuring
   - Caring for Hurts
4. Silly Bones
5. Balloon Walk
6. One Potato, Two Potato
7. Barber Shop
8. Blow Over, Suck Up
9. Back massage
10. Taste Test
11. Feeding
12. Goodbye Song

Agenda 3:

1. Entrance - Dance In on Toes
2. Welcome Song
3. Inventory - What's Special about You
   - Caring for Hurts
4. Body Trace
5. If You're Happy and You Know It
6. Ring around the Rosie
7. Blanket Rock
8. Cotton Ball Blow
9. Cotton Ball Soothe
10. Feeding
11. Goodbye Song

THE DYSREGULATED ANXIOUS OR WITHDRAWN CHILD IN THERAPLAY

At the other end of the behavior spectrum are children who are withdrawn or who dissociate when they feel stress. They tend to react to stimulation, lack of structure, changes in routine, new expectations, or any kind of threatening situation by becoming overly anxious or fearful. They try to avoid these feelings by running away from the situation altogether or in the extreme by retreating inward and becoming unresponsive. They may appear extremely shy, may seem to daydream or appear inattentive. A child like this may cling to a parent and cry if pressured to separate or participate. Where the child has experienced severe trauma at a very young age, before he was able to respond with a physical reaction of fight or flight, he may react to stress by turning inward and dissociating. In effect he has learned to protect himself from harm by separating his core being from what is going on around him. A child like this may appear to be in a dreamlike state or, in the extreme, may seem to be "spaced out" and disconnected from what is going on around him (Perry and Szalavitz, 2006). Sometimes parents or teachers may misinterpret a dissociative response as defiance since in this state a child will be unable to comply when given direction. Instead he will remain frozen and unresponsive until the fear or anxiety subsides.

When a withdrawn, anxious child comes into Theraplay, it is important from the outset to help him feel calm and safe in the therapeutic environment by speaking in a gentle tone of voice and keeping the activity and noise level down. This child may not handle surprises well, so the therapist should give forewarning when the activities are going to change and introduce new things slowly and carefully. It is also important to gauge the level of intrusion so the child does not feel threatened by the close personal contact with the therapist. At the same time, the activities need to be playful and include some gentle surprises to engage the child's interest and help him discover that these kinds of interactions can actually be fun. When working with a very young child, a game like Peek-A-Boo is ideal for enticing and surprising the child in a non-threatening way. For a slightly older child, the therapist could introduce a game like Quiet Parts/Noisy Parts (see appendix). In this game the therapist makes quiet or funny squeaks or pops while tweaking different parts of the child's body (like his nose, ear, or big toe), or makes a squeaky pump sound while raising and lowering his arm, or makes a "whooshing" noise while moving his chin down and up. These are all designed to delight the child, engage his curiosity, and make him laugh. Once he begins to feel more comfortable in the environment, which may take several sessions, the spontaneity, fun, and activity level should slowly increase to build the child's tolerance and help draw him out of his shell (Jernberg and Booth, 1999).

Because one or both of the parents of an anxious child are often anxious themselves, it will be important to work with them to help them feel more at ease, comfortable, and matter-of-fact when doing the activities, both during the sessions and at home. Often these parents have the knowledge and the basic good parenting skills, but are unsure of themselves so don't follow through should they anticipate any resistance or fear from the child. Because their own fears, anxieties, and uncertainties can be transmitted, they need to gain experience in leading activities with an air of confidence, giving clear directions, and ensuring the child follows instructions. They also need to learn how to do these things in a fun and playful manner. Their self-assurance as parents will grow as they practice these skills and they will be better able to present a strong, united front at home. This in turn will help the child feel secure and reduce his anxiety.

The results of the Franke and Wettig study (2007) pertaining to the shy withdrawn child, revealed that over the course of Theraplay treatment, the shyness of these children decreased while their courage and risk taking increased to the levels of the children in the control group. At the same time, their sociability and willingness to make contact with others increased, they had greater empathy and were more trusting. As well, their attention improved considerably and their self-confidence grew to the level of the controls. As was found with the oppositional defiant children, this improvement was maintained two years after Theraplay treatment ended.

A CASE STUDY OF A DYSREGULATED, ANXIOUS, WITHDRAWN CHILD IN THERAPLAY

Lexie (not her real name) was a twelve-year-old girl when she began Theraplay. Her parents were going through a divorce and her mother was concerned about Lexie's tendency to be withdrawn and to keep her feelings inside. She had always been a shy child and was very clingy as a preschooler. Even at twelve she still found it very hard to meet new people. Although her mother felt she and Lexie had a good relationship, she was concerned that Lexie sometimes acted as though she were starved for affection. She said Lexie would sometimes make "such a big deal" out of things that she ruined everyone's fun. Mom did not feel that either Lexie's tendency to be emotionally withdrawn or her sister's acting out behavior had any relationship to the impending divorce.

When the family was first observed interacting together, it was noted that there was not much physical affection shown by either parent toward their daughters and the sisters did not seem to have affection for each other. In fact there was open animosity between the siblings.

During the first few sessions, Lexie was visibly uncomfortable with the closeness and touching that is an inherent part of the nurturing activities in Theraplay. She would pull back from the therapist when her hurts were cared for and would cover her face whenever she received a compliment or a personal observation about what made her unique. She also avoided making eye contact. If an activity or game involved holding hands she would deliberately position herself so that her sister was between her and the therapist so she would not have to take the therapist's hand. When it was her turn to add her ideas or give a response during quiet games she would try to relinquish her turn and pass it on to the next person. In fact, she rarely spoke.

Through the course of Theraplay, Lexie became much more comfortable with the nurturing and gained in self-confidence. Although she still tried to avoid some things, her engagement in the activities improved considerably. She grew to accept having her hurts cared for and would sometimes point them out to the therapist. When paid a compliment, she was able to maintain good eye contact, smile and say thank you. Vocalizing was still hard for her and she continued to shy away from humming or singing the welcome or goodbye songs. Even Silent Scream, where she was to scream into a pillow, was resisted. If she did speak, it tended to be in a babyish voice.

When the parents joined the Theraplay sessions Lexie's mother found it hard to take on the therapist's role and perform the nurturing activities. This was clearly not part of the mother/daughter experience. She did what was asked of her, but in an awkward fashion and needed continual guidance to use a gentle, soothing touch. She did improve in this regard, but it did not seem to be a natural behavior for her, and like her daughter, she never seemed totally comfortable with it.

Other than the caring for hurts, any physical nurturing continued to be difficult for Lexie to accept, even from her parents. If an activity was supposed to end in a hug, she would stand stiffly and wait for her parents to respond, never initiating, moving toward them, or hugging in return. There is no question that the therapy was making progress with Lexie and her parents, but there was still a long way to go. Unfortunately family circumstances, with the impending divorce, made it an untenable situation for the parents to work together as a team. Although it was strongly recommended that the family continue with Theraplay to build on the gains made, they chose to end after only seven sessions.

SAMPLE THERAPLAY AGENDAS FOR THE DYSREGULATED ANXIOUS OR WITHDRAWN CHILD

Agenda 1:

1. Entrance: Chair Ride
2. Welcome Song
3. Inventory - What's Special about You
   - Caring for Hurts
4. Feather Blow
5. Balloon Toss
6. Simon Says
7. Hum Garden
8. Ping Pong Blow
9. Cross the Room in Funny Ways
10. Crisscross, Applesauce
11. Feeding
12. Goodbye Song

Agenda 2:

1. Entrance - Follow the footprints
2. Welcome song
3. Inventory - Paint a Portrait
   - Caring for hurts

4. Balloon walk
5. Untangle Hands
6. Duck, Duck, Goose
7. A Day at the Spa - Hair Combing
   - Back Massage
   - Wash/Dry Feet
   - Toe Polish
8. Feeding - Food Preference
9. Goodbye song

Agenda 3:

1. Entrance - Chair Ride In
2. Welcome song
3. Inventory - Ghost Prints
   - Caring for hurts
4. Cross the Room in Funny Ways
5. Clap Patterns
6. Slip and Grip
7. Marshmallow Toss
8. Silent Scream
9. Blanket rock
10. Feeding
11. Goodbye song

BRAIN PLASTICITY AND THE IMPLICATIONS FOR TREATMENT

Recent years have seen a growing body of research on brain development and plasticity, particularly regarding how messages are transmitted through neural pathways and how these pathways can be modified through life experience and training. The areas of the brain that are stimulated the most will grow and develop more, while the parts that are less stimulated develop less. These changes in the brain continue throughout our lives. Some current research on very young animals has documented changes in the developing brain due to stress and trauma. Rat studies by Dr. Bruce D. Perry and Dr. U'Prichard found that when the animals were at an early stage of development, over-activation of stress hormones, such as cortisol, epinephrine, and norepinephrine, led to abnormalities in many areas of the brain. Stress hormones are released by the adrenal gland during times of perceived threat to prepare the body for fight or flight. The heart races, pupils dilate, breathing quickens, and blood sugar levels elevate, among other physiological responses. The over-activation of stress hormones when these animals were very young actually resulted in changes in the number of brain receptors, as well as their sensitivity and function, in many parts of the brain. Once the brain in these rats was altered, they would overreact to even tiny amounts of stress and forget everything they had learned. Their ability to respond normally to stress and threat from that point on was altered (Perry and Szalavitz, 2006).

This kind of animal research has direct implications for our understanding of the human brain. Dr. Michael Merzenich, a neuroplastician and a leader in brain plasticity research, has concentrated his studies on the human brain. He discovered that exposure to certain kinds of stimulation, such as stress or trauma, during critical periods in the developing human brain leads to a disruption in the way brain maps are differentiated, just as was found in the rats (Merzenich, as cited in Doige, 2007). Children and adolescents who exhibit aggressive, violent, and anti-social behavior have been found to have higher levels of the stress hormone cortisol in their systems. This suggests that their bodies are responding to perceived threat. In addition, magnetic resonance imaging (MRI) on the brains of children and adolescents who have committed violent crimes reveals actual signs of brain damage resulting from early trauma (Perry and Szalavitz, 2006).

When a child has experienced trauma, the same stress hormones that were released during the traumatic event will be released again when something reminds the child of the experience, causing the same feelings of anxiety, fear, or insecurity. The child learns to be constantly wary, watchful, and hypervigilant for signs of impending danger so as to be prepared for self-protection. The body's fight or flight response systems may remain on high alert even when there is no actual danger, and the child may become inattentive, impulsive, have difficulty regulating his emotions, and may respond to seemingly minor events by lashing out or running away.

On the other hand, if the child was very young when the trauma occurred, his reaction to stress or fear may be quite different. A baby or toddler is unable to escape from danger by fighting or running away. When a child is faced with trauma at this young age, the more primitive parts of the brain become engaged and he will respond by curling up, looking as small as possible and crying for help. Instead of speeding up, the heart rate slows and the brain releases endogenous opioids (i.e., endorphins, a natural painkiller), producing a trancelike state where he becomes withdrawn and non-responsive. When he is older, he will be more likely to respond to stress or danger in a similar way, by dissociating or mentally escaping from the situation.

Because of the brain's continuing ability to adapt and change, the maladaptive alterations that developed in the brain as a result of trauma or neglect have the possibility of being modified and improved. An example of this is a recent training program that has been developed by Merzenich and a team of colleagues based on his neuroplasticity research. The program, called Fast ForWord, has been designed to exercise every part of the brain involved with language processing and has greatly improved the functioning of children who are language impaired, those who have difficulty with auditory processing and even those with autism (Merzenich, as cited in Doige, 2007). Extrapolating from this, the brains of children who respond to stress or anxiety in a maladaptive way can also be re-trained to react in a more normal way. The children need to experience what they missed when they were younger, i.e., calm, structure, consistency, and a safe and nurturing environment. The increased equilibrium experienced through therapy helps neurotransmitter levels to become better regulated and even may remap neural pathways, hence the child becomes calmer (Wieland, 2008). Personal attention, communication, gentle touch, and having the physical needs met are all vitally important to help a child feel safe and secure. Frequent positive physical contact and play also help to relax the child, and thereby reduce stress and anxiety (Foxman, 2004).

BRAIN RESEARCH AND THE IMPLICATIONS FOR THERAPLAY

While this brain research does not specifically address how Theraplay can help to change the response style of children with regulation problems, it does provide a window into the science behind the positive changes we see during the therapeutic process. It also gives us an optimistic outlook for children with regulation problems. We now know that we have an opportunity to alter the neural pathways by re-training the brain to respond in a positive, normal, adaptive way. First and foremost, we need to reduce the level of arousal and stress so the child will feel safe. In Theraplay, the child is helped to achieve a feeling of comfort and calm through soft nurturing touch, rocking or holding gently, making soothing, caring comments, and providing unconditional acceptance.

In Theraplay, the child learns through gentle guidance, encouragement, and possibly direct hand over hand modeling, the skills that he needs to learn. All of this is done in a safe, highly structured, predictable, and very nurturing environment to reduce the level of stress or anxiety while engaging the child in a playful and enticing manner. The child experiences total acceptance and the full attention of the therapist, is given positive esteem-building comments, is guided in a non-critical way to perform the activities as directed and is given unconditional praise for accomplishments, all while playing and having fun. In addition, many of the activities in Theraplay are designed to regress the child to an earlier stage of development (e.g., rocking, singing a lullaby, or possibly giving a baby bottle) to help him experience what he may have missed at that point in his life.

By observing how the therapist deals with anxiety, resistance, or aggression the parents' skills improve, their messages to the child become clearer, there is more consistency in the way problems are handled, and the parents more reliably ensure that the child follows through with their requests. All of this increases the child's feelings of safety and security, which allows him to relax and relinquish control to his parents. According to the research, with the experience in Theraplay each week and the incorporation of Theraplay activities into the regular routine at home, the practice of these skills may, over time, help to restructure the neural pathways in the brain so the child is able to respond in a more normal, adaptive way and emotions are no longer dysregulated.

Although there is no way of knowing what is actually happening from a neurological standpoint, many therapists have had cases where a child continues to react explosively or aggressively and can't seem to regulate his responses, even after many sessions, as was the case with Jeffrey mentioned earlier. The parents participate faithfully, exhibit good parenting skills during the sessions, do the homework regularly, but progress appears stalled and only marginal improvements are noted at home. Then suddenly, seemingly overnight, there is a breakthrough and the child just "gets it." Behavior problems at home and at school improve significantly and there is a marked difference in the child's engagement and cooperation in the Theraplay sessions. Even after Theraplay is discontinued, the improved behavior is maintained. This kind of sudden change is Makela's (2003) "moment of attunement between the child and therapist." In light of recent brain research, this breakthrough may in fact be the point at which the neural pathways have re-aligned.

It would be an interesting research project to actually map the brains of children through an MRI before and after Theraplay to see if any differences are observed. Brain plasticity research provides a thought provoking theory as to why this innovative treatment method is so effective in helping children overcome such significant behavior problems in such a relatively short period of time. But whether or not neurological change is at the root of the success, the efficacy of the Theraplay treatment method is clearly supported.

REFERENCES

Carlson, Gabrielle A. (2007). "Who are the children with severe mood dysregulation, a.k.a. 'rages'?" *The American Journal of Psychiatry Editorial* (164: 1140–1142, August 2007).

Doige, Norman. (2007). *The Brain That Changes Itself.* New York: Penguin Group Inc.

Franke, Ulrike, and Herbert H. G. Wettig. July 2007, "Theraplay therapeutic treatment process." (Paper presented at The Third International Theraplay Conference, Chicago, IL).

Foxman, Paul. (2004). *The Worried Child.* Alameda, CA: Hunter House Inc.

Greene, Ross W. (1998). *The Explosive Child.* New York: HarperCollins Inc.

Jernberg, Ann M., and Phyllis B. Booth. (1999). *Theraplay.* San Francisco, CA: Jossey-Bass Inc.

Makela, Jukka. (2003). "What makes Theraplay effective." *The Theraplay Institute Newsletter* (Fall/Winter, 2003).

Perry, Bruce D., and Maia Szalavitz. (2006). *The Boy Who Was Raised as a Dog*. New York: Basic Books.

Wieland, Sandra. (2008). "Therapy: The brain's second chance." The Centre for Counselling and Therapy, Victoria, British Columbia, Canada. www.sandrawieland.com/centre.htm.

4

Theraplay with Overtly and Passively Resistant Children

Shirley Eyles, Maria Boada, and Catherine Munns

Our motivation to write this chapter stems from our own experiences in working with challenging children and their families. These families are a mosaic of the types of resistance we faced in our clinical work and we hope you find the information useful. We conceptualize resistance on a continuum, from the impulsive, high-octane child to the immutably stoic child.

We feel it is imperative to reframe how we talk about *resistance*. This term is synonymous with expressions of adult frustration, such as non-compliant, uncooperative, defiant, or oppositional; however, these latter terms imply the problem lies solely within the child. Traditional thought regarding non-compliant behavior typically sees an adult giving an instruction, which the child is expected to follow. When the child does not follow through with adult-determined expectations she, over time, may be labeled "defiant" or "oppositional" and become the focus of treatment. This does not take into account a myriad of factors, which may have an effect on the adult-child relationship and may influence the child's continuous refusals.

Maag (1999) states, ". . . successfully managing resistance requires attending to the behaviours of the child and adults alike" (p. 161). In this view, resistance is not exclusively the domain of the child, but also includes how the adult responds to the child. The main focus of the intervention needs to be the adult-child interaction. Through Theraplay®, if adults and children are given the opportunity to experience new ways of interacting together, then adult perceptions of the problem behaviors may change and therefore lead to positive changes in adult-child interactions. Approaching the interaction, activity or situation in a calm, nurturing, and respectful manner increases the opportunities for successful outcomes for the child. She/he needs to receive a clear message that the adult will keep her/him safe during the interaction by being finely attuned to her/his responses, and adjust the approach when necessary.

Knowles and Linn (2004) categorize resistance in either behavioral terms, "the act of withstanding influence," or motivational terms, "as an oppositional force" (p. 4). They identify several faces of resistance, the most relevant being reactance and distrust. "The clear core . . . is that it is a reaction against change" (Knowles and Linn, p. 4). Reactance is initiated when influence is perceived to threaten one's choices. Adults and children alike become guarded or distrustful when faced with a message to change. This framework allows us to view resistance as a defense mechanism, which attempts to maintain homeostasis.

Adult-child interaction is a significant contributing factor to resistance; however, there are several others. It is important to explore physiological, developmental, and environmental factors in order to understand the function of the resistance and, ultimately, to help manage it more effectively. For example, explore the parent's own cognitive bias of their child. If a parent perceives their child as "difficult," they may anticipate that their child *will* be difficult, and this bias sets the stage for a less than optimal interaction. A negative interaction history is a perpetuating cycle. Practitioners working with families and children may find it beneficial to increase their knowledge of predictors for behavior problems in children, which have been demonstrated in recent research articles (Shipman, Sneider, and Sims, 2005; Ronnlund and Karlsson, 2006; Pierrehumber, Miljkovitch, Plancherel, Halfon, and Ansermet, 2000).

Theraplay focuses on the parent-child interaction. Theraplay takes into account where the child is at and structures an environment/situation in a way that enables the child to be successful, and feel good about herself. At the same time, through the adult-child interaction, therapists help change their mental representations and the parents are also able to see their child differently. As a result, the pattern of interactions will change and therefore, enable the internalization of a new lived experience. Jernberg and Booth (1999) state, ". . . in Theraplay . . . we give [children] a new view of the world and how people can respond to them. . . . We change the child's picture of herself and the world and therefore change the way she behaves and the kinds of responses she evokes from others" (p. 54).

CASE STUDIES

Case 1

The two case studies in this chapter involved children displaying some of the challenging behaviors presented to us along with interventions used to elicit therapeutic responses. The first family (where overt resistance was demonstrated) involved Ms. Smith and her two adopted children, 6-year-old Rhona, and her 4-year-old brother, Leon. They were adopted at ages three years and eighteen months respectively. Ms. Smith and her husband separated a year after the adoption, leaving Ms. Smith as a single parent. He has had no contact with the children. Ms. Smith reported that the children's histories involved domestic violence and deprivation of basic physical and emotional needs. Both children were described as having the following presenting problems: verbal and physical aggression, emotional and regulatory issues, and difficulty expressing emotions.

The initial treatment plan was to work with Ms. Smith and both children together as that was their lived experience. Ms. Smith required help to increase her awareness of the exceptional needs of her children and how to adjust her parenting approach to meet those needs. However, after several sessions it was evident that the high needs of both children necessitated individual time with their adoptive mother. Also, as Ms. Smith became more trusting in our relationship, she divulged more about her own attachment history, which was interfering with her ability to form healthy attachments with her children. Given all these factors, after several sessions together, we separated the children and had individual sessions back to back with each child.

Initially, while working with both children in the same session, they arrived into the session highly dysregulated, bursting into the playroom, running around, often yelling and then hiding under a shelf in the room. We discovered early on that we actually had to start our structuring practically from the car door, because Rhona and Leon played off of each other's excess energy and negative resistant behaviors. We coached Ms. Smith on playing a "Follow the Leader Game" (see appendix) when they got out of the car. We locked the playroom door, as a way of slowing down their energy. At first, Rhona responded to this new boundary effusively by banging on the door with her hands and kicking it with her feet, wanting to enter the playroom immediately. Her behavior spoke to her tremendous need to be in control, and this had been challenged. We started a Morse code–like tapping on the opposite side of the playroom door in response to her banging, effectively joining with her and leading her into a reciprocal, playful communication through the door. The therapist then opened the door and praised her ability to do Morse code. This became part of the opening routine with each session. Acknowledging their previous need to hide under the shelf, we immediately initiated joining type activities right from the door (i.e., a magic carpet ride, a rolling chair ride) bringing them over to that special space.

Initially we stayed with the child if there was active resistance (i.e., moving away and refusing to join), but we found this increased Rhona's anxiety and Leon also became dysregulated. It was apparent that we needed to give them time to join us. We adjusted our approach and always started the activity with an invitation to join us. A verbal invitation worked best with Leon, whereas with Rhona it was the challenge of the activity that would capture her interest. Due to their difficulty with singing (singing the welcome song), we adjusted our agenda and instead greeted them with a creative handshake. Our flexibility grew a great deal while working with these children.

We learned that nurturing touch served to ground the children and regulate their behaviors. Once Rhona became more comfortable with the therapists she sought physical contact, albeit initially through rough and rather aggressive means. This included bumping into the therapists purposefully and sometimes jumping on their backs. Her sensitivity to redirection made it important that we took much care in how we dealt with the roughness. It was important that she was aware that her actions hurt, but at the same time the focus needed to be on the therapists' joy of connecting with her in order not to trigger her deeply rooted trust issues. It was important to be proactive and have activities that could be pulled in, in the event of resistance, particularly ones that had previously evoked a positive response from the child. In Rhona's case, it was back massage or simply sitting and rocking back and forth. The rhythmic movement allowed her to feel connected to someone and served to ground her. Creativity and spontaneity were key components in this work. On one occasion, Rhona jumped on the therapist's back unexpectedly and could not be swayed from this position. This momentarily reduced us, two experienced therapists, to feeling incompetent and uncertain. Fortunately, our creative instinct surfaced and one of the therapists spontaneously proceeded to make exaggerated sounds and movements like a dump truck backing up and dumping its load. This enticed Rhona to eagerly participate, allowing herself to be dumped gently off the therapist's back into the other therapist's lap.

In the initial sessions, we were still getting to know the children and assessing their needs and how to best respond to them. Rhona and Leon proved to be great teachers. We quickly learned to keep any distractions, even our supplies, hidden away. We also discovered that trying to make a game out of cleanup after all the cotton balls were recklessly tossed about the room, only increased resistance. The best way to refocus the children was with individual time. We learned to tighten our transitions, and offered more individual nurturing, and engaging activities. We learned about the impact of past deprivation of food as the children slapped or grabbed food from our hands on various occasions, even greedily grabbing it up off the floor. As a result we began to include feedings throughout the session, as well as recommending that their mother provide them with a snack on their drive to Theraplay. Toward the end of the individual sessions each child's emphasis on food subsided significantly.

In one session, Rhona started running around wildly trying to entice a chase that we knew would end up with her in charge and likely escalate her behavior. To help contain and decrease the potential for Rhona becoming increasingly more dysregulated, the therapist exaggerated a crouching, tiptoeing step toward her, all the while being aware of her response to make sure she was going to be okay with the closeness. The therapist then wrapped her arms around Rhona as if she was caught. Rhona giggled delightedly and accepted the closeness for a lengthy period as the therapist moved into looking for wiggly parts/stiff parts, which was part of the original agenda. Instead of backing away, Rhona smiled broadly as she accepted the close, intimate contact she so needed, but guarded against.

Transitions were difficult for Leon in that he would often become dysregulated at those times, and ran around the room grabbing lotion and squirting it on the floor. We proactively put the lotion out of reach prior to his entrance into the room. We used animal movements, counting, and cue words to help structure the transitions. We would structure the transition by saying a combination of "okay we're going to hop like bunnies to the center," "when I say rabbit we are going to hop to the center," "on count of three we will . . . " We often engaged in a containing, physically close game of horseback ride with him, whinnying like horses as we moved to begin our next activity. We also attempted to empower Leon's mother in the structuring by dialoguing with her as to what she had found helped to ground and regulate Leon. From this dialogue we discovered that she used to do an activity she called "Planting a Garden" with Leon and Rhona to help settle them at night. When we began using this activity in the sessions, Leon and Rhona's mother began using it at home again and felt more positive about her contribution. We also used video-taped sessions to play back to their mother to help her identify her strengths as well as how she could have responded differently to make a more positive outcome possible.

After approximately eight sessions it was apparent that working with both children at the same time was not a fruitful exercise due to the amount of control that Rhona had over her younger brother and the high needs they both had for nurturing and individual attention. In spite of significant issues with trust, especially with Rhona, we made some connection with them individually, so we decided to hold separate sessions for the two children.

During the individual sessions with Leon things progressed quite quickly. He no longer had his sister's defiant example to follow, made connections with the therapists, and trusted the adults around him. This generalized to home with his mother and school as well. He made more friends, had them come over after school, and in general did develop his own personality and sense of self separate from his older sister. Rhona, on the other hand, took longer to gain our trust, but this happened more quickly as she was the focus of attention in individual sessions. She became gentler in her interactions and readily accepted and began to seek out physical touch in appropriate ways. In spite of the progress she made in her relationships in Theraplay, home, and school, the extent of her deep seeded trust issues again surfaced. The trigger for this was her perception that as school ended so would Theraplay. When she found that this was not so, she jumped to the conclusion that if she had to come to Theraplay during the summer she would miss out on going to overnight summer camp. She also verbalized quite clearly that she wanted to feel like a "normal kid with a normal family" and not have to attend "therapy" during the summer months. She felt betrayed and her trust issues resurfaced full tilt. She hid under the shelf glaring at the therapist and her mother, and tried to kick out at the therapist when she went over to speak to her. The therapist remained physically present, but at a safe distance and empathized with her painful feelings. Slowly Rhona decreased her ranting and swearing in the midst of a respectful, accepting, and empathic approach. She, at last, verbalized her feelings. The therapist coached her mother to approach at this point and hold her. Rhona readily went into her mother's arms and began to sob uncontrollably. This was a significant moment as it took a great deal of trust to be that vulnerable, something that she had never been able to do before. Her anger dissipated and she was able to feel what was really under all the rage: her sense of betrayal. She talked about her perceptions, and her feeling that she had been deceived. The progress her mother had made was truly evident at this point, as she was fully attuned to Rhona and able to meet her need to be nurtured. This was a turning point for her mother, who had never had the opportunity to see Rhona as a vulnerable little child. At last she understood Rhona's deep need for connection and was able to see behind Rhona's rejecting, defensive, and aggressive responses for the first time. We problem-solved this issue and decided to meet every other week instead of every week over the summer months. We also assured Rhona that she wouldn't miss summer camp. Although this seemed to be an acceptable plan at the time, when Rhona was to come for her next session she was very resistant. She would not come into the room and when she finally did she was swearing, yelling "I hate you," and became destructive by pulling at the blinds in the room and pulling things off the shelf. Attempts to deescalate were ineffective, and we felt her safety, as well as that of others in the room, was at risk. We coached her mother to hold her and as before, she sobbed and was able to more readily verbalize her feelings. When she was calmer and released from her mother's hold, although she would not sit with us, she participated at a distance as she verbalized her feelings, while the adult's listened empathically. What she needed at this time was to be listened to in a safe and structured environment.

In spite of our efforts to come to some kind of compromise and respect Rhona's wish not to attend "therapy" during the summer months, she absolutely refused to return to Theraplay for her next session. We also suspected that her increased positive rapport with us perhaps began to scare her thus resulting in her need to push us away. As we felt it would be counterproductive to force the issue given Rhona's strong oppositional response, we decided to follow up with her mother every other week by phone to support her in continuing Theraplay activities at home. We did bi-monthly checkups with Leon and his mother emphasizing the need to continually focus on nurturing and structuring with Rhona. We coached her on ways to continue to bring Theraplay activities into her day-to-day interactions with both children to help decrease power struggles and increase positive interactions. Rhona was much more receptive to limits set by her mother and more responsive and accepting of nurturing touch.

Case 2

Our work with the second family illustrates dealing with passive resistance. Jenna, seven years old, lived with her mother who was very strict and emotionally unavailable to her daughter. She was a single parent and Jenna's father had sporadic involvement. At an early age Jenna learned to take care of herself, because of her mother's limited attention. Presenting problems included concern over her emotional state due to an emotionally absent parent, physical aggression toward people and animals including hitting and kicking at home and at school, defiance, tantrums, and throwing objects. Although overt behaviors were displayed at home, in Theraplay we encountered passive resistance.

Jenna demonstrated her passive resistance by shaking her head "*NO*," withdrawing, stepping back, lowering her gaze, and putting her head down, crossing her arms or putting them behind her back. To help reduce her anxiety around challenging and/or new activities, we often modeled the activity first, so she knew what to expect and then made attempts to invite her into joining us in the activity. When she shook her head (indicating no) and refused to attempt the activity, we learned the importance and power of meeting her where she was, thereby joining her. For example, in "Silly Bones" (see appendix), she initially refused attempts to participate, standing awkwardly and lifting and holding her foot with her hand, which appeared to be an anxious response. After several attempts to try to engage her in the activity we realized that the solution was right before our eyes. It became clear to us that she was not ready for the physical aspect of silly bones with touching body parts. As she was already touching her feet, the therapist spontaneously said "Simon Says touch *your* feet." Using the posture she was presenting us with, helped Jenna to come out of her anxious state and allowed her to engage successfully in the activity. Once she felt safe enough to proceed with that activity she could be playfully engaged in it for a lengthy period of time. Modifying the activity into more of a "Silly Bones/Simon Says" activity made it less intrusive and more acceptable and comfortable for Jenna. Later we slowly increased the more intimate touching interactions using "Silly Bones" format. Eventually she accepted even touching heads together.

With Jenna, as with other children, seizing those spontaneous moments in interactions required being finely attuned to the child and also listening to one's own therapeutic intuition. For example, during Cotton Ball Soothe while the therapist was soothing Jenna's arm, Jenna suddenly and abruptly pulled down her sleeve. The therapist responded empathically by commenting "oh that (the cotton ball) was too itchy for you" and then moved to soothing her hand. Immediately after that, Jenna put her hands behind her back. The therapist then began soothing Jenna's face. Although this may be seen as counterintuitive, the therapist chose to do this because previously Jenna had allowed the therapist to tuck her hair behind her ear. Fortunately Jenna accepted this, spontaneously moved her face forward toward the therapist, and even closed her eyes indicating her comfort with this interaction.

When Jenna's parents joined the sessions to participate, initially Jenna wouldn't play and instead stood at the side with her hands behind her back watching tentatively. She resisted attempts to be engaged, so the therapists proceeded with the first activity with her parents. While playing ball with her parents, the therapist tried to continually include Jenna by talking to her casually, for example, "oops your Dad missed that one! I wonder if he will catch this one." All the while the therapist observed her facial expressions, and made brief eye contact with her. As the activity progressed, the therapist noted Jenna's facial expression soften and she indicated that she was more interested in what we were doing. For example, not turning away when the therapist spoke to her, making more sustained eye contact, overall more relaxed body posture. In response the therapist quietly signaled Jenna's mom to toss the ball to Jenna. This effectively opened the door for Jenna to participate fully, which she did. This was an example of meeting the child where she was at, while giving her the opportunity to join without eliciting a power struggle. Sometimes a simple strategy worked best to engage and provide opportunities for the child to join in. For example, during the goodbye song, which Jenna did not normally sing, we either deliberately paused in the song or whispered or mouthed a word or name in the song to non-verbally invite Jenna to join in. This strategy effectively caught her off guard, surprised her and enticed her to join in, which she did.

In summary, what was achieved with these families? All of the children increased their emotional regulation and trust. With two of the three children there was an increase in accepting and seeking out nurturing touch. There were increased positive interactions within the family units as a whole, and two of the three children increased in verbalizing their thoughts and feelings and decreased in acting them out. All of the children increased their peer interactions at school and at home. Jenna, for the first time, played with her peers at school and at home, while Leon actually brought a friend home. Rhona dropped her pseudomature façade, relaxed, laughed, and generally became more spontaneous and verbal in her interactions. All of the parents saw more positive aspects of their children and in turn responded in a more empathic and positive manner with them. As well, there was increased flexibility and spontaneity on the part of all caregivers to different degrees.

What did we learn? Firstly, we were reminded of the importance of attuning to the child and particularly to *work with* their responses. Paradoxical responses caught these children by surprise and interrupted their usual patterns of responding. This gave them the opportunity to identify on a physiological level that it was safe to respond and allow the adult into their emotional space. It took time and patience to earn the trust of these children as their defensive walls had served to keep them safe from real or perceived harm and they weren't going to drop their guard easily. We learned to be *proactive* when planning our sessions and to *anticipate* that when making some headway with the child who seemingly had accepted us into her physical and emotional space, the resistance might heighten, later on.

Video-taping sessions and reviewing them, particularly as a beginning therapist, is a very good way to pick up on cues that the child gives. In the midst of impulsive/resistant behaviors one can miss important information about how the child responds, so reviewing a video-tape can be helpful to both therapist and parent in ensuring success in future sessions.

Last, but by no means least, it is *crucial* that the therapist be aware of her own triggers. The behaviors of overtly resistant children can very easily derail the most competent therapist and interfere with being able to fully attune to the child. Children, especially resistant children, have built in radar for negative responses and will react to a therapist's triggered emotions. Identifying issues in our own attachment histories minimizes the risk of transference and counter transference. The more conscious we are of that potential, the easier it is to help parents also identify how their own triggers from families of origin, may interfere with their ability to be more effective parents. Of course, ongoing supervision is very important, increasing the opportunity to process one's own responses.

AGENDAS

Here are examples of three agendas for beginning, middle, and ending sessions, as well as changes made, dependent upon responses elicited by the child(ren) described in our previous case studies (see appendix for descriptions of activities):

Beginning Sessions: **These have a lot of structure, engagement, and rapport building through fun and playfulness.**

Entrance: Magic Carpet Ride

Greeting Song: "Here we are together, together" (Rhona responded negatively to the singing, covered her ears, ran under a shelf.) Given her history, we hypothesized that this response stemmed from her need for control, which made her feel safe. As a result, we struggled to come up with a solution by which she had some sense of control while minimizing dsyregulation. Initially we had Ms. Smith and her children make up their own welcome song for the following week. When this failed we changed the activity to a secret handshake, which elicited a positive response.

Inventory (special things): This activity was accepted by Jenna but not by Rhona, as she was not able to hear positive things about herself that didn't fit with her internal view of herself. We kept it very brief and interspersed noticing positive things about her throughout the session. Done in a more spontaneous manner she was able to accept it.

Lotioning: As this was rejected initially by all of the children, decorative children's Band-Aids were readily accepted for their hurts.

Feather Blow; Motor Boat Motor Boat; Ping Pong Blow; Feather Guess; Feeding

Goodbye Song: Baa Baa Baa Baa Boom. From experience with many other children we thought that Rhona too would be engaged in the boisterous nature of this song, but she rejected being sung to with her usual flair for clearly demonstrating her displeasure. She did however engage in "High 5 Goodbye."

Middle Sessions: More nurturing activities; parents come in and participate

Entrance: Wheelbarrow (a challenging activity which engaged them immediately and began the session on a positive note); Hello Secret Handshake (Hello Song with Jenna);

Inventory: more formalized and focused now as increasing level of trust and slowly feeling more comfortable with hearing positive comments; Lotion Hurts: by this session the children are accepting nurturing and actually pointing out hurts and inviting them to be taken care of by mom; Measuring Muscles;

Paper punch and Basketball; Over/Under with ball; Redlight/Greenlight; Handstacking; Taco Roll

Cotton Ball touch (while still in blanket in mother's lap); Cotton Ball soothe; Feeding; Goodbye High 5

Ending Sessions: Parents leading activities and therapist coaching.

Entrance: Dancing in on mother's feet; Hello Secret Handshake; Inventory (face portrait with pretend paint and soft brush); Lotioning; Butterfly/elephant/Eskimo kisses; Mother May I; Peanut toss; Shapes on Back; Toe touch under blanket (natural progression to Rocking); Rock in Blanket

–"My (*child's name*) lies over the ocean" or "Rock a Bye (*child's name*)." With Leon and Jenna we sang the latter. However, for Rhona we used the former, anticipating her need to maintain dignity coming from a pseudomature stance; Story (Rhona)/Lullaby (Leon and Jenna) and juice (in juice box with mother holding); Feeding; Goodbye Song

ACKNOWLEDGMENTS

We wish to acknowledge the assistance we received from Jamie Sherman and John Breuer and to thank them both for all of their guidance.

REFERENCES

Jernberg, Ann M., and Phyllis B. Booth. (1999) *Theraplay: Helping Parents and Children Build Better Relationships through Attachment-Based Play.* 2nd Ed. San Francisco, Cal: Jossey-Bass Inc.

Knowles, E., and Jay Linn. (2004) *Resistance and Persuasion*. Mahwah, N.J.: Laurence Erlbaum Associates, Inc. knowles.socialpsychology.org. (7 Feb.2008).

Maag, John W. (1999) "Why They Say No: Foundational Precises and Techniques for Managing Resistance," *Focus on Exceptional Children* 32, no. 1 (September): 159–174.

Pierrehumbert, Blaise, Raphaele Miljkovitch, Bernard Plancherel, Oliver Halfon, and Francois Ansermet. (2000) "Attachment and Temperament in Early Childhood; Implications for Later Behaviour Problems." *Infant and Child Development* 9, 17–32.

Ronnlund, M., and Erika Karlsson. (2006) "The Relation Between Dimensions of Attachment and Internalizing or Externalizing Problems during Adolescence." *The Journal of Genetic Psychology* 167, no. 1, 47–63.

Shipman, Kimberly, Renee Schneider, and Sims Chandler. (2005) "Emotion Socialization in Maltreating and Nonmaltreating Mother-Child Dyads: Implications for Children's Adjustment." *Journal of Clinical Child and Adolescent Psychology* 34, no.3, 590–596.

5

Theraplay with Adopted Children

Sandra Lindaman and Dafna Lender

INTRODUCTION

Theraplay®'s goal is to create a healthy connection between parent and child, and its methods are the very kinds of interactions that promote secure attachment. Therefore, Theraplay treatment is extremely useful for preparing and assisting adoptive and foster families to connect and interact. Even children adopted as newborns or during the first year of life may display attachment problems when they join their new families. Older children with histories of loss, neglect, and/or abuse are even more likely to have difficulty establishing new relationships. Parents often are surprised that providing what had been missing in their child's life: a safe environment, affectionate attention, stimulation, and loving provision of basic needs are rejected by the child.

In our experience, children in new adoptive or foster relationships have four basic social-emotional needs on their path to attachment to the primary caregivers: to feel safe; to become physically and emotionally regulated; to experience attuned responsiveness; and to change the negative internal working model of self and others that formed during inadequate care. These needs can be met by their parents through learning the Theraplay philosophy and techniques.

The Uses of the Theraplay Model in Adoption and Foster Care

Theraplay treatment has been used successfully to facilitate new adoptive and foster parent-child connections in many settings and cultures (Lindaman, 1998; Vierikko, 2007). In addition to the direct treatment of parent-child dyads described in this chapter, Theraplay principles have been used as the basis for educational and experiential programs for pre-adoptive parents (Lender and Lindaman, 2007), preventive intervention when children first arrive in their new homes (Walton, 2007), ongoing adoptive parent counseling groups (Bone, 2007), and family group activities in specialized retreat programs (Lindaman 2005).

Even foster children should receive Theraplay services stemming from the belief that a child should not have to wait for permanency to experience security, attunement, co-regulation and a more positive internal working model from a caregiver. In our experience, participation in Theraplay with a foster parent can stabilize a child's placement, thereby reducing relational trauma. Infants and toddlers receiving Theraplay were found to make smoother transitions from foster to adoptive families (Fesperman and Lindaman, 1998.) A Theraplay treatment and research project with long-term foster families in the SOS Children's Villages program in Finland found reduction of the children's internalizing and externalizing problems; parents felt more skilled and children liked the treatment (Makela and Vierikko, 2004).

The Theraplay Treatment Model

Theraplay for all types of children and families provides four essential aspects of healthy parent-child relationships: Structure, Engagement, Nurture, and Challenge. To review, Theraplay provides Structure because it is the basis of safety and internal organization and regulation. Theraplay provides Engagement because it is the essential personal, focused, and attuned connection with the child. Theraplay provides Nurture because all children need it to feel worthy, cared for, and soothed. Theraplay provides developmentally appropriate Challenge because children need it to experience mastery and competence. From the beginning of Theraplay in the 1960s, its intention was to provide positive interpersonal experiences that would change the client's behavior because of a more positive view of the self and world. This view of self and other is now referred to as an internal working model. Theraplay provides the child interpersonal experiences that are non-congruent with their (insecure) internal working model. The mind is then challenged to develop new, healthier knowledge of what it is like to be in a relationship (Lender 2006). Who needs this more than a child who spent her early years in an impersonal orphanage, a chaotic birth family, or multiple foster placements?

Modifications of Theraplay in Adoption and Foster Care

Treatment Choice

A variety of treatment modalities will be helpful to the child and family across the life span to deal with adoption/foster concerns. The therapist should help families to understand treatment options and goals and to decide which issues are prominent at the beginning of treatment. Theraplay is often an appropriate first treatment to work on strengthening relationships. It can be used in combination with or preceding other treatments such as narrative therapy, Eye Movement Desensitization and Reprocessing Therapy (EMDR), and Dyadic Developmental Psychotherapy (DDP). A consideration of the nature and extent of the child's problematic behaviors will help determine whether Theraplay alone or in combination with other methods will be needed to help the child to deal with possible shame he or she has and to be able to heal. Another chapter in this book describes how to combine Theraplay and DDP.

Treatment Length

Theraplay is a "short term" treatment model and indeed often produces changes in behavior patterns quickly, especially in biological families with mild to moderate problems. Overcoming the challenges of complex adoptions, however, takes longer, and therefore the Theraplay treatment period may be lengthened to six to twelve months. Even when the child and parents quickly become adept at the Theraplay interactions, they need an extended period of intense focus on the playful Theraplay philosophy and techniques in order for new healthy brain patterns to be firmly established. In addition it is important to allow adequate time for parent discussion, reflection, and practice.

Inclusion of Parents

The original Theraplay model had parents observing and discussing several sessions with an interpreting therapist before entering the treatment room and interacting with the child. With newly adopted children (less than 6 months), however, parents usually are present in sessions from the start.

Discussing the Child's History

Theraplay was originally designed to focus on the "here and now" without reference to or processing of past events. In treatment sessions with adoptive families, we verbally acknowledge the child's early situation (of deprivation, loss, neglect, abuse, etc.) as the opportunity arises. This frequently happens during nurturing activities, but could happen during any activity. Furthermore, a more overt explanation of the purpose of treatment is offered right from the beginning, e.g., learning how to be part of a family, learning to be a son to this mother.

Working with Parents

Since parenting an adopted/foster child is very challenging, parent work is critical. Adopted/foster children need a more therapeutic environment than many families are aware of, or, in some cases, are able to provide. Parents need to learn about attachment and brain development, the effect of relational trauma, the importance of attunement, as well as how to understand the intentions and needs of their specific child. They also need to understand that raising a child with attachment issues may trigger their own attachment history. Time must be set aside for parents to discuss these issues with the therapist outside of the child's direct treatment sessions. Parents can be referred for additional help, if necessary. The parents' willingness and ability to learn to carry out attuned, structured, and nurturing interactions on a moment to moment basis at home is critical to the success of treatment.

The Theraplay Dimensions Applied to the Needs of Adoptive or Foster Families

The Need for Emotional Safety

The question: "Does the child feel safe?" should be considered by the parents and the therapist during the intake interview. It may be difficult for a parent to accept that a child who has been living in a caring adoptive home for some time feels unsafe, but behaviors such as verbal and physical aggression, tantrums, running away, hiding, unresponsiveness, and trying to control can be related to a child's fear. Trauma researcher Perry reminds us,

"If a child has been exposed to extreme or pervasive threat or trauma, his stress system may become sensitized and he may respond to ordinary experiences as though they are threatening"(Perry, 2007, p. 249). The child's responses may move along a continuum in the direction of dissociation or arousal. The more distressed or threatened the child is, the more primitive the level of brain functioning, behaviors, and response. Trauma researchers now recognize that "Complex Trauma," defined as multiple traumatic events that occur between a primary caregiver and child, cause seven primary domains of impairment: attachment, biology, affect regulation, dissociation, behavioral regulation, cognition, and self-concept (NCTS, 2003). Perry advises, "To help traumatized children these responses must be taken into account and their stress response systems calmed so they can feel safe enough to rely upon their higher brain functions and reduce the amount of time they spend on the arousal continuum" (2007, p.250). Adoption expert Purvis reminds us that "fear will bully your child into poor behavior" (2007, p. 49). Purvis describes the appropriate intervention as "Disarming the fear response with felt safety" (2007, p. 47) and the following concepts as contributing to "felt safety": "The parent is a kind, but firm and confident leader; Shows emotional warmth and affection consistently; Offers positive emotional responses and praise often; Responds attentively and kindly to the child's words and actions; Interacts playfully with the child; Physically matches child's voice and behavior; Sensitive to child's tolerance for sounds, touch, distance" (2007, p. 52).

The structure of the Theraplay session and Theraplay's overall emphasis on the adult as the leader provides the child with the experience of felt safety. Theraplay sessions are organized, calming, and reassuring, and contain the right amount of stimulation for a given child. The therapist and the parent are the leaders in a warm, kind, and responsive way. Activities are simple. The level of challenge is manageable and done in a cooperative spirit, ensuring that the parent-child play is enjoyable. If a child becomes dysregulated in a session, the incident can be dealt with on the spot. For example, voices become louder in play and the child suddenly turns away. The adult responds, "I think that got so loud it bothered you, let me see if I can do it again quietly—let's see if that is more comfortable."

Parent education includes the stressful effect of relational trauma on brain development and function. We teach parents to recognize that the child's difficult behaviors are related to triggers of stressful past experiences. We advise adoptive/foster parents to provide younger forms of structure in daily activities such as using simple rules, reducing choices, setting clear limits, keeping the child physically close and monitoring behavior, recognizing the difficulty of transitions, and offering interactive assistance rather than only verbal directions.

Physical and Emotional Regulation

Theraplay meets the most basic need of an adopted child: the provision of a self-regulating other. Children who have experienced a loss of a caregiver and/or inadequate early caregiving require a responsive and attuned caregiver to co-regulate their physical and emotional states. Theraplay interactions provide multiple opportunities for such co-regulation. The therapist co-regulates with the child and the parent, and helps the parent to establish these rhythms with the child.

> What we do in Theraplay is to intervene at the appropriate physiologic level to connect with this type of child and capture the "attention" of his right brain. For example: grabbing a child's hand and making a game of "ring around the rosy" out of a child who was previously running around the room chaotically, and then quickly placing him in your lap, facing out, and making finger prints in play dough or feeding him something chewy, is a common Theraplay sequence. What happened on a regulatory level is that the therapist met the child at his highly aroused level and helped to organize it, and then quickly provided

> both the structure and the engagement to help him calm down and focus his attention on a more soothing level, being ever mindful that because the child's whole system is overstimulated and reactive, it is best not to insist on face to face contact but use body contact, which is less intense. (It is possible that with certain sexually or physically abused children, body contact, even with the child facing out, can also be too interpersonally intense. This needs to be determined on a case by case basis by the therapist.) (Lender, 2006, p. 2).

The Experience of Attuned Responsiveness

Theraplay's dimension of engagement, or attuned connection with the child, provides many opportunities for attuned responsiveness. We achieve this attuned connection by focusing exclusively on the child and not on toys, games, or symbolic objects; using simple preverbal, physically interactive play; noticing the child's special attributes; and reacting to feeling states by soothing distress and amplifying pleasure. Children with inadequate early caregiving have not had enough of these critical experiences. The response is often just an attuned statement of having noticed, but being noticed makes all the difference. For example: At the beginning of a session of a very self-sufficient three-year-old child in foster care, the therapist begins to check "what the child brought with her today," finding ten warm fingers and toes that wiggle. The child raises her hands to her own eyes and the therapist says "oh you brought your hands for playing peek a boo" and rounds of gentle peek a boo with the child's hands and feet follow.

Theraplay also creates opportunities for intense interpersonal experiences that involve many moments of surprise, For example:

> You are quietly studying a child's face in Theraplay and he reaches out to touch your nose and you make a resounding "BEEEEEP" sound, the child is suddenly completely alert and, looking straight into your eyes, the child giggles spontaneously at the surprising, funny shared event between the two of you, and you laugh in turn. The discrepancy between what the child expected and what actually happened is surprising. This element of surprise, so important in Theraplay, is the growing edge for a child to learn that new things can happen, but that these new things can be both fun/exciting *and* safe. (Lender, 2006, p. 2)

Parents are guided to initiate simple routines using the nonverbal paths to attachment: facial expression, eye contact, affect, touch, voice, and play to demonstrate to the child that "You are no longer alone and I understand you."

Changing a Negative Internal Working Model

Here we arrive at the change in the child that allows him to no longer rely on his dysfunctional behaviors. Children often develop coping behaviors such as the avoidance of intimacy or the need to control others, in order to deal with the negative experiences they have endured before reaching their adoptive families. Parents experience these behaviors as intentional and manipulative on the child's part. The Theraplay therapist helps parents empathize with the child's need for such behaviors and helps the child move beyond them.

> For example, when a child is struggling in a Theraplay session and pushes you away with his legs, you say "Boy you've got strong legs! I bet you can't push me over with these legs on the count of three!" and then hold his two feet in the palm of your hand, count to three, the child pushes and you rock backwards with a big "OOOOHHHH" sound. When you come back up, you see the child's face has changed from defensive fear to a moment of proud delight. What just happened? By reframing and organizing his resistance into a moment of reciprocal play, you have given the child an opportunity to experience himself as strong, clever and most importantly still *connected* to the adult rather than bad, rejected and isolated. You have given him new meaning for what it means to be him. (Lender, 2006, p. 1)

CASE EXAMPLE

Consider how the Theraplay model met the needs of an adoptive child and parent through a clinical vignette from the treatment of Heather and her adoptive mother Melissa.

Heather was a five-year-old girl with a history of emotional and physical neglect prior to placement with her adoptive mother at three years of age. When she was first adopted, she was small and weak, and her speaking skills were underdeveloped, suggesting significant neglect in her previous placements. Behaviorally, she displayed severe behavioral problems. After two years in her adoptive home, Heather's motor and verbal skills greatly improved, but she continued to display emotional dysregulation with frequent tantrums, aggression, difficulty with transitions, and low frustration tolerance. Heather especially resisted letting anyone touch her. When her mother tried to cuddle her, Heather would subtly push Melissa away by poking her eyes or pulling her hair. Heather appeared purposefully reckless, often walking wildly and falling to the ground. At these times, she did not cry or look to her parent for soothing or reassurance. After doing an extensive intake and MIM, Heather's therapist chose to focus on the following goals: helping the mother engage in simple activities that would capture Heather's interest and lead to genuine moments of playful connection between mother and child. The simplicity and interpersonal nature of the activities would allow the mother to attune to Heather's reactions and regulate her affect as needed. Another goal was to find ways to soothe, calm, and nurture Heather in ways she could accept. Helping Heather feel more relaxed while interacting with her parent, would lead to a greater sense of comfort and trust, a sense that she was a pleasure to be with and she could depend on mom. It was hoped that these changes would lead to a lessening of Heather's problematic behaviors. Furthermore, the therapist would work with the mother on understanding Heather's younger needs and managing daily routines to accommodate those needs.

With a big smile on her face, Heather bounded into the therapist's waiting room. She ran up to the therapist, looked into her eyes very intently and followed her down the hall without hesitation, while mom followed behind. At the treatment room entrance, the therapist pointed to the seat she had prepared and said, "Okay Heather, hold your mom's hand and I'll count how many big steps it takes you to get to that pillow." At the pillow the therapist took their hands and declared, "On the count of three we're going to sit down, one-two-three!" Heather sat down before she realized she had complied. Sitting across from Heather, with her mom sitting to her side on another pillow, the therapist said, "Heather, you've come here to play with Mom and me so that you can learn how to have fun and let your mom take care of you. I'm going to be playing these games with you too. But just because I play these games with you, doesn't mean that I'm going to be your Mom. This (pointing) is your Mom." Heather looked quizzically at the therapist and nodded her head. The therapist proceeded to engage Heather in some typical first-session Theraplay games: she counted her fingers, found a "beep" when she touched her nose, cared for small hurts on Heather's hands, blew a cotton ball back and forth, and shaped aluminum foil around her hands and feet to make special prints.

Just as the session was about to end, Heather jumped up and off her pillow seat and opened the therapist's supply cabinet. Heather's mom, still sitting on her pillow, shouted across the room "No Heather, that's not our stuff, don't touch that!" She then got up and walked over to Heather and gave her a long explanation about other people's personal belongings and asking permission to do things. Heather pouted momentarily, and then melted into a crying tantrum. These were the kinds of dysregulated behaviors she typically displayed at home. The therapist got up, put her hand on mom's shoulder and said gently "Heather can't be reasoned with right now, because she's so upset. Can you try just scooping her up and holding her without saying anything?" Melissa gave the therapist a worried look and responded "I've tried doing that, but she kicks and punches me so hard that I get hurt. It seems to make things worse." With Heather's screaming continuing, the therapist quickly pulled out some play dough and bent down to Heather's level. "LOOK!" she said, pushing Heather's thumb into it, making a print. Heather stopped for a brief second to inspect the thumbprint, and then continued wailing. The therapist pulled out a juice box from her bag and slipped in the straw, then handed it to Heather. Heather pushed it away with a frown, but looked interested. The therapist set the juice box down in front of Heather and moved away. Heather then tentatively picked it up and began drinking, sniffling and rubbing her eyes. With a heavy sigh, Heather began to calm down from her tantrum. The therapist then said "Heather, I think you wanted to know what was in my closet. I think it's good to check things out when you're in a new place. I'm sorry I didn't tell you what was in my closet." The therapist proceeded to open the closet door and generally described some items inside. Heather nodded and looked weary. Heather's therapist then suggested a special way to end the session by doing a "Sock and Shoe Race." The therapist instructed Heather, "You get to say 'READY, SET, GO!" Heather hesitated and then said the signal words, and the race began. The therapist let mom win and Heather seemed mildly amused by the process. The session now over, Heather's therapist arranged a phone appointment with Melissa to talk about the session.

Later that day on the phone, the therapist explored Melissa's assumptions about why Heather ran and opened up the supply closet. The therapist guessed that Heather wanted to know what was behind the closed doors so she could know what to expect would happen in the sessions. In other words, to increase her sense of control. The therapist discussed the important idea that children with Heather's background typically feel very unsafe when they do not know what is going to happen, and will try to do anything to increase their ability to predict their uncertain world. Furthermore, the therapist explained that children with Heather's profile feel a lot of shame when they are given the slightest reprimand, and become very dysregulated in response. This explained why Heather became so uncooperative and miserable after Mom gave her the long lecture about not touching other people's stuff. They then discussed more developmentally appropriate strategies such as prevention, distraction, or a mild reprimand with an opportunity for a quick repair of the relationship, after the incident occurred.

These types of debriefing conversations occurred frequently over the course of treatment and were instrumental in helping Melissa learn to understand, deeply, the underlying motivations for Heather's troubling behaviors. Over the course of time, Melissa became much more empathic to Heather's need for safety and found many ways to meet them, before Heather's anxiety prompted her to engage in inappropriate behavior.

Over the course of treatment, the therapist modeled these kinds of reparative interactions for Melissa in the Theraplay sessions. For instance, the first time the therapist placed a bean bag on her own head and told Heather to hold out her hands and catch it on the count of three, Heather did not succeed in catching the bean bag, so she grabbed it and threw it across the room. The therapist said, "I think you weren't sure what was going to happen, I'll show you." The therapist slowed her pace and repeated the activity in an easier way, until Heather was successful.

In the Nurture dimension, there was much work to do to get Heather to accept care from her mother. Lotioning hurts was an activity that was initiated from the first session onwards. At first the therapist demonstrated the activity, but from the second session onwards, Heather's mother was always the one to look for and put lotion on Heather's hurts. Heather tried to deny that she had any hurts at the beginning of treatment, saying, "That's not a scratch, that's marker." The therapist instructed Mom not to argue about Heather's statements, but simply to say, "I'm going to put some lotion on it anyway." After several sessions, Heather no longer denied having "owwies" and let her Mom lotion them.

Because it was so hard for Heather to accept care and comfort from her mother in the form of food, a special ritual was developed to initiate the feeding at the end of the session. The therapist made a "special delivery" of Heather to her mother's lap. She scooped her up in a cradled position and swung her to her mom while singing, "I have a little Heather, and she's going to her Mommy, one-two-three." The therapist would place Heather gently in her Mom's lap. Feeding, juice, and the Twinkle song ("Twinkle, Twinkle, little star, What a special girl you are"—see appendix) would take place in this position. While Heather was not pressured to look at her mom or even face her, Mom fed Heather the animal crackers and gave her the juice. At first Heather protested, wanting to hold the bag. But the therapist matter-of-factly reassured her: "We know that you can feed yourself, but in here Heather, remember that you're practicing how to be a daughter to your mom." Heather would look at the therapist as though she was letting this message sink in. The therapist would continue: "Because when you were a baby, you didn't get to be fed a lot by your first mom." The therapist waited and watched Heather's face to *gauge* the effect of this statement on Heather. Heather looked focused and interested. "See Heather, your first mom was so young that she didn't know how to take care of you so well. That's why we practice in here, so you know what it feels like to be taken care of." Heather looked at her Mom, who looked tenderly back. Melissa held up a cracker to Heather's mouth and Heather opened her mouth and ate it. From then on, Heather accepted Melissa's feeding her crackers.

Heather and Melissa participated in 26 sessions over 6 months of treatment. Throughout, Melissa and the therapist communicated to Heather through their leadership of the session activities and their pleasant facial expressions, warm voice, and calm touch, that they enjoyed being with Heather, they had ideas for pleasant things they could do together, and they were confident that they could help Heather calm down if she was upset.

The Theraplay sessions taught Melissa how to stay connected with Heather and provide nurturing, soothing experiences. In turn, Heather became much more accepting of her mother's physical contact and began to turn to her for comfort and support. Melissa told of one triumphal moment when Heather turned six and got a bike without training wheels. Heather had almost completely mastered riding the bike and Melissa was no longer running beside her. Melissa looked down for a second as Heather was several yards away and heard Heather fall. Melissa ran to Heather and saw her knee had been mildly scraped. Heather looked up at Melissa and started to cry, reached her arms up and let Melissa pick her up. Heather put her head on her mom's shoulder and rubbed her nose, and then became quiet. Melissa described this as "a moment in heaven."

SUMMARY/CONCLUSION

Theraplay is uniquely suited to meet the relationship-building needs of families created through adoption and fostering. These needs can be substantially met by the parents through Theraplay-guided awareness and interactions: to feel safe, to experience attuned responsiveness, to become physically and emotionally regulated, and to change the negative internal working model of self and others that formed during inadequate care. Additionally, parents need to understand and empathize with the child's underlying emotional needs and have ways to therapeutically respond to those needs. Theraplay therapy provides adoptive parents with these experiential and educational opportunities to master these parenting skills.

REFERENCES

Bone, A. (2007). SAFE: Strengthening Adoptive Families-England. Poster session at the 3rd Annual International Theraplay Conference, Chicago, IL, July 2007.

Booth, P. B. and Lindaman, S. L. (2000). Theraplay as a Short Term Treatment for Enhancing Attachment in Adopted Children. In H. G. Kaduson and C. E. Schaefer (Eds.) *Short Term Play Therapy for Children*. New York: The Guilford Press.

Complex Trauma in Children and Adolescents. White paper from the National Child Traumatic Stress Network. www.NCTSNet.org.

Fesperman, L. and Lindaman, S. L. (December 1998/January 1999). Theraplay Reaches Difficult to Engage Children in Foster Care. In *Bulletin of Zero to Three: National Center for Infants, Toddlers, and Families, 19*, 3, 34–35.

Makela, J. and Vierikko, I. (2004). From Heart to Heart: Theraplay Research at SOS Children's Villages Finland. Espoo, Finland: SOS Children's Village Association.

Perry, B. D. (2006). Applying Principles of Neurodevelopment to Clinical Work with Maltreated and Traumatized Children: The Neurosequential Model of Therapeutics. In N. B. Webb (Ed.), Working with Traumatized Youth in Child Welfare. NY: Guiford, p. 27–52.

Lender, D. (2006). What's Behind These Theraplay Activities: A Window into Attachment." TTI Newsletter. Summer 2006.

Lender, D. and Lindaman, S. (2007). Attachment-Based Parenting Skills for Newly Adoptive Parents. Curriculum developed for Presentation August 25, 2007, The Theraplay Institute, Wilmette, IL.

Lindaman, S. (1999). Theraplay for Children Who Have Been Adopted or in Foster Care in Jernberg, A. M. and Booth, P. B. *Theraplay: Helping Parents and Children Build Better Relationships Through Attachment Based Play*, Second Edition. San Francisco: Jossey-Bass. p. 291–334.

Lindaman, S. (2005). Theraplay Goes to Family Camp. Article in TTI Newsletter Summer 2005, pp. 4 and 11.

Vierikko, I. (2007). Theraplay as an International Intervention; Training Theraplay Tutors in Botswana, Africa. Presentation at the 3rd Annual International Theraplay Conference, Chicago, IL July 2007.

Walton, L. (2007). Proactive Use of Theraplay with Adoptive Families. Presentation at the 3rd Annual International Theraplay Conference, Chicago, IL, July 2007.

6

Theraplay Approaches for Children with Autism Spectrum Disorders

Paris Goodyear-Brown

A nine-year-old boy with Asperger's Syndrome bemoans his difficulty making friends and sums up his resulting self-perception with the statement "I guess I'm a jerk." A four-year-old boy with Pervasive Development Disorder NOS is days away from being moved to a more restrictive learning environment for extremely destructive behaviors. The mother of a 7-year-old boy diagnosed with autism cries in my office, grieving the lack of connectedness she has with her own son. All of these children have Autism Spectrum Disorders (ASDs) and all of them can be helped through Theraplay®.

The Autism Spectrum Disorders are neuro-developmental disorders characterized by deficits in three main areas: impairment in social interaction, impairment in communication abilities, and unusually restricted interests, behaviors, and play patterns. These clients may also have some rigidity in their need for routines and some perseveration on topics that they care about. These clients are usually social outliers in their peer groups, because of their differences from typically developing peers. While the specific causes of ASDs are unknown, the incidence of these disorders is 10 times what it was 10 years ago. Although the onset is usually within the first two years of life, the average age of diagnosis is between 3 and 4 years of age. Autism is 4 times more common in males than in females. A new case of autism is diagnosed every 20 minutes and 24,000 new cases are diagnosed each year (Stats from the Center for Disease Control and Autism Speaks websites, September, 2007).

When autism first began to be diagnosed, the cause was often and regrettably ascribed to lack of nurture in the parent. As the knowledge base for these disorders has grown, this damaging assumption has been dismantled.

However, the pain that a parent feels at the lack of connectedness she may have with her child cannot be over-estimated.

One of the hallmarks of all ASDs is impairment in areas of social relatedness. Children with these diagnoses face many challenges in building relationships, first with their parents and later with the expanding microcosms of childhood. Early social development is reliant on the interplay between the "self" and the "other." Typically, developing infants come equipped with neurologically pre-determined preference for human interaction. For example, a newborn baby is able to focus his eyesight between 8 and 12 inches away from his face. This is the distance between the crook of a caregiver's arm and the caregiver's face. Infants are generally fascinated by faces and begin reacting to emotional changes in a caregiver's face very early in life. The baby coos and the mother responds with her own "babytalk." The baby learns that he can impact his world. Babies at 6 weeks old begin practicing social smiles.

Imagine a mother who comes into her baby's room in the morning, leans over the crib rail, and says "Good morning, sweet boy!" while smiling warmly at him. Her baby (whose mirror neurons are being activated) smiles back at her with a sweet drooly grin and begins to kick his legs gleefully. The baby's response is gratifying for the mom who experiences spontaneous delight in her ability to engender joy in her baby. The baby too is delighted with his newfound abilities and may experiment by initiating a smile and lifting up his arms to be held. This signal is quickly and correctly read by mom who picks the baby up and holds him close while nuzzling his head and murmuring sweet baby talk in his ear. These circles of communication are opened and closed by baby and caregiver alike. It is the thousands upon thousands of repetitions of these early interactions that set the developing person on a path toward social proficiency. The success of this cycling is reliant, at least in part, on the neuro-developmental platforms in the developing infant that make him hungry for social interaction.

In contrast, consider the baby who may later be diagnosed with an ASD. Mom comes into the room, leans over the crib rail and says "Good morning, sweet boy!" with a big grin on her face. The baby may turn toward the noise, but stares at a particular facial feature instead of making eye contact. The baby may have almost no change in affect or may even become agitated by the interruption and may quickly return to staring at his mobile. The mother may feel inadequate and puzzled. She may even internalize the baby's response as rejection. Although her own desire may be to reach for her baby and pull him close, he appears to be most soothed by remaining in his crib and watching his mobile. By leaving the child to self-soothe, the parent is accurately reading the child's cue and giving the child what he wants, but not necessarily what he needs.

Whereas typically developing children are soothed and restored through the physical touch and nuture of a caregiver, children with ASDs may find touch to be overstimulating or even aversive. Since they may not have the neurological scaffolding to encode touch positively, children with ASDs may become dysregulated, arching away from parents who attempt to physically connect with them. A parent whose efforts to lovingly connect with her child are met with screams may understandably choose the path of least resistance and pull back from physical overtures of affection. When a child is underresponsive to the social bids of a parent, the treatment plan is counterintuitive. The child needs more intense dosing of relationally connecting experiences in order to compensate for his natural tendency toward isolation. The neurological differences of the child with an ASD sets up a scenario in which the "dose" of relational experiences provided by the parent is not satisfactorily absorbed. Theraplay allows for a more intense and focused "dosing" of health-promoting dimensions of the parent/child relationship.

The mnemonic device "Every Child Needs Something" is useful in remembering the four dimensions of Theraplay.[1] The "E" stands for Engagement, the ability that the parent has to catch and extend the attention of a child through fun. The "C" stands for Challenge, the ability of the parent to gauge the child's current level of mastery and encourage him or her toward activities that allow for growth and result in a sense of success, competence and increased self-esteem. The "N" stands for Nurture, the Theraplay dimension aimed at helping parents provide safe, positive, contingently responsive caretaking experiences for the child. The "S" stands for Structure, the ability of the parent to order the environment, set clear expectations and boundaries and enforce appropriate limits with the child. The mnemonic device "Every Child Needs Something" begs the question "What does the child with an ASD need?" Of course there is no single definitive answer, but treatment often begins in the context of activities that heighten engagement between parent and child.

While more research is needed on the effectiveness of Theraplay with children with ASDs, some preliminary data exists. Wettig, Franke, and Fjordbak (2006) conducted two separate studies evaluating the effectiveness of Theraplay interventions. Fifty-six children who evidenced "autistic like lack of social mutuality" on the German validated CASCAP-D showed a reduction in symptoms and an increase in social mutuality after 26 thirty-minute sessions of Theraplay. It is important to note that significantly more sessions were needed to affect this social mutuality deficit than were needed for many other externalizing or internalizing behavior disorders.

The DIR/Floortime model created by Stanley Greenspan and explicated in the book *Engaging Autism* (2006), utilizes an approach with aspects that are very similar to Theraplay. DIR/Floortime interventions begin by following the child's lead, but then move into a series of games and activities aimed at promoting engagement in much the same way as the directive interventions prescribed in Theraplay. The book reviews Greenspan and Weider's research on 200 cases of children with ASDs who received two or more years of Floortime Intervention. In their outcome summary, 58 percent of patients moved into the "good to outstanding" range as evidenced by their shift into the nonautistic range on the Childhood Autism Rating Scale. These childrens' abilities to engage, reciprocate social bids and solve social problems all improved dramatically. Another 25 percent made moderate gains in these same areas. Based on this preliminary data, it can be hypothesized that the pleasurable engagements with caregivers that occur during Theraplay and Floortime activities provide the scaffolding for successful growth in areas of social relatedness.

Case 1

By selectively using the Theraplay activities that promote engagement, children with ASDs can access their parents more effectively and learn to find basic social interactions pleasurable. The case of Ethan, a 4-year-old with Pervasive Developmental Disorder NOS illustrates this point. When Ethan came to treatment, his mother was desperate for any kind of help. Ethan was having extreme acting out behavior in his classroom, consisting of hitting other children, biting, pulling off all his clothes and running around the classroom in circles. On a number of occasions Ethan had actually run out of the classroom. In one such instance, he was halfway across the parking lot before a teacher caught him! He had severe speech and language delays, and was receiving Speech Therapy, but mom reported little improvement.

During our initial session together, the client merely grunted and avoided any of my attempts to engage him. He would let mom touch him, but did not respond affectively or gesturally to her attempts at engagement. He was not yet potty trained, and his interest in the toys was restricted to carefully arranging them. He was not able to engage in joint attention tasks with mom and ignored all attempts on her part to set limits.

The parent was originally given skills for reflecting and describing the child's play. Ethan began to play in the dollhouse and Mom consistently reflected his play behaviors. Ethan proceeded to organize the toys in the dollhouse without sharing his attention with Mom in any way. Typically developing children will elaborate verbally on behavioral descriptions made by the parent. The parent says, "You put the baby in the bed." The child gives more information by saying, "She's taking a nap." The child might draw the parent's attention to a toy by pointing and saying "Look mommy, a pretend potty!" Ethan did none of these things. He seemed to be completely unaffected by Mom's attempts to verbally connect with him. Mom persevered for several minutes and then turned to me with a helpless countenance and a resigned shrug of her shoulders. Mom needed intervention that would heighten engagement with Ethan.

Ethan shifted his focus to the sandtray and began burying his hands. Children with ASDs often have sensory integration issues, and can be calmed and grounded by the kinesthetic sensations of running their hands through sand. I said to mom, "Let's try something different. The next time that he buries his hands in the sand, you ask "Where are Ethan's hands?" and move your own hands through the sand until they find his." Mom followed my directions and exclaimed with delight as she touched his fingers under the sand, "There is Ethan's hand! I found it!" Ethan's demeanor did not change, he did not look up and make eye contact with Mom, and he made no verbalizations. However, he stuck his hands deliberately back under the sand again in a way that communicated, "Do it again!" Mom and Ethan played this game several more times and the engagement became more pronounced each time. Ethan would tense his body as she searched for his fingers and then giggle when she found them. After several rounds of this hide-and-seek hand game, Mom turned to look at me and said "You know, we used to play count the piggies before bed every night when he was little."

Ethan climbed up into the sandtray and buried his feet. I said to mom, "Oh, look, Ethan's feet want to play, too." Mom played the game with Ethan's feet several times. I asked mom to take a little longer to find the toes the next time in order to build the client's anticipation. Mom slid her hand under the sand and right up to his toes while asking the same question "Where are Ethan's TO-OOO-oooes?" and in the pause between her asking and her finding, Ethan looked at her and smiled. This was the first spontaneously connected moment in treatment for mother and child. The quick delight in playing one of his "baby games" was clear. For homework, Mom and client were instructed to play "count the piggies" and have some rocking and singing time each morning.

At their second session, I began by having Mom and Ethan play the "Slippery, Slippery, Slip" game (see appendix). I had Mom rub lotion on the child's arm, hold it firmly while saying "Slippery, Slippery, Slip" and pull her hands down Ethan's arm. Ethan slipped away and Mom fell back in an exaggerated way. It was once again in the moments of anticipation that Ethan looked at Mom intently, and when he pulled free he squealed in a high pitch tone and giggled. After each round of the game, he would thrust his arm out again, sending the non-verbal message, "I want more please.'" I gave voice to his non-verbal gesture by saying, "Looks like his arm is saying 'More, please,'" and I highlighted for Mom how much Ethan was enjoying playing with her. My conscientious attempt to pair words with the client's gestures was aimed at stimulating his expressive language abilities.

Later in the session, mom held Ethan on her lap and fed him a lollipop while telling him a story about when he was a baby. Although Ethan clearly enjoyed the lollipop, he showed no sign of attending to the story. He stared off to the side of mom's head and seemed not to hear her. After telling part of her story (a very sweet story about how he put his whole face in his birthday cake and had an icing beard) and getting no noticeable feedback from him, Mom turned to me bleakly and said, "Well, I tried." What struck me most about this was Mom's clear sense of inadequacy and rejection in the face of Ethan's apparent indifference. One of the unique dynamics involved in Theraplay is the support and nurture that the Theraplay therapist can provide to the parent at a time like this. The Theraplay therapist can help the parent press in to relationship even in the face of unresponsiveness in the child.

Once again I said, "Let's try something different." I then instructed Mom to sit on the floor with the client facing her on her lap. I showed her a high intensity, high movement version of "Row, Row, Row Your Boat." Mom began to rock Ethan almost all the way to the ground and back up onto her lap in time to the rhythm of the song. As I was continuing to test my hypothesis that Ethan's engagement was most intense when he was anticipating what came next, I asked Mom to pause in the rocking and singing at an unexpected interval. Mom and child rocked as mom sang, "Row, Row, Row your boat, gently down the—." She paused in both her words and her rocking and was instantly rewarded with eye contact from Ethan. His eyes stayed glued to hers with an ever-widening smile as she grinned with anticipation and finally said "stream." He squealed with delight and the process began again. For Ethan, the power of the pause was his hook into engagement with his mother. This revelation informed the rest of our sessions. Whichever Theraplay activities I chose, I would help mother and son into a comfortable rhythm and then interrupt it to catch Ethan's full attention.

During the third session, Ethan spontaneously began to repeat words that mom was saying. Mom said "Do you want to color?" Ethan said "color." Mom made a simple shape and Ethan copied it. I suggested that mom draw his hands. Ethan looked at mom and said, "I . . . want . . . hands." Mom and I both celebrated Ethan's communication success, saying, "You did such a good job using your words. Your mom knows exactly what you want, and she's going to give it to you." Ethan kept his hands still and his eyes focused on the paper as I structured the intervention by making comments like, "Now mom's moving the marker around your thumb; she knows just how to draw your hands!" At the end of the activity, the client lifted his hands and smiled. Mom and Ethan were both on their tummies with their heads close together. After seeing his hands drawn, he suddenly moved his face in toward Mom's and, much to Mom's amazement, Ethan rubbed his nose against hers. This was the first spontaneous gesture of affection that Ethan had initiated since the start of treatment. Mom was in tears later as she talked about how unexpected and touching his gesture had been. Mother and son were sent home with more Theraplay activities that were high in engagement and nurture.

By the fifth session, Ethan looked significantly different. He and Mom played an attunement game. Ethan played in the sandtray with his back toward mom. He would make a sound and Mom would respond with a matching sound. Then Mom would make a sound and he would repeat it. Frequently he glanced over toward her and smiled. At one point Mom commented on his play in the sandtray, and he surprised us both by saying, "You can play, too, mommy." The rapid expressive language gains were astonishing.

The connectedness to Mom and the suprisingly pleasurable rewards of interpersonal interaction triggered an explosion in his verbal communication abilities. In essence, Theraplay helped to activate Ethan's non-verbal communication which provided the foundation for expressive language. His forays into one-word articulations were rewarded with more engagement and fun with Mom, creating a positive feedback loop that led to the quick expansion of his speech. Theraplay increased mom's awareness of her child's non-verbal cues and taught her how to extend the moments of connection, while the intrinsic delight that Ethan experienced, sparked his spoken communication.

The social deficits of children with ASDs manifest themselves in many different ways as children age: lack of eye contact, lack of reciprocity and turn taking, difficulty understanding and responding to the social bids of others, difficulty in accurately perceiving non-verbal cues, and difficulty understanding and utilizing social conventions. Structuring interventions in which the cues are based on eye contact and other non-verbal communications have been extremely effective in helping clients with ASDs to make treatment gains in the social arena. The magic of Theraplay is that the challenge and engagement of the dyadic game play induces high motivation for attending to social cues. Another case example will illustrate the use of Structuring/Challenging interventions.

Case 2

John, age 9, presented with all of the impairments listed above and perseveration on the subject of the Titanic and how it sank. Many children with ASDs have a restricted range of interests (in John's case, books about the Titanic) combined with limited awareness that their fascination is not shared by peers. I did an experiment during John's first session to see if he could accurately perceive or respond to my non-verbal cues. He began talking about the Titanic and after 15 minutes of perseveration on this topic, I began to look at my watch in an obvious way. John kept on talking. I yawned and stretched my arms over my head. John kept on talking. I got up from my seat and went to look out the window. John kept on talking.

The treatment plan for John was heavy on interventions that required accurate cue reading. Successive approximation was used to shape the games from word-based cues to non-verbal cues. We began with the Bean Bag Drop, but instead of a bean bag we used an object that fit within his restricted range of interests (a toy boat that we called the Titanic). After I modeled the game, mom put the boat on her head and chose a cue word: Titanic. Mom looked at John, who had his hands outstretched to catch the boat. Mom said two or three other words that started with similar sounds, requiring John to employ self-control until the correct word was given. Mom said, "Tickle . . . tiny . . . Titanic!" and let the boat slide off her head and into John's eager hands. John caught it and smiled widely. I reinforced both mom and John for working so well together and highlighted how patiently John waited for the right cue word.

John asked to play again. This time we shifted from a verbal cue to a non-verbal cue. Mom chose a wink as her cue, requiring John to make eye contact with her. Mom wiggled her nose, puckered her mouth, and then winked. John again caught the boat and was reinforced for his close attention to Mom's non-verbal cues. Parent and child then switched roles and John got to choose the cue word and later a non-verbal signal. Interestingly, John wanted his non-verbal signal to be one of his stereotypic movements. Repetitive movements or stereotypy is another symptom that a child with an ASD may manifest.

John's sterotypic behavior was the rapid movement of his eyes from side to side instead of making eye contact with people. He could move his eyes so quickly that it looked as if they were jiggling. We helped John come up with a non-verbal signal that approximated a longer gaze. John jiggled his eyes for a moment, then forced himself to gaze at mom solidly for one second to communicate that he was dropping the boat. Mom successfully caught the boat and was thrilled to have several experiences of prolonged connectedness through John's extended gazes. The other activities for the session included a "bubble popping game," the "Newspaper Punch" activity, and the "Dyadic Dance" (see appendix), all of which we played first with word cues and then with more and more subtle non-verbal cues. As John's finesse in accurately reading mom's cues increased, so did the size of his smile. After one iteration of the Dyadic Dance, I commented on how well they moved together and how much they seemed to be a real team. John spontaneously hugged Mom tightly and said, "I love you Mom."

Often, I will intensify the non-verbal cue even more by structuring it with a verbal count. If John is currently making eye contact for 1/2 a second with Mom before dropping the boat, I might say "O.K. Mom, we're going to surprise you this time, so watch carefully." I then whisper to the client, "I'm gonna count to three and then you drop it." Slowly increasing the challenge by increasing the length of time the gaze is held prior to the release of the object can help shape a child's tolerance for and enjoyment of eye contact.

Another activity I created to help with non-verbal cueing is the "Eyeball Toss." John sat at one corner of an invisible triangle while Mom and I sat at the other points. I gave John a squashy, gooey ball that resembled an eyeball. His job was to make eye contact with the person to whom he was going to roll the ball. The game continued with everyone signaling through eye contact. The speed of play and the distance between people can be varied to make the game more challenging. John asked to play this game repeatedly and his eye contact increased significantly over the course of treatment.

A child's impairments in reciprocity and turn taking can be helped by all of the above mentioned activities and several specific activities listed below. In the game "Mirror, Mirror on the Wall" the parent and child face each other. The parent slowly moves her body and the child moves his body with hers so that each looks like a reflection of the other. The parent and child can later switch roles. This game requires the child to become aware of his body in space and in relationship to his caregiver. Moreover, he must use his peripheral vision and try to take in the overall movement of the parent's body instead of hyperfocusing on one attribute of the non-verbal communication, which is their natural tendency.

Another useful game is called "Instrument Attunement." For this game, both the child and parent have a maraca or other musical instrument. The parent plays a simple rhythm and the child copies it. The rhythms can increase in complexity as long as the child remains successful in his reciprocation of the rhythm. The parent can also vary the speed or the loudness of the instrument. This game requires the child to pay attention to the communication being sent by the parent and replicate it. Then the child can set the rhythm and have the parent repeat it.

Typically developing children intuitively internalize the unspoken rules that apply to physical proximity and appropriate physical boundaries. Children with ASDs, however, often have to be taught appropriate boundaries didactically. I use Twizzlers and long ropes of licorice as measuring tools when assisting children with Asperger's Syndrome to grasp these concepts. The child sits on the parent's lap and we see how much licorice fits in between them. The parent then gets to feed it to the child. Next the parents and I line up with the child as if we are in the child's classroom, an environment in which social difficulties are often exacerbated.

We let the child play with the distance between people while measuring the space with the treats. Once the child is able to accurately assess appropriate distances from others in various settings, we practice recognizing when someone is saying with his body, "That's close enough." We do this while playing a version of Red Light, Green Light. We generate a list of non-verbal communications. Gestures such as raising a hand in front of one's body are included as well as movements like someone scooting sideways after being bumped. The client then stands several feet away from the parent and begins to walk slowly toward them. Each of the non-verbal gestures that usually mean "That's close enough" function as the Red Light. When the child accurately reads the cue and self-monitors by stopping, the parent and I cheer.

Finally, the sensory integration issues that children with ASDs grapple with can be addressed through Theraplay. Theraplay activities can be modified to give the sensory seeking child and the sensory defensive child the kinds of experiences that promote health and a positive relationship with the parent. Each client must have his or her sensory needs individually assessed so that the "dose" of sensory exposure is titrated accurately for each child. Clients who are sensory seeking may respond best to more intense pressure in the lotioning tasks, whereas sensory defensive children may respond better to the use of baby powder, or hand tracing.

For children who need more experiences of pressure or containment in their physical bodies, games like (see appendix) "Tunneling" and "The Toilet Paper Bust Out" can be helpful. Games like "Push Me Over," "Pull Me Up" and the "Pillow Push" can be customized to provide extra stimulation for sensory seeking children. Conversely, the "Cotton Ball Touch" or a gentle game of "Pass the Touch" might be most appropriate for a sensory defensive child. "The Blanket Swing" can be a gentle containment experience or a boisterous exciting game depending on the child's needs. Feeding games that allow for the client to experience the slow melting of an M&M in his mouth or the intense crunching of a carrot can be handpicked based on a child's sensory needs.

In closing, the use of Theraplay techniques with children with ASDs is based on a careful dyadic assessment with an aim toward using each of the four dimensions to stimulate a child's desire for interpersonal connection. The child's current developmental level, his interests and the areas of social interaction that need shaping should be considered when customizing Theraplay activities to successively approximate healthy social interactions. For children with ASDs, Theraplay can become a vehicle for breaking out of isolation and into the world of social connectedness.

Below is an agenda for each phase of Theraplay with Ethan. In most activities the therapist models the game once with the child and then facilitates the child and parent playing it together, increasing the challenge level from verbal to facial cues as they play. "Peek-a-Boo," feeding, and the "I Remember When" stories are parent led, with elaborations facilitated by the therapist if necessary.

Theraplay activities (see appendix) used in Session 1:

1. Check in and Helping Hurts (Therapist/Parent/Child)
2. Measuring with Fruit Roll-Ups (Therapist/Parent/Child)
3. Peek-a-Boo games (in the sand) (Parent/Child)
4. Bean Bag Game (Therapist/Parent/Child)
5. Pop the Bubbles (Therapist/Parent/Child)
6. Finding Powder Shapes in Hands, (Therapist/Parent/Child)
7. The Blanket Swing, (Therapist/Parent/Child)
8. Feeding (Hide and Seek) and "I Remember When" Story (Therapist/Parent/Child)

Homework included lotioning and rocking at night time, as well as "Peek-a-Boo" with the covers at bedtime. In the mornings, mom spent extra time doing the "This Little Piggy" game with client's toes before putting on his socks and shoes. Mom was instructed to check-in every morning at wake-up time and to make a game out of seeing if all his freckles, fingers, etc., were still there.

Theraplay activities used in a middle session:

1. Check in and Helping Hurts (Therapist/Parent/Child)
2. Stack of Hands (Therapist/Parent/Child)
3. Tracing Hands (Therapist/Parent/Child)
4. Row Row Row Your Boat (Parent/Child)
5. Push Me Over-Pull Me Up (Therapist/Parent/Child)
6. Slippery, Slippery, Slip game (Therapist/Parent/Child)
7. The Blanket Swing (Therapist/Parent/Child)
8. The Doughnut/Pretzel Challenge (Therapist/Parent/Child)
9. More Feeding and an "I Remember When" story (Therapist/Parent/Child)

Homework included lotioning and singing before bed every night and simple reinforcements of reciprocal interactions through turn-taking games.

Theraplay activities used in a final Session:

1. Check in and Helping Hurts (Therapist/Parent/Child)
2. Final Measuring (to see how much he'd grown) (Therapist/Parent/Child)
3. Cotton Ball Touch (Therapist/Parent/Child)
4. Instrument Attunement (Therapist/Parent/Child)
5. Mirror, Mirror on the Wall (Therapist/Parent/Child)
6. Slippery, Slippery, Slip (Therapist/Parent/Child)
7. Row Your Boat (Therapist/Parent/Child)

8. The Blanket Swing (Therapist/Parent/Child)
9. Feeding Celebration with an "I Remember When" story (Therapist/Parent/Child)

Children feel safer when they have rituals and routines that remain consistent over time. Theraplay sessions can be structured with beginning and ending rituals that remain the same across sessions. In this case, Check-In and Handling Hurts marked the predictable start of each Theraplay session. The end of each session was signaled by the Blanket Swing and the parent feeding the child while telling an "I Remember When" story. The repetitive beginning and ending activities serve as book-ends that provide predictability for the child and parent, while the middle activities of each session can change to match the growing edge (structure/nurture/engagement/challenge) for each dyad. The role of the therapist is mainly to model each new activity and then to undergird the parent/child dyad as they experience the intervention together. The therapist makes many comments to both child and parent that affirm their together identity and the way they complement each other in their individual roles. In the final session, the "I Remember When" story time can be expanded. The remembering focuses on the most important moments from the Theraplay process and all three participants (parent, child, and therapist) can all tell stories, helping them build a coherent narrative of treatment that will continue past termination.

NOTE

1. The mnemonic device "Every Child Needs Something" was created by Dr. Linda Ashford, assistant professor of pediatrics at Monro Carell Jr. Children's Hospital at Vanderbilt.

REFERENCES

Greenspan, Stanley I., and Weider, Serena. (2006). *Engaging Autism: Using the Floortime Approach to Help Children Relate, Communicate, and Think*. Cambridge, MA: Da Capo Lifelong Books.

Wettig, H., Franke, U., and Fjordbak, B. S. (2006). "Evaluating the Effectiveness of Theraplay." In C. E. Schaefer and H. Kaduson (Eds.), *Contemporary Play Therapy* (pp. 103–135). New York: The Guilford Press.

WEBSITES

www.autismspeaks.org
www.cdc.gov/ncbddd/autism/

7

Theraplay: The Powerful Catalyst in Residential Treatment

Karen Doyle Buckwalter and Annette L. Finlay

One of the most powerful applications of Theraplay® may also be one of the most overlooked; the highly successful use of Theraplay to treat adolescents in Chaddock's residential setting demonstrates that this therapeutic intervention is full of potential benefits. The benefits are seen in the quality of the therapeutic relationships between the children and staff and the children and their families. They are also seen in the confidence and level of satisfaction staff gain from their work, as evidenced through interviews with direct care staff who have worked in both behavior modification or level system residential milieus and within Chaddock's therapeutic model. The confidence gained by staff in the use of Theraplay has also been noted in families who are preparing for the return of their children to their care. Families who struggled to understand what their troubled children needed from them were able to find confidence in their ability to effectively parent their children.

This chapter will first explore the benefits of Theraplay in establishing therapeutic rapport early in treatment. Second, it will discuss the benefits of Chaddock's program structure and treatment phases, which are based upon the typical progression of treatment when utilizing Theraplay (Jernberg and Booth, 1999). Finally, it will explore the impact of its use upon the confidence and attitudes of direct care staff and families. To illustrate this therapeutic process, we will follow a typical client named Josie Petersen (not her real name) and her family as they journey through treatment at Chaddock.

BUILDING INITIAL RAPPORT

Mr. and Mrs. Petersen sought treatment for their fourteen-year-old adoptive daughter, Josie, when they were no longer able to manage her escalating behaviors in the home. Josie had been diagnosed with Bipolar Disorder, Post-Traumatic Stress Disorder, and Attention Deficit Hyperactivity Disorder. She exhibited physical and verbal aggression toward her parents and a sibling, who continued to reside in the home. Mr. and Mrs. Petersen also reported Josie's refusal to allow her parents to touch her, as well as excessively controlling behaviors, poor impulse and anger control, and poor self-esteem. Her parents reported Josie did not have friends at school or in the neighborhood, and she had a history of hurting the family pets.

Prior to being admitted to Chaddock, Josie had been receiving outpatient therapy services through her local mental health center, but was not responding to treatment in that setting. Although Josie had previously been placed in a psychiatric unit for out-of-control behavior and physical aggression, Chaddock was her first residential placement. Mr. and Mrs. Petersen voiced anxiety about their decision to place Josie in a residential treatment program so far from home. Yet they stated they were no longer able to safely parent Josie in their home and knew she needed specialized care.

Josie appeared angry and defiant throughout her admission into Chaddock and refused to speak with staff. Chaddock's first priority for Josie, as with all clients, was to establish a therapeutic rapport with her. In order to accomplish that goal, Chaddock utilizes Theraplay in the program structure and in the interactions between Josie and her individual counselor and therapist.

Chaddock's treatment model utilizes direct care staff with Theraplay training called individual counselors who work closely with an assigned child. Their role is to act as the child's "practice" attachment figure while they are in treatment. The role of individual counselor was developed because many families live too far away to participate in weekly family therapy. Clearly, the preference would be to have the parent present in therapy sessions, but distance and the responsibilities of home represent difficult barriers. The individual counselor assigned to Josie was Maria, who worked closely with Josie's assigned therapist, Sarah. Maria also attended therapy sessions with Josie. As Sarah worked with Josie and Maria, a relationship began to grow, enabling Maria to be more effective in her work with Josie in the milieu. The fun, enjoyable experiences they shared in therapy sessions using Theraplay provided a foundation for Maria and Josie. From that foundation, Maria was able to support Josie through difficult situations in the milieu with empathy and compassion. As Josie's individual counselor, Maria shared experiences with Josie that were engaging, structured yet balanced with accepting nurture and, as Josie was able, challenging, to enable her developmental and emotional growth. Maria did not wait for Sarah, the therapist, to establish a therapeutic rapport with Josie before she began engaging her, as so much of her critical work occurred within the milieu between therapy sessions. Bruce Perry noted in his book, *The Boy Who Was Raised as a Dog* (Perry and Szalavitz 2006):

> . . . my experience as well as the research suggests that the most important healing experiences in the lives of traumatized children do not occur in therapy itself. (p. 231)

Although Josie's interactions with her therapist, Sarah, were critical, her daily interactions with Maria and the other staff provided the consistent emotional and physical safety Josie needed as a catalyst in her treatment. A part of Maria's training had been to teach her to utilize the four dimensions of Theraplay to create that emotional and physical safety for Josie. Maria focused on interventions designed to help her engage Josie in telling her about her home, school, and what she liked to do. Structure was woven into the fabric of Josie's day through routines and Maria's directions to accomplish tasks. Maria received extensive training focused upon therapeutic boundaries in order to allow her to define appropriate nurturing touch to be utilized with Josie. Tiffany Field noted in her book, *Touch* (Field 2001):

> . . . children need touch for survival. Their growth and development thrive on touch. And how will they learn about affection if not through touch? (p. 5)

A pat on the back, a high five, or holding Josie's hand were all appropriate nurturing touches that Josie began to accept. Maria provided challenging moments for Josie that were fun and in the context of games, which made it easier for Josie to accept them.

Theraplay's four dimensions are powerful tools in parenting, treating, and educating children and adolescents. Children like Josie often feel afraid and alone when they arrive in treatment centers. Establishing therapeutic rapport quickly provides a springboard for treatment by allowing them to feel safe and cared for as quickly as possible. Rapport is defined in Wikipedia as ". . . one of the most important features or characteristics of unconscious human interaction. It is commonality of perspective, being in 'sync,' being on the same 'wavelength' as the person with whom you are talking." Maria's primary focus in her work with Josie initially was to strive to be in sync and on the same wavelength with her. Maria was also Josie's special staff during the evenings she was assigned to work. Once Josie began to demonstrate basic reciprocal behaviors with Maria she was encouraged and challenged to generalize those same behaviors to her family.

Maria spent a lot of time with Josie in those first days of her placement talking about the expectations of the program, some of the activities she might participate in and what she could expect from staff. When it was time for Josie to do her daily chore of sweeping and mopping the kitchen floor, Maria worked with her to complete it. By working side by side with Josie, Maria was able to provide structure and support to her. As expected, Josie responded alternately with openness and anger throughout her chores. When Maria asked Josie to sweep crumbs she had missed under the table, Josie responded by throwing the mop on the floor and using profanity. Maria encouraged Josie to use her words to articulate her feelings. Josie responded initially with expletives then was able to talk about feeling sad she wasn't at home and angry Maria was telling her what to do. Maria's response was to acknowledge how difficult it must be for her to be in a residential placement (nurture) while calmly restating what was being asked of Josie (structure). Josie was tearful, but able to complete her chore with Maria's help.

Through structured moments such as this one, children are given limits, parameters, and boundaries within which they are expected to live. As children grow to trust that the adults in their lives will consistently maintain those boundaries, they can begin to trust.

Josie was not willing or able to explore her feelings of fear and sadness nor her traumatic experiences until she felt emotionally safe. As Bruce Perry noted in *The Boy Who Was Raised as a Dog* (Perry and Szalavitz 2006):

> One of the few things I knew for sure by then about traumatized children was that they need predictablility, routine, a sense of control and stable relationships with supportive people. (p. 61)

Emotional safety stems from a strong, healthy, therapeutic rapport with an adult who has the resources to manage the verbal or emotional outbursts that may occur. Historically, therapists and direct care staff would tell the child they were safe, but utilizing Theraplay activities allowed the child to experience that safety rather than simply accepting a statement as fact. Therapeutic rapport was achieved more rapidly because Maria was engaging and nurturing in her interactions with Josie, while providing her the consistent daily structure she needed.

Critical to the successful use of structure is an equal balance of nurture that allows the child to know she is accepted, respected, and cared for. Structure and nurture must be perfectly balanced to be effective. Many facilities err on the side of focusing on structure exclusively. Theraplay's emphasis on both structure and nurture is a constant reminder of the importance both dimensions play in the overall health and well-being of children (Jernberg and Booth, 1999). During Josie's first therapy sessions her therapist and individual counselor used gentle humor and unexpectedly fun activities to engage her in interacting with them (engagement). They incorporated safe touches into the activities they chose (nurture) while ensuring the adults were responsible for the focus and direction of the session (structure). Those early sessions did not focus on trauma resolution, but rather on building relationships and establishing a therapeutic rapport that allowed them to later process the grief, loss, trauma, and anger that existed. Josie did not know it, but blowing bubbles (structure, challenge, and engagement), cotton ball races (structure, challenge, and engagement), and row, row, row your boat (structure, engagement, and nurture) led to a rapport that yielded a level of trust that allowed her to find healing.

The use of Theraplay provides the fertile soil in which therapeutic rapport may grow and accelerates the child's progress through treatment. The use of the four dimensions works as a road map to allow the individual counselor and therapist to confidently engage the child while being attentive to his other needs of structure, nurture, and challenge.

TREATMENT PROGRAM PHASES

Chaddock utilizes five distinct phases of treatment through which children and their families pass. These phases represent the entirety of the child's treatment at Chaddock, which typically lasts twelve to eighteen months. These phases of treatment are Invitation, Tentative Acceptance, Resistance, Growing and Trusting, and Separation/Transition and are based upon the typical progression of Theraplay treatment (Jernberg and Booth, 1999).

> Although it is not invariable, most children go through a predictable sequence of phases in their response to treatment. (p.141)

The Invitation Phase

When Josie and her family entered treatment at Chaddock they entered the Invitation Phase of treatment. Both Josie and her parents were invited to enter the treatment process and begin working on their lives, both individually and as a family. This was a time of anxiety and fear for both Josie and her parents. They sought assurances that this was the best decision for Josie and their family. While Mr. and Mrs. Petersen expressed hope when speaking of Josie's future, they also voiced concerns about her prognosis.

The therapeutic milieu is often overwhelming for both the parents and their child when they arrive. As previously noted, Maria's focus was upon establishing therapeutic rapport with Josie to engage her in the treatment process. At the same time, the family service coordinator, Helen, began establishing a therapeutic rapport with Josie's family. Helen had received Theraplay training in working with both children and their families. Helen's focus with Mr. and Mrs. Petersen was to provide both counseling and education in order to help them understand the treatment process and what was needed and expected of them. Helen established at least weekly contact with Mr. and Mrs. Petersen in order to communicate Josie's progress and struggles in treatment as well as information about her treatment plan. Helen sought information from Mr. and Mrs. Petersen in order to provide more effective interventions for their family and establish their role as part of the treatment team. Sarah, Josie's therapist, asked Josie and her family to participate in a Marschak Interaction Method (MIM). The MIM was an important tool in understanding Josie's relationship with her parents and predicting how she would likely interact with staff, at least initially in her treatment. So often, children reenact their parent/child relationships with particular staff and reenact sibling relationships with other children placed in the residential treatment program. Watching the interactions between Josie and her parents also allowed the therapist to gain information that was helpful in supporting them to modify their approaches with her. The family service coordinator also worked with Mr. and Mrs. Petersen to evaluate their interactions with Josie and help build upon their strengths as well as explore any weaknesses noted in each of the areas of structure, engagement, nurture, and challenge.

The Tentative Acceptance Phase

The second phase of treatment is the Tentative Acceptance Phase. In this phase of treatment, both Josie and her parents expressed anxiety and tentativeness regarding the treatment program. While there appeared to be an outer acceptance of the program and the expectations therein, the trust that would eventually develop was not yet present. As Ann Jernberg and Phyllis Booth noted:

> There is a period of tentative acceptance in which the child seems to be saying, "This is interesting, a bit strange, but it could be fun." (p.141)

Helen worked closely with Mr. and Mrs. Petersen during this time providing education about the program. Mr. and Mrs. Petersen were encouraged to allow staff to provide the structure Josie needed, while they were to focus on interacting with her in ways that were engaging and nurturing. Frequently, by the time children require placement out of their homes in a residential treatment center, the parents struggle to feel enjoyment when spending time with them. The focus of therapeutic interventions with Josie and her family during this phase of treatment was to allow them to once again have positive experiences with one another. Josie's first visit with her family after placement consisted of blowing bubbles into the wind and watching them float away then running to catch them. They put lotion on each other's hands; played row, row, row your boat while holding hands, and had cotton ball races with straws and cotton balls. Her mother wrapped her arms around Josie and sang a familiar lullaby to her. Each smile, hug, and moment of pleasurable acceptance between Josie and her parents marked a step forward in building a trusting, reciprocal relationship. Josie's parents were asked to call her often, visit a minimum of every six to eight weeks, or more frequently if possible, and send frequent cards and letters to her. They were also asked to send special items that helped provide an emotional connection between themselves and Josie. Mrs. Petersen sent a small photo album with family pictures and an envelope full of hearts with handwritten messages to Josie, which were hidden in her bedroom to be found over time. These nurturing connections with their child continued throughout treatment.

The Resistance Phase

The Resistance Phase of treatment is often stormy and characterized by outbursts and tremendous amounts of emotion for both the children and their families.

> Following this (tentative acceptance) comes a period of resistance (the negative reaction phase) . . . . At this point the child may pull out all the stops in his efforts to resist becoming involved with the therapist. It is as though he were saying, "I never trusted anyone before, so why should I trust you?" (Jernberg and Booth, 1999, p. 141)

In this phase of treatment Josie began to grasp that Maria was committed to developing a real relationship with her. It was important that Maria communicated to Josie that she would remain invested and involved in her life even when she wasn't "being good" or compliant. Parents have often stated that this phase of treatment seems endless as they watch helplessly and wonder if their child will ever improve. Children with attachment and trauma issues in treatment have stated they are afraid to open their hearts to someone else. It is as though they are afraid that what is in their heart is too horrible or too scary for anyone to accept. Due to Josie's life experiences, she needed to be assured that Maria and her colleagues were able to physically manage the behaviors she exhibited, no matter how extreme or severe. She also needed to trust that Maria would not ridicule her or reject her for the thoughts and feelings she held within her heart. The fear of being rejected often leads clients to push everyone away in order to protect themselves emotionally.

In therapy and in the milieu, the entire staff consistently utilized the four dimensions of Theraplay by providing structure, engagement, nurture, and challenge with Josie. Visits and family therapy sessions also focused on

Theraplay activities to provide additional enjoyable experiences for Josie and her parents. During this phase of treatment, it was important for Maria, Sarah, and the other staff to provide the structure Josie needed rather than placing her parents in that difficult role. Helen continued to provide counseling and education to Josie's parents and guided them as they interacted with Josie. In this way Theraplay activities were a consistent part of therapy, the milieu, and visits between Josie and her parents.

The Growing and Trusting Phase

The fourth phase of treatment is the Growing and Trusting Phase. In this phase of treatment, the child begins to report feelings of enjoyment when interacting with others. The child begins to demonstrate confidence in daily living experiences and in interactions with others.

> . . . this is a phase of increasing trust in which the child seems to be saying, "Well I guess you really are all right. I think I can trust you." (Jernberg and Booth, 1999, p. 141)

During this phase of treatment Josie began to look at many of the deeper issues that were beneath the surface. Josie was challenged to explore her feelings of sadness, loneliness, grief, despair, shame, resentment, and anger. During the Growing and Trusting Phase of treatment Josie began to demonstrate reciprocal behaviors with Maria. Mr. and Mrs. Petersen voiced frustration and resentment during this process as they stated they felt hurt and pushed aside by Josie. They worked with Helen and Sarah to address those feelings. During this time, Helen provided both nurture (encouragement and empathy) and structure (suggestions about what they could do) to Josie's parents in order to guide them. Josie had been practicing reciprocal behaviors with Maria for many months, and her parents were practicing those same behaviors with her during visits with the support of the treatment team. Over time, Josie's focus shifted to her parents and that focus led to an attachment.

Josie's parents were guided to provide greater levels of structure for Josie during this phase of treatment. Maria began fading into the background of the visits with Josie and her parents, allowing them to find their rhythm in providing structure, nurture, challenge, and engagement. Helen worked with the family prior to their visits to help them plan activities within each of the four dimensions to provide Josie balanced interactions that met her needs.

The Separation/Transition Phase

The last phase of treatment is the Separation/Transition Phase (referred to as termination by Ann Jernberg and Phyllis Booth), and is characterized in Theraplay (Jernberg and Booth, 1999) as:

> When this phase (Growing and Trusting) is well established and the parents have become part of the playful interaction of treatment sessions and are able to carry on at home, it is time to plan for termination. (p. 141)

In this final phase of Josie's treatment, both she and her parents at times questioned if they were ready to live together. At the same time they voiced confidence and hope about the future. Josie talked about her sadness of leaving Maria, Sarah, and the other staff who had worked with her. The staff supported her through her grief and challenged her to strengthen her relationship with her parents. Mr. and Mrs. Petersen worked with Helen to prepare the framework of daily life that enabled Josie to successfully transition home. Helen helped the family identify daily activities and routines that met Josie's needs within all four Theraplay dimensions. Helen challenged Josie's parents to establish consistent times and routines for sleeping, awaking, meals, homework, physical activity, and fun activities (structure). Within the framework of this structure, Josie's parents were also challenged to identify times and methods of providing Josie the nurture she needed on a daily basis. They identified activities that would challenge Josie and help her grow and develop. Her parents also worked closely with Josie's treatment team to identify methods of engaging her when she would attempt to isolate herself from them or push them away in the home setting. Helen also worked with Josie's parents to identify plans for them to care for themselves and one another, thus providing the parents the nurturing moments they might need. A plan was developed to maintain contact with Mr. and Mrs. Petersen after Josie was discharged from treatment in order to provide them support, guidance, and encouragement. Josie was successfully discharged to the home of her parents and has remained there with support from their hometown treatment team.

THERAPLAY IMPACT UPON DIRECT CARE STAFF

Theraplay has had a significant impact upon Chaddock's residential treatment program. That impact has been noted upon the program framework and with the attitudes and skills of the staff and families. Staff receive Theraplay training and advanced opportunities to develop skills in their challenging work with children and their families. Yet, one of the major challenges of any residential treatment center is burnout and turnover among direct care staff. Typically, as in most of the child care field, they receive low wages and also must work evenings, weekends, and holidays. When coupled with working long shifts with children and adolescents that are challenging, aggressive, and typically do not reciprocate the positive emotions that care staff extend to them, maintaining a team of professional and committed staff can be challenging. Few people would deny the work is emotionally exhausting and it is imperative to find ways to help staff find enjoyment in their work and know they are making a difference. Incorporating the playfulness of Theraplay into the environment improves the satisfaction and enjoyment of staff as evidenced through interviews with staff. One staff noted, "Theraplay gives me the opportunity to play simple games with the child while making a true connection with them." Bruce Perry noted in *The Boy Who Was Raised as a Dog* (Perry and Szalavitz, 2006):

> . . . in normal childhood . . . nurturing human interactions become intimately and powerfully connected with pleasure. It is through the thousands of times we respond to our crying infant that we help create her healthy capacity to get pleasure from future human connection. (p. 89)

This same response could be expected in the interactions between staff and child. As staff experience positive feelings in their work, they can be expected to remain in that work over a longer period of time. One staff noted, "As adults, we can forget to play, and many of our clients never learned how to play. As a result, they missed out on the sense of accomplishment and connection that healthy play can inspire."

When staff at Chaddock were asked how Theraplay has changed the way they work with children, the benefits they noted fell into four categories. First, the staff expressed that the use of Theraplay increased their level of empathy and understanding of the children, their needs, and issues. One staff noted, "If we can see the pain, fear, and loneliness in our clients' eyes, hopefully they will see the care, compassion and empathy in ours." Another staff reported, "Theraplay training opened my eyes to the importance and value of touch. Sometimes even the slightest touch can calm and soothe a client who is struggling."

Second, the staff expressed increased confidence that they were able to meet the children's needs. "Theraplay has the amazing power of helping children build trust and accept care from adults which in the end, brings healing and makes the difference between despair and hope," shared one staff.

Third, many staff stated they were encouraged by the development of new skills. When focusing on how Theraplay has changed the way she works with children, one staff member commented, "Overall it is much easier to work through their resistance and do the unexpected, which allows you to connect with them."

Finally, many staff reported feeling a connection with the children they had not previously experienced when utilizing more traditional methods of interacting with children in a residential treatment center. "The most significant impact that Theraplay has had on me is it lets me be myself and not have to be the residential staff that all of these kids have had to deal with most of their lives," noted one experienced staff person. "Knowing what I now know after the training, I would never go back to more 'traditional' therapeutic approaches."

SUMMARY

Theraplay has radically changed the face of residential treatment services at Chaddock. The dimensions of Theraplay have provided a framework and the tools not only for the staff, but also for parents who enter the treatment process. Staff who have worked in traditional residential programs have voiced increased confidence in their work and their ability to make a difference in the lives of severely traumatized children as a result of utilizing Theraplay. The power of Theraplay to change interactions and develop positive relationships where none previously existed is inspiring to witness. For those who have experienced compliance based treatment programs, the use of Theraplay in treatment has led to a passionate belief that its use is the best hope for these children and their families.

AGENDAS

Theraplay Session 1: (This session would use a great deal of challenge and structure and less nurture until the child knows the staff better)

- *Check up* (Done by using pieces of string to measure arms, legs, etc. If child is comfortable something as intimate as a smile could be measured)
- *Jump the river* (Take pieces of string that were used for measuring and put them on the floor at various intervals for the child to jump across)
- *Tic Tac Spit* (Similar to seed spit except using tic tac mints. One person spits a tic tac and then the other person sees how closely they can spit a tic tac to the first one that was spit. This makes it more cooperative than competitive by seeing how far each person can spit.)
- *Newspaper punch that becomes newspaper basketball* (Take pieces of newspaper that are ripped up from newspaper punch and crumble it into balls to shoot baskets through a "basket" that the therapist makes by putting their arms in a ring for balls to be thrown through)
- *Sharing of a drink and snack* (Therapist would attempt to feed the child the snack and drink while sitting across from them adding some sort of challenge to it such as taking a bite of a cookie ring while trying not to break it.)
- *Goodbye Secret Handshake* (Child will be given the lead in making up that hand shake. The hand shake will become a ritual to end each

session so the therapist may need to write it down so they do not forget it!)

Theraplay Session 25: (At this point in treatment the therapist would be incorporating more nurture and engagement with the child since the child will now feel more comfortable with closeness having known the therapist and milieu staff for more than two months and experiencing many impromptu Theraplay activities in the milieu environment.)

- *Check up and Lotioning hurts* (Typical check up as described in appendix . . . noticing eyes, hair, smile, lotion any hurts)
- *Lotion Handprints*
- *Cotton Ball and Feather touches* (Child closes eyes if willing, if not can do with eyes open and guess if therapist is touching them with a cotton ball or feather)
- *Balloon Volleyball* (structured by only being able to hit balloon with body parts the therapist specifies)
- *Balancing Bean Bags on Head* while crossing the room
- *Pretend face painting*
- *Feed snack and drink* (the hope would be that by this point in treatment the adolescent could accept this)
- *Twinkle song*
- *Goodbye secret handshake*

Theraplay Session 50: (Parents would now be actively involved in Theraplay session so this session would occur when there is a parent visit.)

- *Foil prints/mold* (Therapist makes foil prints of child while parent hides their eyes. Parent then guesses what parts of child the molds are by feeling them.)
- *Hand stack*
- *Peanut butter and jelly* (Parent in the lead so the client is following the structure the parent sets with the game)
- *Marshmallow fight* (Chaddock therapist and individual counselor on one team and parent and child together on other team to build relationship between them.)
- *Progressive Touch Pass*
- *Feed snack and drink while cradled in parents arms* (If the child feels safe and comfortable to do this, otherwise they can just sit close beside each other)
- *Goodbye secret handshake* (Chaddock staff and child would teach the hand shake to the parent to include them in this ritual.)

REFERENCES

Field, T. M. (2001). *Touch.* Cambridge, MA: Massachusetts Institute of Technology.

Finlay, A. (2005). *Parent Guide.* Quincy, IL: Chaddock.

Jernberg, A., and Booth, P. (1999). *Theraplay. Helping Parents and Children Build Better Relationships through Attachment-based Play,* 2nd ed. San Francisco: Jossey-Bass.

Jernberg, A. M., Booth, P., Koller, T., and Allert, A. (1991). *Manual for the Administration and the Clinical Interpretation of the Marschak Interaction Method (MIM): Preschool and School Age (revised).* Chicago, IL: Theraplay Institute.

Marschak, M. (1960). "A Method for Evaluating Child-Parent Interaction under Controlled Conditions." *Journal of Genetic Psychology* 97:3–22.

Perry, B., and Szalavitz, M. (2006). *The Boy Who Was Raised as a Dog: And Other Stories from a Child Psychiatrist's Notebook: What Traumatized Children Can Teach Us about Loss, Love, and Healing.* New York: Basic Books.

III

THERAPLAY AND CULTURAL DIVERSITY

8

Theraplay and Aboriginal Peoples

Linda Perry and Patti Sutherland

INTRODUCTION

Attachment theory and subsequent methodologies have had an impact on the way many clinicians assess and intervene with families. Bowlby (1969) believed that all humans have a biological drive to form attachment relationships and these relationships have evolved because they enhance our potential for survival. The application of Ainsworth's (1978) strange situation and the categorization of attachment classifications (secure; insecure ambivalent/resistant; insecure avoidant; and disorganized) provided a way of describing the reciprocal relationship between a parent and child dyad. However, recent research indicates that a homogeneous approach to understanding attachment and parent-child relationships often negates the diversity of families based on variables such as history, culture, and socio-demographics (Haight, Kagle, and Black, 2003; Letourneau, Hungler, and Fisher, 2005; Neckoway, Brownlee, and Castellan, 2007).

Attachment theory has been influential in informing our work with Aboriginal families. However, the applicability of attachment theory to Aboriginal culture and parenting practices has not been addressed (Neckoway et al., 2007). In the absence of research, clinicians have had to forge ahead and work with Aboriginal families using models of intervention that they believe, based on their clinical experience, will be beneficial to the families. It is our experience that models of intervention based on attachment theory, such as Theraplay®, have to be adapted to take into consideration historical and cultural factors relating to Aboriginal people.

In this paper we first provide a brief description of the history of colonization of Aboriginal people and the profound impact this has had on family life and parenting practices. Then we discuss considerations related to clinical work with Aboriginal families and the implications for Theraplay. Finally, we present a case study that illustrates how these considerations influence Theraplay practice.

It should be noted that both writers are non-Aboriginal and therefore acknowledge a bias based on their own history, culture, and socio-economic contexts as Caucasian social workers.

HISTORICAL CONTEXT

In an attempt to understand the nature of attachment interventions with Aboriginal parents and children it is crucial that we consider the historical context of colonization and its impact on Aboriginal families in Canada. One of the greatest losses experienced by Aboriginal people, the loss of childhood, was perpetuated through the installation of reserves, residential schools, and the apprehension and adoption of First Nation children into non–First Nations homes. Residential schools first appeared in Western Canada in 1883–1884. The last one closed about 100 years later (Heritage Community Foundation, 2002).

Residential schools resulted in the separation of many Aboriginal children from their homes and families, often at an early age. They were forbidden to speak their language or to observe their cultural practices (Bruce, 1998; Haig-Brown, 1998). They grew up in an institution, far from the love and care of family and community (English-Currie, 1990; Dumont-Smith, 1995). As a result, they did not experience cultural integration, and family life was destroyed (English-Currie, 1990; Miller, 1997b). Not only was family life destroyed, but it was replaced with an institutionalized, and often abusive, alternative. The children in residential schools were not allowed to be playful or spontaneous, and they were not allowed to explore their world. For most students, daily life meant hard work, rigid structure, and physical abuse (Miller, 1997b). Further, children living in residence were often physically, sexually, and emotionally abused (Bruce, 1998; Dumont-Smith, 1995; Hughs, 1999; Miller, 1997b; O'Hara and Treble, 2000; Ross, 1992)

Another major historical event that contributed to the loss of family was the apprehension of Aboriginal children by the child welfare system. During the "sixties scoop," an enormous number of children were apprehended and placed in foster care or adopted into non-Aboriginal Canadian and American families. These children usually had no further contact with their birth family (Green, 1997). According to York (1990), the child welfare system essentially replaced the residential school system. As the residential schools began to close in the 1950s, more and more Aboriginal children were apprehended. A review of foster care and adoption in Canada (McKenzie and

Hudson, 1985) indicates that in 1980 Aboriginal people accounted for 12 percent of the population of Manitoba, but Aboriginal children represented approximately 60 percent of the population in care or adopted. More recent data indicate that during the fiscal year 2005–2006, of the 6,629 children in care in Manitoba, 85 percent were Aboriginal (Manitoba Family Services and Housing, 2005–2006). These statistics suggest that the legacy of colonization continues to have a profound impact on Aboriginal families.

INTERGENERATIONAL TRANSMISSION OF TRAUMA

The historical trauma experienced by Aboriginal people is an important consideration in understanding the challenges faced by Aboriginal parents today. Lane, Bopp, and Bopp (2003) state that historical trauma has led to intergenerational trauma, which has been passed on for as many as seven generations through Aboriginal family and community systems. They describe this trauma as physical and sexual abuse, abandonment, alcohol and drug dependency, suicide and loss, the withholding of intimacy and affection, persistent fear, violence, and racism and prejudice. The result is the transmission from one generation to the next of a pattern of thinking and human interaction that reflects symptoms of post-traumatic stress and codependency. Included in this is a culture of violence in which family violence and abuse have become the norm.

In their discussion of a framework for interventions aimed at eliminating intergenerational trauma, Lane et al. (2003, p. 92) suggest, "The most potent force for attracting Aboriginal families to involve themselves in long-term programs may be the love they feel for their own children."

CLINICAL PRACTICE WITH ABORIGINAL FAMILIES

Our experience suggests that it is important not to generalize or make assumptions about the impact of historical trauma when working with a particular Aboriginal family. Aboriginal cultures in Canada are not homogeneous, but rather have characteristics specific to their geographic regions and social networks (Neckoway et al., 2007). However, our experience working with Aboriginal families in Manitoba has identified some factors that are important to consider when assessing and developing a treatment plan for a family.

Referral Source

There is no typical story or typical response from families when they come to their first meeting with therapists. However, some of the Aboriginal families who participate in Theraplay have been referred by a child welfare agency. Participating in Theraplay is sometimes a condition of their family reunification contract. Feelings of powerlessness and frustration, together with experiences of trauma, racism, and internalized shame can sometimes lead a parent to present as hostile or non-communicative. We recognize the context of their response and move slowly and respectfully toward building a therapeutic relationship.

Not all families are referred for clinical intervention by a child welfare agency. Many voluntarily seek out our services and are eager to participate in an intervention that will improve their relationship with their child. Sometimes parents, after they have had the opportunity to understand and heal from their own traumatic experiences, are encouraged by staff in community agencies, including Aboriginal agencies, to participate in Theraplay.

Culture and Parenting

Although there is relatively little research looking at parenting practices that has been conducted with Aboriginal Peoples, there is some evidence that parenting practices in Aboriginal culture differ from Western norms (Letourneau et al., 2005; Neckoway et al., 2007). Neckoway et al. (2007) identify three core patterns of parenting that are evident in different cultures. They are hypersensitive parenting, where the parent is very involved and intensive in meeting the infant's needs, selective parenting, which is less intensive in meeting infant's needs, and shared parenting, where there are multiple caregivers in a significant role in caring for the infant. They suggest that Aboriginal parenting is often characterized by shared parenting and selective parenting. They further note the importance that Western culture, and attachment theory, place on the parent-child relationship is not relevant for Aboriginal culture, which is based on a broad definition of family that could involve extended family, clan, and community, all of whom share responsibility for caring and nurturing the child. As a result, the bond between the child and the parent and other caregivers in Aboriginal culture is multi-layered rather than dyadic, and creates a dense network of relationships.

A distinction sometimes made between Aboriginal and non-Aboriginal parents is that Aboriginal parents tend to be less hurried parents, to observe their child rather than participate, and to prefer child initiated learning (Letourneau et al., 2005). The communication patterns include prolonged periods of silence and non-directive communication. Aboriginal parents believe that their role is not to shape and create behavior, but rather to provide a context for its expression. As such, children are allowed to make many decisions and are free to explore their own environment. Hamilton and Sinclair (1991) state that in comparison to Canadian mainstream parenting practices, Aboriginal values and parenting practices would be wrongly interpreted as passive, permissive, and lacking control of children's behavior.

Socio-economics

In a recent study that compared Canadian Aboriginal parent-child interactions and Canadian non-Aboriginal parent-child interactions within low income families, Letourneau et al. (2005) found that parent-child interaction scores did not differ between Aboriginal and non-Aboriginal families. While Aboriginal parents were less verbal with their children and used fewer instances of praise and encouragement in teaching, the overall quality of their interactions with their children did not differ from that of non-Aboriginal parents. An important finding of this study is that both groups of parents scored low (i.e., below the 10th percentile) on the Nursing Child Assessment Teaching Scales and had what were considered to be "worrisome scores." The researchers suggest that the low scores by both groups were more likely related to low socio-economic status than to ethnicity. That is, poverty may have as much impact on the nature of the parent-child relationship as does culture. We know that 52 percent of Aboriginal children in Canada live in poverty and that children in poverty have more than twice as many physical, social, and emotional health disabilities than children who do not live in poverty (Letourneau et al., 2005; Dumont-Smith, 1995). Haight et al. (2003, p. 201) suggest that factors related to socio-economic stress, such as lack of food and housing, and living in violent communities may "over-ride maternal sensitivity" to their children. They further suggest that sometimes a parent's insecure attachment with a child living in these conditions is adaptive and provides the child with the vigilance he or she may need to survive in a violent community.

Separation and Loss

It is important to consider the context of separation and loss when we are observing interactions between parents and children. The impact of involvement with child welfare and out-of-home placements often results in multiple losses and sometimes trauma for the children. James (1994) suggests that because children experience their primary attachment figure as necessary for survival, the loss of this person "represents a loss of everything to a child—loss of love, safety, protection, even life itself"(pg 7). These separations are painful, and behavior that on the surface looks like rejection, may be indicative of multiple experiences of loss.

In her work with Native Americans, Brave Heart and Wakiksuypi (2000) discusses that one of the outcomes of historical trauma is "historical unresolved grief." She suggests that this complicated bereavement may be passed down through generations of children carrying on the legacy of pain. This contention is supported by research that suggests that attachment patterns tend to be perpetuated across generations (Benoit, 2002a; Zeanah, Danis, Hirshberg, Benoit, Miller, and Heller, 1999; Fonagy, Steele, and Steele, 1991).

Trauma and Attachment

Increasingly researchers are focusing on the connection between trauma and attachment (Busch and Lieberman, 2007; Perry, 2001). There is evidence that trauma impacts on the attachment relationship (Kaufman and Henrich, 2000), and the quality of the attachment relationship influences a child's ability to recover from traumatic experiences (Busch and Lieberman, 2007; James, 1994). A child who has a secure attachment relationship is more likely to trust that adults will be available to him or her in a time of need, and seek out assistance. Conversely, a child with an insecure attachment may lack the inner resources and emotional support to cope with the trauma, and therefore is more vulnerable to the impact of trauma (Belsky and Fearon, 2002). The link between attachment and trauma is further illustrated in the case of domestic violence (Busch and Lieberman, 2007). Domestic violence is a strong risk factor for disorganized attachment (Zeanah, Danis, Hirshberg, Benoit, Miller, and Heller, 1999). Based on attachment theory, Busch and Lieberman (2007) hypothesize that witnessing domestic violence shatters the child's trust that the parent will not physically hurt them and will protect them. Further, a child who sees their caregiver hurt or injured may be overwhelmingly terrified, and that fear may then disorganize the attachment relationship.

The connection of trauma and attachment is an important consideration in our clinical work with Aboriginal people. Benoit (2002b) indicates that the most significant factors predicting the development of a disorganized attachment pattern are family violence, unresolved mourning, and unresolved trauma. Unfortunately, historical circumstances suggest these experiences are all too common for many Aboriginal people, and have been for the last several generations. The experience of traumatic events can impact on a parent's ability to recognize or respond adequately to their child's needs, or on a child's ability to express needs or respond to the adult (Levendosky and Graham-Berman, 1998; Radke-Yarrow et al., 1994; Slade, 2007; Spacarelli et al., 1994).

THERAPLAY AND ABORIGINAL FAMILIES

There are several factors that give credence to Theraplay as an appropriate intervention with Aboriginal families. First, Aboriginal culture values a circular, rather than a linear, approach to life (Bopp et al., 1985). According to Manery (2000) the ebb and flow of reciprocity between the parent and child in Theraplay is a nonlinear process. Second, Theraplay focuses on facilitating attunement between parents and children, and attunement is universal regardless of culture (Hall, 1976). Third, Theraplay is play-based and does not involve processing trauma. Benoit (2002b) suggests that when there are attachment difficulties, children cannot wait for their parent to process trauma. Theraplay works in the here and now and is experiential in nature, allowing for shifts in the parent-child relationship without resolution of trauma (although trauma resolution might be recommended following Theraplay therapy). Provided therapists are sensitive to cultural and historical factors, Theraplay can be a respectful intervention to assist Aboriginal parents to develop healthier interaction patterns with their children.

MICHELLE AND TYLER: A CASE STUDY

Family History

Michelle, a 26-year-old single Aboriginal mother of three boys (8, 6, and 4 years old), was referred for treatment by her child welfare worker. Each of her children had a different father, none of whom were involved with the children.

Michelle's childhood involved frequent moves back and forth between the city and her First Nations Community. She was the oldest of five children. Her mother was alcoholic. Her father also drank and was abusive to her mother. Michelle and her siblings witnessed family violence and drinking parties, and she and her younger sister were sexually abused by an extended family member. Michelle was often left to care for her siblings.

Michelle and her siblings were apprehended when Michelle was 12 years old. The children were placed in different foster homes and saw each other infrequently. Over the years Michelle was moved to about six different foster homes and group homes, and she lost contact with her family. When she was 18 years old she found her parents. They were still drinking and were not able to be a support to her, and in fact demanded money from her. For some Aboriginal people, there are cultural expectations regarding helping others and sharing that can place large demands on their time and financial resources.

Michelle became involved with the father of her first child when she was 18 years old. He became abusive to her after the birth of their son, and left her when the baby was less than a year old. Her subsequent relationships with men also were abusive. At the age of 19 she was diagnosed with Bipolar Disorder and had been taking medication on and off since then.

Michelle reports that she did some heavy drinking after the father of her four-year-old left her, but stopped when a child welfare agency threatened to apprehend her children. She started attending a community agency for Aboriginal women and children and she and her children participated in their healing circles. This agency referred Michelle and her son specifically for Theraplay.

Presenting Problem

Michelle's middle child, Tyler, was having difficulties at school (i.e., poor attendance, not listening to the teacher, non-attentive, poor social skills, and aggressive with peers).

Michelle reported having little control over her children at home. She indicated that they did not listen to her. They refused to go to bed when told, there was a high level of aggression between the children, they were destructive and left the house without permission (i.e., left the house through an upstairs window and on one occasion were brought home by the police at midnight). Staff in the Aboriginal agency who had referred the family for Theraplay described Tyler as a little boy "who did not know where his belly button was," suggesting he had difficulty being grounded in the moment, seemed disconnected from relationships (peer or adult), and would move from task to task quickly with little affect or interest.

Assessment

On intake Michelle presented with symptoms of depression. She spoke with little affect, reported that she slept a lot, but often felt tired and lethargic. She talked about the violence she experienced from her partners. The stories were short, but demonstrated the magnitude of the trauma. She had an understanding of the impact of the traumatic events on her children, and on her own depression.

Aboriginal parenting practices have implications for how we interpret the parent and child interaction observed in a Marschak Interaction Method (MIM) assessment (Jernberg, Booth, Koller, and Allert, 1991). In the MIM Michelle presented as tired, uninterested, and perhaps dissociative. Mothers who are depressed often demonstrate anxiety, sadness, irritability, and a sense of helplessness that can lead to being self-absorbed and emotionally unavailable to their children (Radke-Yarrow, Zahn-Waxler, Richardson, Susman, and Martinez, 1994; Maughan, Cicchetti, Toth, and Rogosch, 2007). Tyler attempted to take charge and engage his mother in activities, but she seemed to simply be going through the motions rather than enjoying the interaction with him. Tyler began to escalate and run around the room. Michelle made some ineffectual attempts to get him to sit down.

The research relating to Aborginal parenting suggests that Aboriginal parents are more likely to observe their children rather than to lead, and that this may appear, according to Western standards, to be passive parenting (Hamilton and Sinclair, 1991). However, Tyler's behavior suggested that his mother's response made him uncomfortable and anxious. While Michelle appeared to be observing Tyler, she did not respond to his attempts to involve her and he clearly did not feel that she was present or able to respond to his needs.

In the nurturing activities it was observed that Tyler was comfortable being nurtured by his mother, but Michelle rushed through these activities and was task oriented.

An important consideration following the assessment is to determine what approach would work best for a family. Given that Aboriginal parents are often quiet observers and guides for their children's exploration and learning, it is important that the therapist be sensitive to this parenting style.

Theraplay

Based on the assessment information, the goals of intervention were to enhance Michelle's ability to engage in playful activities with Tyler, to provide him with more structure and guidance, and to be more attuned to his need for nurture (Jernberg and Booth, 1999).

Engagement

Two key factors were taken into consideration in our attempt to address this goal. First, the idea of engagement for Aboriginal parents may be somewhat less intrusive and include observation and curiosity, rather than verbalizations of praise and heightened energy. Second, Michelle's symptoms of depression and dissociation relating to her history of trauma necessitated that we proceed slowly and assist her to be more effectively attuned to Tyler's need for stimulation and attention.

Intervention involved helping Michelle to understand that Tyler was not an inherently difficult child, but rather that he was attempting through his behavior to have her respond to his needs. Over time, Michelle was able to find her own way of engaging Tyler, one that was gentle and encouraging. Booth (2005, p. 35) indicates that the "emphasis on attunement to the child's feelings and emotional needs has shifted our focus from the playful activities themselves to a focus on reading the child's responses."

Nurture

Discussion with Michelle about her own childhood indicated that she had been forced to be independent at a young age, and had received little nurture from her own parents. She said that her mother grew up in a residential school, and was unlikely to have experienced nurturing. Miller (1997b, p. 423) states, "Overwork, harsh punishment, and abuse were merely the tip of the iceberg of inadequate care that included poor food, lack of nurturing, shoddy clothes and cold formality." Michelle acknowledged her discomfort with nurturing, and she wanted to change this legacy for her children.

In Theraplay, Tyler presented as being worried about his mother, and it was difficult for him to relax and accept nurturing from her. However, with gentle reminders that his mother was able to care for him, and therapists' support for Michelle to be persistent in her attempts to nurture him, he gradually became more accepting of the nurturing she offered. This coincided with noticeable decreases in Tyler's level of anxiety.

Structure

There is evidence that in traditional Aboriginal communities, parenting took the form of shared parenting and children often had multiple caregivers. This form of parenting does not require that a parent be solely responsible for supervising and guiding their children, but rather these tasks are shared by all the caregivers of a given child (Neckoway et al., 2007). However, colonization has left communities with widespread family violence and abuse, and consequently without a healthy infrastructure to support this cultural approach to shared parenting (Lane et al., 2003). As a result, Aboriginal parents today need to be supported to learn a different approach to parenting that will ensure the safety and healthy development of their children.

One of the primary concerns of the referring agency was that Michelle struggled in her attempts to supervise her children. This concern related to the lack of supervision in the home, as well as in the community. Inadequate supervision had sometimes placed Michelle's children at risk. Part of the intervention included modeling for Michelle strategies for setting boundaries for the children, and when they tested the boundaries, to use distraction, engagement, reminders about the rules, and praise for positive behavior. When these strategies were not effective, she was encouraged to use more directive strategies, such as holding them on her lap or taking away of a toy.

It was particularly helpful for Michelle to learn about the ebb and flow of Tyler's energy and excitement level. Video tapes of sessions were reviewed with Michelle to help her to understand that when Tyler became excited and active, she could guide him by first matching his level of excitement, then bringing the activity level down, thereby assisting Tyler to learn to calm himself and improve his ability to self-regulate. Makela (2003) suggests that this interaction represents a resonant hum of emotions which provides a corrective experience that supports the child's ability to regulate, and enhances the quality of the parent-child relationship.

Challenge

Tyler presented as an anxious child who tended to avoid taking risks within Theraplay. New activities and activities that were more challenging intimidated him and he sometimes refused to participate or his problematic behaviors escalated. Intervention involved assisting Michelle to understand Tyler's reaction, and that it was rooted in his fears and anxiety. Within Theraplay sessions the therapists reduced the element of surprise, and increased predictability by repeating activities and ensuring he was successful when he did take risks. Michelle also reported that she now understood Tyler's behavior as rooted in the violence he witnessed and his insecurity about her safety and ability to care for him, and she was able to develop strategies to help him to feel more secure during times he was separated from her. While some improvement in his ability to take risks was noted, overall this continued to be difficult for him.

As we were ending Theraplay, Michelle said she had gained confidence in her ability to have a healthy, enjoyable relationship with her son. She recognized that her depression was directly related to her trauma experiences and in consultation with her doctor stopped taking medication related to the bi-polar diagnosis. She continued to struggle with depression, and there were still times when she struggled to meet Tyler's physical and emotional needs. However, overall she was more awake and attuned to his unique spirit. He was now able to attend for longer periods, seemed to experience more "now moments" in his relationship with his mother, and, as per the referring agency, demonstrated an ability to form reciprocal relationships. These changes suggested that he had "found his belly button."

SUMMARY AND CONCLUSION

This paper has highlighted the importance of working within a framework that takes into consideration the interplay between culture, trauma, and attachment and has suggested some necessary modifications when using Theraplay with Aboriginal people. Theraplay can be an effective and respectful intervention to enhance attachment and assist Aboriginal parents to have health-promoting interactions with their children. However, it is essential that clinicians working with this population have a thorough understanding of the historical context of colonization and its impact on Aboriginal families, as well as knowledge of Aboriginal parenting practices. Perhaps the most significant adaptation required is in relation to the interpretation of parent and child interaction and our expectations of parents. It is crucial to be mindful of assumptions about healthy parenting practices and attachment that may be based on a Western perspective. It is the multilayered lens of culture, trauma, and attachment that will assist Theraplay to remain a vital and evolving intervention that supports Aboriginal families.

AGENDAS: MICHELLE AND TYLER (6 YEARS OLD)

First Session

Opening song

Inventory. Check to see what the child brought with them, such as a smile, warm or cold fingers or toes, bright eyes, curly hair, Superman t-shirt; count fingers and toes.

Measuring. Using a measuring tape, measure the child's height, length of arms, legs, feet, hands, and so forth. Also measure surprising things, such as the child's smile, muscles, length of ears, and how high he can jump. You can write down the measurements and keep them for later comparisons.

Balloon tennis. Hit a balloon back and forth, trying to keep it in the air. You can make this more challenging by seeing if you can hit it back and forth a specified number of times, increasing the number on further trials if you are successful.

Balloon between two bodies. Hold a balloon between you and the child (such as between hips, legs, foreheads, elbows) and move across the room without dropping or popping the balloon. You can make this more challenging by returning to your start position by going backwards.

The Grand Ol' Duke of York. Hold hands standing in a circle:

> The Grand Ol' Duke of York.
> He had ten thousand men.
> (As you sing this, walk in a circle.)
> He marched them up to the top of the hill,
> (Holding hands, everyone walks toward the center of the circle, moving your hands up in the air.)
> And he marched them down again.
> (Everyone steps back and lowers their arms.)
> And when they were up they were up,
> (Everyone moves back to the center of the circle and raises their arms.)

And when they were down they were down.
(Everyone steps back and lowers their arms.)
And when they were only half way up, they were neither up nor down.
(Everyone raises their arms half up, then fully up, then fully down.)
He marched them to the left.(Everyone moves to the left.)
He marched them to the right. (Everyone moves to the right.)
He marched them all around the town, and he marched them out of sight.
(Let go of each others hands and turn around. Clap at the end.)

Push me over, pull me up. Sit on the floor in front of the child. Place the child's palms against yours. On a signal, such as a word or eye blink, have the child push you over. Fall back in an exaggerated way. Stretch out your hands so that the child can pull you back up.

Foil prints. Using aluminum foil, shape a piece of foil around the child's elbow, hand, foot, face, ear, and so forth. It helps to place a pillow under the foil and have the child press her hand or foot into the soft surface to get impressions of the fingers and toes.

Caring for hurts. Check the child's hands, arms, legs, feet, and so forth for scratches, bruises, "hurts," or "boo-boos." Apply lotion or salve to or around each hurt. Ask the child if they have any more hurts. Check for healing in the next session.

Feeding. Have a small snack and drink available. Have the child sitting comfortably against pillows, facing you, or take the child on your lap. Feed the child, listening for crunches, noticing whether the child likes the snack and when the child is ready for more. Encourage eye contact.

Closing song

Middle Session Agenda

Opening song

Inventory

Measuring

Peanut butter and jelly. Say "peanut butter" and have child say "jelly" in just the same way. Repeat five to ten times, varying loudness and intonation. For young children it might work better to have them repeat say "peanut butter" back to you.

Hokey Pokey. Sing and act out the motions:

You put your (right hand in),
You take your (right hand out),
You put your (right hand in),
And you shake it all about.
You do the hokey (Action: shake your hands in the air)
And you turn yourself about (Action: turn around)
That's what it's all about. (Action: clap hands).

Repeat with different body parts, such as foot, head, butt, whole self.

Pop the bubbles. Blow a bubble and have the child pop it with a particular body part, such as finger, elbow, toe, or by clapping.

Mountain of bubbles. Use a large plastic bowl or basin. Fill the bowl about two-thirds full with water. Add several squirts of dish soap. Give each participant a straw. On a signal challenge them to make a "mountain of bubbles." They can also "blow the mountain down" after by gently blowing air at the suds.

Zoom-erk. Sitting in a circle, the word "zoom" is passed around the circle quickly. When one person stops the action by saying "erk," the "zoom" reverses and is sent back the way it came.

Shaving. Sit the child on a stool or chair facing a mirror. Pretend you are a barber and are giving the child his first shave. Place a towel around the child's shoulders. Apply shaving cream to the child's cheeks and chin and pretend to shave it off with a popsicle stick. At the end, admire the smoothness of the child's face.

Straw Wars. Use milk shake straws and Q tips. Give each participant one straw and several Q tips. You "load the straw" by inserting the Q tip in the end closest to the mouth. Give a signal for everyone to shoot the Q tip across the room. You can make it more interesting by challenging them to hit a target, such as a door or mirror. (This activity was invented by Jennifer Curtis, Winnipeg, MB, Canada.)

Blanket swing. Spread a blanket on the floor and have the child lie down in the middle. The adults gather up the corners and gently swing the child while singing a song. Position the parents so they can see the child's face. At the end, bring him down gently. (We then direct the parent to sit down so they are comfortable. The therapists wrap the child in the blanket and swing the child into his mother's arms.)

Ring pop and lullaby. Parent feeds the child a ring pop (candy sucker shaped like an infant's soother) while singing a lullaby.

Closing song

End Agenda (second last session)

Opening song

Inventory

Measuring with fruit tape. Use Fruit by the Foot to measure parts of the child's body. As you measure, tear off the fruit tape and feed it to the child.

Free throw. Divide into two teams (the child and parent are always a team). Using masking tape, make a line on the floor and have each team facing each other across the line. Place small piles of cotton balls on each side of the line. When you give the "go" signal, each team throws the balls at the other team, trying to get rid of all the balls on their side. When you give the "stop" signal, direct players to freeze in position.

Musical pillows. Have each participant sit on a pillow in a circle. As the music plays (or you sing a song) everyone stands up and walks around the circle. When the music stops, everyone stands on a pillow. Remove one pillow each time you stop. Inform participants that there can be more than one person on a pillow. At the end there is one pillow and everyone must try to stand on it for a group hug.

Head and Shoulders, Knees and Toes. Sing this song while pointing to the body parts while you name them:

Head and shoulders, knees and toes
Knees and toes, knees and toes.
Head and shoulders, knees and toes
Knees and toes, knees and toes,
Eyes, ears, mouth and nose.
Head and shoulders, knees and toes
Knees and toes, knees and toes.

Hide notes. Write questions about the child on small pieces of paper. Examples of questions are: "What is your child's favorite color," "What is your child's favorite food," "What is your child's favorite movie/tv show/book." Lay the child down on his back on pillows. Ask the parent to hide his or her eyes. Hide the notes on the child and direct the parent to find them and answer the questions as they find the notes.

Soft and floppy. Have the child lie on the floor and help him get "all soft and floppy," like spaghetti. Gently juggle each arm and leg and let it flop to the floor. If the child has difficulty getting floppy, have him get "stiff like a board" and then let go. Once the child is relaxed, ask him to wiggle just one part of his body, such as his tongue, big toe, baby finger, and so forth.

Pass a silly face. Everyone sits in a circle. The first person makes a funny face and "passes" it to the person sitting next to them, who passes it to the next person, and so on until it comes back to the first person. Participants can take turns starting off and passing the funny face.

Blanket swing. Spread a blanket on the floor and have the child lie down in the middle. The adults gather up the corners and gently swing the child while singing a song. Position the parents so they can see the child's face. At the end, bring him down gently. (We then direct the parent to sit down so they are comfortable. The therapists wrap the child in the blanket and swing the child into his mother's arms.)

Ring pop and lullaby. Parent feeds the child a ring pop (candy sucker shaped like an infant's soother) while singing a lullaby.

Plan closing session. Ask the child and his parent to name their favorite activities and choose party food for the last session.

Closing song

REFERENCES

Ainsworth, M., M. C. Blehar, E. Waters, and S. Wall. (1978) *Patterns of Attachment.* Hillsdale, NJ: Lawrence Erlbaun Associates

Belsky, J. R., and M. P. Fearon. (2002) "Infant-Mother Attachment Security, Contextual Risk, and Early Development: A Moderational Analysis." *Development and Psychopathology,* vol. 14, 293–310.

Benoit, Diane. (2002a) "Transmission of Attachment Across Three Generations." *Attachment. Contributions to Infant Mental Health,* special issue (January 2002a): 16–17.

Benoit, Diane. (2002b) "The Importance of Nurturing Babies." Conference in Winnipeg, Canada, March 11–13.

Booth, P. (2005) "Current Theraplay Best Practice: Focussing on Attunement and Regulation in Play." *The Theraplay Institute Newsletter* (June).

Bopp, J., M. Bopp, L. Brown, and D. Lane. (1985) *The Sacred Tree.* Alberta: Four Worlds Development Press

Bowlby, J. (1969) "Attachment and Loss." *Attachment,* vol.1. New York: Basic Books.

Brave Heart, M., and Y. H. Wakiksuypi. (2000) "Carrying the Historical Trauma of the Lakota." In *Disaster and Traumatic Stress Research and Intervention,* ed. M. J. Zakour, pp. 245–266. New Orleans, LA: Tulane University, School of Social Work.

Bruce, L. (1998). "A Culturally Sensitive Approach to Working with Aboriginal Women." *Manitoba Social Worker,* vol. 30, no. 2, (Summer): 7–10.

Busch, A., and A. Lieberman. (2007) "Attachment and Trauma: An Integrated Approach to Treating Young Children Exposed to Family Violence." In *Attachment Theory in Clinical Work with Children. Bridging the Gap Between Research and Practice,* eds. David Oppenheim and Douglas F. Goldsmith, pp. 139–171. New York: The Guilford Press.

Dumont-Smith, C. (1995) "Aboriginal Canadian Children Who Witness and Live with Violence." In *Ending the Cycle of Violence,* ed. E. Peled, P. Jaffe, and J. Edelson, pp. 275–283. Thousand Oaks, CA: Sage Publications.

English-Currie, V. (1990) "Vickie English-Currie." In *Writing the Circle,* ed. J. Perrault and S. Vance, pp. 47–60. Alberta: NeWest Publishers Ltd.

Fonagy, P., H. Steele, and M. Steele. (1991) "Maternal Representations of Attachment During Pregnancy Predict the Organization of Infant-Mother Attachment at One Year of Age." *Child Development,* vol. 62, 891–905.

Green, H. (1997) "May I Walk in Beauty." *Guidance and Counselling,* vol.12, 22–27.

Haig-Brown. (1998) "Warrior Mothers." *Journal for Just and Caring Education,* vol. 4, no. 1, 96–109.

Haight, W. L., J. D. Kagle, and J. E. Black. (April 2003) "Understanding and Supporting Parent-Child Relationships During Foster Care Visits: Attachment Theory and Research." *Social Work,* vol. 48, no. 2, 195–207.

Hall, E. T. (1976) *Beyond Culture.* Garden City, NY: Anchor Press/Doubleday,

Hamilton, A. C., and C. M. Sinclair. (1991) *Report of the Aboriginal Justice Inquiry of Manitoba: The Justice System and Aboriginal People.*

Heritage Community Foundation. (Nov. 5, 2007). *Residential Schools: The Background.* 2002. www.albertasource.ca/treaty8/eng/1899_and_After/Implications_and_Contentions/residential_schools.html.

Hughs, A. (1999) "Disturbing Revelations." *New Internationalist,* vol. 309, 6–8.

James, B. (1994) *Handbook for Treatment of Attachment-Trauma Problems in Children.* New York: The Free Press.

Jernberg, A., and P. Booth. (1999). *Theraplay.* San Francisco: Jossey-Bass Publishers.

Jernberg, A., P. Booth, T. Koller, and A. Allert. (1991) *Manual for the Administration and the Clinical Interpretation of the Marschak Interaction Method (MIM) Preschool and School Age.* Chicago, IL: The Theraplay Institute.

Kaufman, J., and C. Henrich. (2000) "Exposure to Violence and Early Childhood Trauma." In *Handbook of Infant Mental Health,* ed. C. H. Zeanah, pp. 195–208. New York: Guilford Press.

Lane, Phil, Jr., J. Bopp, and M. Bopp. (2003) *Aboriginal Domestic Violence in Canada.* Ottawa, Canada: Aboriginal Healing Foundation.

Letourneau, N. L., K. M. Hungler, and K. Fisher. (2005) "Low-income Canadian Aboriginal and Non-Aboriginal Parent-child Interactions." *Child: Care, Health and Development,* vol. 31, no. 5, 545–554.

Levendosky, A., and S. Graham-Berman. (1998) "The Moderating Effects of Parenting Stress on Children's Adjustment in Woman-Abusing Families." *Journal of Family Violence,* vol. 13, no. 3, 383–397.

Makela, Jukka. (2003). "What Makes Theraplay Effective: Insights from Developmental Sciences." *The Theraplay Institute Newsletter* (Fall/Winter).

Manery, G. (2000) "Dual Family Therapy with Withdrawn Children in a Cross-Cultural Context." In *Theraplay: Innovations in Attachment-Enhancing Play Therapy,* ed. Evangeline Munns, pp. 151–194. Northvale, NJ: Jason Aronson Inc.

Manitoba Family Services and Housing. *(2005–2006) Annual Report.*

Maughan, A., D. Cicchetti, S. L. Toth, and F. A. Rogosch. (2007) "Early-occurring Maternal Depression and Maternal Negativity in Predicting Young Children's Emotion Regulation and Socioemotional Difficulties." *Journal of Abnormal Child Psychology,* vol. 35, no. 5 (Oct 2007), 685–703.

McKenzie, B., and P. Hudson. (1985) "Native Children, Child Welfare, and the Colonization of Native People." In *The Challenge of Child Welfare,* eds. K. Levitt and B. Wharf, pp. 125–141. Vancouver, Canada: University of British Columbia.

Miller, J. R. (1997b) "Shinwauk's Vision/Aboriginal Nightmare: An Assessment." In *Shinwauk's Vision: A History of Native Residential Schools,* ed. J. R. Miller, pp. 406–438. Toronto, Canada: University of Toronto Press,

Neckoway, Raymond, K. Brownlee, and B. Castellan. (2007) "Is Attachment Theory Consistent with Aboriginal Parenting Realities." *First Peoples Child & Family Review,* vol. 3, no. 2, 65–74.

O'Hara, J., and P. Treble (2000) "Abuse of Trust." *McLean's,* vol. 113, no. 26, 16–22.

Perry, B. (2001) "Bonding and Attachment in Maltreated Children." *The Child Trauma* Academy. www.ChildTrauma.org.html. (5 Nov., 2007).

Radke-Yarrow, M., C. Zahn-Waxler, D. Richardson, A. Susman, and P. Martinez. (1994) "Caring Behaviour in Children of Clinically Depressed and Well Mothers." *Child Development,* vol 65, 1405–1414.

Ross, R. (1992) *Dancing with a Ghost.* Markham, Ontario: Webcom Ltd.

Slade, A. (2007) "Disorganized Mother, Disorganized Child: The Mentalization of Affective Dysregulation and Therapeutic Change." In *Attachment Theory in Clinical Work with Children. Bridging the Gap between Research and Practice,* ed. David Oppenheim and Douglas F. Goldsmith, pp. 226–250. New York: The Guilford Press.

Spaccarelli, S., N. Sandler, and M. Roosa. (1994) "History of Spouse Violence Against Mother: Correlated Risks and Unique Effects in Child Mental Health." *Journal of Family Violence*, vol. 9, no. 1, 79–99.

York, G. (1990) *From Manitoba to Massachusetts: The Dispossessed. Life and Death in Native Canada*. London, England: Vintage, United Kingdom Publishers.

Zeanah, C. H., D. Benoit, M. Barton, C. Regan, L. M. Hirshberg, and P. Lipsitt. (1993) "Representations of Attachment in Mothers and Their One-Year-Old Infants." *Journal of the American Academy of Child and Adolescent Psychiatry*, vol. 32, 278–286.

Zeanah, C. H., B. Danis, L. Hirshberg, D. Benoit, D. Miller, and S. S. Heller. (1999) "Disorganized Attachment Associated with Partner Violence: A Research Note." *Infant Mental Health Journal*, v. 20, 77–86.

9

Theraplay for Chinese Children

Angela Siu

Cultural sensitivity has always been acknowledged in therapeutic work. The greater the extent to which a therapist knows the meaning of a child's culture, the better the therapist's ability to achieve cross-cultural identification (Glover, 2001). When applying Western approaches in working with Chinese clients, caution must be taken since Western psychology and values might be rather different from those held by the Chinese people. As Bond (1991) put it, the psychotherapeutic process as practiced in the West is verbal, focused on the self and on the disclosure of personal information, change oriented, and non-directive. This may not be compatible with Chinese culture as Chinese people are less willing to disclose personal problems. Hence, efforts need to be devoted to selecting and modifying different Western therapeutic approaches to best serve clients from the Chinese culture. The purpose of this chapter is to evaluate the potential of Theraplay® in working with Chinese children. Modifications of Theraplay activities, aiming at enhancing its effectiveness for working with Chinese children and their families, are discussed.

CHINESE CULTURE AND THERAPLAY

In a review of counseling with the Chinese population, Leong (1986) highlights that Chinese clients tend to have less tolerance for ambiguity, and prefer structured counseling sessions with practical, concrete, and immediate solutions to their problems. Different counseling approaches are making adaptations to meet the needs of Chinese people. The following is a discussion on some of the characteristics of Chinese people and how

Theraplay can address those characteristics as an intervention approach for Chinese children and their families.

Relationships with People

Interpersonal harmony is an important characteristic of Chinese communication. Emotional restraint and indirect communication as opposed to confrontation are often preferred (Huang, 1994; Smith and Wang, 1996). Chinese people are more reluctant to express themselves verbally or emotionally. They see family problems as "secrets" and one will make the family lose face if family problems are brought up to a third party for help. As Theraplay is an action-based type of therapy and its focus is more on activities versus talk, Chinese people may find this approach less "intrusive." In addition, the collectivist cultural values of the Chinese coincide with Theraplay's core element on attachment and interdependence. To the Chinese, the nuclear family, as well as the extended family, is often valued more highly (Homma-True, 1990). In Theraplay, the core element is to enhance relationships among different family members (Jernberg, 1979).

Warmth

Most of the Chinese families nowadays are dual earners' families. Babies experience a lot of parental warmth, including physical affection, in the family when they are born. However, very soon after that, babies are moved from their parents to other caregivers (probably nannies) in the family or in the day care center where it's likely that there is a strong demand for obedience, control, and restraints, rather than affectionate cuddling. The so-called parental warmth has changed its component. Some research (e.g., Patrick, Synder, Schrepferman, and Synder, 2005; Siu, in press) suggested that parental warmth maybe an important factor relating to the development of children's behavior problems in later life. As Theraplay activities include a lot of positive physical contact, such as cradling and touching, this may provide children with one of the important factors in creating a sense of security that is needed as a protective factor for their psychological development.

Control

For Chinese children, control of movement is exercised physically all along their childhood years. Due to parents' beliefs that young children might get hurt if they are allowed to move around freely, babies are commonly put in physically restricted areas and preschoolers are often discouraged from exploring and manipulating their accessible environment. Apart from physical restriction, Chinese children are also taught to restrict themselves verbally, especially outside the family circle. As suggested by Ho, Spinks, and Yeung (1989), Chinese infants are less vocal, less active, and more apprehensive in social and separation situations; they are quieter, stay closer to the mother, and play less when they are with unfamiliar children. For the "control" of expression, Chinese parents discourage fights among their children by putting pressure on the older children to concede to their younger siblings, and demonstrating what's called "responsibility of the senior." Children's problematic behavior might stem partly from these kinds of "restrictions" and suppression from parents. The freedom of literally moving around as well as the freedom to "be themselves" can be addressed in the various components of Theraplay activities.

Emphasis on Achievements

Chinese parents, in general, place high pressure on academic achievement for their children and put socio-emotional development as a secondary concern. There is strong pressure for obtaining a high academic performance and more pressure to work hard. Achievement is seen as the benefit of a group rather than the individual (Yang, 1988). This kind of pressure may lead to problems for children, including constant self-criticism as well as lowered self-esteem, even if they attain relatively high levels of success, and shame and alienation if they fail to achieve as expected (Csikszentmihalyi, 1997). Some parents, may interpret their children's academic failure, especially in homework, as their failure in parenting. Issues on school achievement are often a common source of problems leading to poor parent-child relationships. Theraplay provides a means for parents and children to put school work aside and be "playful" and have fun together. In Theraplay, especially in nurturing activities, children are unconditionally accepted and are made to feel valued and loved. This is important for building up a child's self-esteem. When he/she feels accepted just for being who he/she is, the sense of self is less dependent on achievements.

MODIFICATIONS OF THERAPLAY FOR CHINESE CHILDREN

Theraplay focuses on fostering healthy attachment, relationships, and trust. The main emphasis is on playful, physical interactions between, first, the therapist and the child while the parents observe, and later, parents participate directly with their child under the guidance of the therapist. There is a strong focus on the positive attributes of both child and parent so the therapy sessions are very rewarding and self-esteem building. The therapist conveys feelings of unconditional acceptance to the child and helps the child to view himself/herself as worthy and important. Parents are guided not only to see and accept their child in a new, positive light, but also to be attuned and responsive to their child's needs. Although these Theraplay characteristics are seen as universal across cultures, some techniques and procedures have to be modified to better meet the needs and characteristics of Chinese families (Manery, 2000). The following is a list of issues that the writer has adapted while practicing Theraplay in Hong Kong.

Building a Cooperative Working Relationship

Many parents are eager to look for "instant" methods to help their children deal with their problems in a direct way. Frequently, children's presenting problems are related to school and achievements. Theraplay, to these parents, may look irrelevant to the context of the problem(s) and seems to take up a long time to "note" the progress relevant to their children's difficulties. Hence, the therapist needs to be patient with the parents, be attentive to nonverbal cues and gestures from them and be ready to involve parents in the discussion for clarifying concerns and queries regarding this approach. A Theraplay session, just with the parents at the beginning of the intervention process, may enable parents to get a feel of what Theraplay activities are like and may also help parents understand these activities better. Also, more time has to be spent with parents in teasing out the elements of Theraplay (such as playfulness and fun) in relation to children's problems (especially relating to academic issues).

Clarifying the Importance of Nurturing and Touching

With reference to the different elements in Theraplay, Chinese children and parents find it easier to adapt to structuring, challenging, as well as engaging activities. At times, nurturing (feeding and touching) activities are difficult for them to accept. To the Chinese, activities like holding hands with the child, looking into the child's eyes are acceptable; however, activities of feeding and combing, especially of older children, are seen by both parents and children as "babyish." Parents need more understanding on the rationale behind these activities before these activities can be effectively carried out both during the session and at home.

Getting Fathers' Involvement

In the Chinese culture, the father is usually seen as an authority figure in the family. The father is the final decision maker for major issues, while the mother is the key person looking after the children and doing most of the parenting work. Although fathers also care about their children very much, they usually take a less active role in parenting and are sometimes reluctant to join in the intervention process, because of many reasons. From the author's experience in working with families, it has been easier to have the father come for the MIM assessment and the follow-up discussion. Session work with mother and child are videotaped. Mothers are encouraged to view the videotapes at home with the fathers and to discuss observations and progress made. Some fathers eventually come at later sessions.

Modifications of Theraplay Activities

Most of the Theraplay activities can be used directly for working with Chinese people. Games like " three-legged walk," "stack of hands," and "tangle-untangle" (Munns, 2000) are very familiar to Chinese children and families. Songs such as "Ring around the rosy," "Row, row, row your boat," "Hokey Pokey" and "This is the way the baby rides" are familiar tunes to them as well. Other activities such as "Red light, green light," "Mother may I" and "Patty cake" have the traditional Chinese version for the lyrics and hence can be well adapted for use. Names of some of the activities can be modified to meet cultural needs. For example, "Cotton Ball Hockey" can be renamed as "Cotton Ball Ping Pong." The melody of a traditional song "You are my sunshine" is used to replace "Twinkle, twinkle little star" for singing out the special (physical) characteristics of the child.

Some of the adaptations discussed above can be illustrated in the following case example.

CASE STUDY: A 7-YEAR-OLD CHILD WITH IMPULSIVE TENDENCY

Background

Felix was a grade-two student. His school performance was, in general, very poor. His motivation to study was low and he often underachieved in academic subjects. Psychological assessments indicated that he had no major problem in his learning abilities. Teachers described Felix as a child "who was always on the go." It was really hard for others to calm him down. He did not relate well to others. He went easily into arguments when interacting with his peers. He was described as having poor coping skills in handling frustrating situations. In the family, Felix's parents put strong emphasis on his academic learning. The poorer results Felix got, the more frustrated the parents were, as they worried that Felix would not be able to finish his schooling. Hence, there was a lot of tension in relating to Felix. In the daily interaction, mother was very caring toward him and he enjoyed the accompaniment of his mother. However, when Felix had temper tantrums, mother, in trying to stop him from anger outbursts, would often give in to his demands. Mother was eager to explore different ways, including this Theraplay approach, to help Felix in reducing his problematic behavior.

Assessment

Felix's problem behavior was assessed using a number of tools including the Child Behavior Checklist—Chinese version (CBCL, Achenbach, 1991; Leung, Ho, Hung, Lee, and Tang, 1998). Felix also completed a self-reported measure on self-esteem—Culture Free Self-Esteem Inventory-III (CFSEI-III; Battle, 2002). The results before intervention were as follows: the CBCL externalizing score, as reported by mother, was at the borderline range (total score = 17). He scored particularly high in items like *Argues, Fights, Screams, Temper,* and *Loud.* The score on General Self-esteem, as measured by the CFSEI-III, was 16. This score was at the 70th percentile when compared to his peers. Upon interview, Felix complained that parents and teachers felt that he was not good enough and that he was often "picked on by adults."

The relationship between Felix and his mother was assessed using the MIM, a standardized method used in assessing adult-child interactions by the underlying dimensions of Theraplay: structure, challenge, engagement, and nurture (Jernberg and Booth, 1999). Overall, the dyad seemed to have some fun together. Mother tried hard to be in charge of the session and frequently gave a message to child that he had to work diligently on schoolwork or else he would be left alone. Limited physical touch was noted. Focus was given to completing tasks and educating the child on the proper ways to behave, instead of acknowledging the child's effort in completing the tasks. In fact, Felix needed more external support from adults to negotiate tasks, because he had difficulty experiencing a calm, focused state of optimal arousal necessary for learning. In addition to his difficulty in "connecting" to his mother, he also had unmet attachment needs that were necessary to soothe him. Finally, Felix's difficulty in adjusting to his learning requirements was understandable as his significant others (including parents and teachers) expected more from him than he was capable of performing and handling.

It was felt that Theraplay could play a role in helping children like Felix to increase their adaptive control of behavior. It can help children regulate their excitement and activity level (Jernberg and Booth, 1999) and to alternate between appropriate stimulation and a state of calmness. As the child moves his body through different activity levels, he is learning self-regulation by being in charge of his own sensory and motor experiences. Specifically for Felix, strategies in Theraplay could be applied to regulate self across situations. (i) Structuring—offer a predictable and safe environment with clear guidelines; (ii) Engagement— provide optimal stimulating and exciting interactions between the dyad; (iii) Nurturing—able to calm the child when he/she is becoming too excited as well as providing warmth, acceptance, and caring; and (iv) Challenging—help the child practice self-regulation by controlling frustration, as well as building self-confidence and self-esteem.

Felix attended 10 Theraplay sessions, 2 MIMs, and a follow-up session. Below is a brief overview of different sessions at various stages of the intervention.

Selected Theraplay Sessions

Session 2

In Felix's early Theraplay sessions, he could be distracted very easily. There was excessive running and fidgeting throughout. He reacted very positively to some challenging tasks such as "balancing on pillows." He could occasionally be calmed down by nurturing tasks like "lotioning" and "powdering." He seemed very interested in being powdered and would try to pretend to be a "flour-man." He reacted in a surprising manner when the special song was sung to him. He laughed and giggled a lot. Overall, he attended well to the therapist's instructions, but needed frequent reminders.

Session 6

By the middle sessions, Felix entered the "working through" stage. He enjoyed games like "motor boat" and was particularly excited with the acceleration on "going faster and faster." The therapist helped Felix to experience a calm and focused state before he accelerated again. He was learning to self-regulate. He started to work well on slow movements such as "motor boat goes so slow" and "mirroring" (i.e., copying of slow movements of the therapist). He was experiencing a calm physiological state within an emotionally calm context. Soothing activities were followed by a big hug and some nurturing activities like feeding. Felix began to be more interactive in the sessions and was more willing to participate and to follow instructions.

Session 10

As the sessions continued, Felix reacted better in structuring, nurturing, and engaging tasks. He reacted in a more normal way and could follow instructions better (i.e., fewer reminders needed). He particularly enjoyed the special time together for calming down and hugs. The sessions continued to involve parents for conducting activities that helped Felix calm down, stay focused, learn to modulate his emotional and physical responses, and to enjoy the new nurturance and engagement he found with his parents. He was particularly interested in the "cotton ball blow" and the "cotton ball touch." He could follow rules easier and could initiate in more planned activities. His impulsivity decreased.

Post-intervention Assessment

The MIM done in the post-intervention showed that Felix was in better control of "himself"—less running and fidgeting in the session and more cooperation in following mother's instructions. Mother seemed to enjoy the games more with Felix and she was less focused on "educating" him during play. Although the CBCL-externalizing score (as measured by the mother) and the self-esteem score of CFSEI (as reported by the child) did not differ significantly between pre- and post-intervention, qualitative feedback from both mother and child reported that they enjoyed each other and there were many gains. The element of affectionate nurturing (e.g., spontaneous touching, hugging between mother and child) was noted throughout the post-assessment. Mother was observed to be more relaxed when being with Felix. She became more confident in her ability to "manage" Felix's situation despite Felix's hyperactivity. She described her relationship with Felix as "improving" and that she found some good directions to follow in managing Felix's impulsive behavior. Most importantly, the mother started to accept Felix as a person in his own right.

CONCLUSION

Theraplay promotes family ties and reciprocal interaction between people. The nature of Theraplay meets the characteristics of the Chinese as a collectivistic group which puts high emphasis on interpersonal relationships. With modifications in techniques and some of the procedures, it can be used successfully, from a clinical perspective, as an alternative approach for working with Chinese children and their families, not only in enhancing healthy attachments, but also in increasing self-esteem, self-regulation, and parental confidence.

AGENDAS OF THE SESSIONS DESCRIBED IN THE CHAPTER

Session 2

Key purposes: have fun; follow instructions, start forming a trusting relationship with adult

Opening:

- clear message of acceptance
- greeting song

Inventory:

- body part sound—touch different body parts, making a funny sound for each
- check things where child sees growth—i.e., height

Activities:

- imitate hand clapping
- powdering handprints
- lotioning hurts
- row, row, row your boat
- balancing on pillows
- guess number/letter traced on back
- funny way to cross the room
- stop and freeze

Closing:

- say some nice things about the child
- feeding activity—food share
- goodbye song—connect with mother

Session 6

Key purpose: mom takes a more leading role in structuring, engaging, and nurturing her child and enjoys playing with her child

Opening:

- clear message of acceptance
- greeting song

Inventory:

- check-ups: describe facial features in a positive way
- measure height
- What I remember when you were a baby . . .
- Caring for hurts

Activities:

- silly bone says . . .
- keep feather in the air
- mirroring
- motor boat
- trace shapes/numbers on back (body massage)
- imitate clap patterns
- thumb wrestling
- partner pull-up

Closing:

- say some nice things about the child
- feeding activity—food share
- goodbye

Session 10

Key purpose: termination leaving child with an increased positive self-image, greater self-regulation, and stronger connection with a parent attuned to his needs

Opening:

- clear message of acceptance
- greeting song

Inventory:

- describe positive special features of child
- caring for hurts

Activities:

- imitate hand clapping game
- cotton ball blow
- cotton ball touch
- balloon between two bodies walk
- mirroring each other
- drawing around body with positive comments
- tangle and untangle

Closing:

- feeding activity—food share of special party food
- what I most liked about Theraplay and why
- big hug and goodbye song

REFERENCES

Achenbach, T. M. (1991). *Manual for the Child Behavior Checklist 4–18*. Burlington: University of Vermont, Dept. of Psychiatry.

Battle, J. (2002). *Culture-free Self-esteem Inventories Examiner's Manual*. 3rd ed. Texas: Pro-ed.

Bond, M. H. (1991). *Beyond the Chinese face: Insights from psychology*. Hong Kong: Oxford University Press.

Csikszentmihalyi, M. (1997). *Finding Flow: The Psychology of Engagement with Everyday Life*. New York: Basic Books.

Glover, G. (2001). "Cultural Considerations in Play Therapy." In G. Landreth (ed.) *Innovations in Play Therapy: Issues, Process, and Special Populations*, pp. 34–42. Philadelphia: Brunner-Routledge.

Ho, D. Y. F., Spinks, J. A., and Yeung, C. S. H. (1989). *Chinese Patterns of Behavior: A Sourcebook of Psychological and Psychiatric Studies*. New York: Praeger.

Homma-True, R. (1990). "Psychotherapeutic Issues with Asian American Women." *Sex Roles*, 22, no. 7, 477–486.

Huang, L. (1994). "An Integrative Approach to Clinical Assessment and Intervention with Asian-American Adolescents." *Journal of Clinical Child Psychology*, 23, no. 1, 21–31.

Jernberg, A. M. (1979). *Theraplay: A New Treatment Using Structured Play for Problem Children and Their Families*. San Francisco, CA: Jossey-Bass.

Jernberg, A. M., and Booth, P. B. (1999). *Theraplay: Helping Parents and Children Build Better Relationships through Attachment-Based Play*. 2nd ed. San Francisco, CA: Jossey-Bass.

Leong, F. T. (1986). "Counseling and Psychotherapy with Asian-Americans: Review of the Literature." *Journal of Counseling Psychology*, 33, 196–206.

Leung, W. L., Ho, T. P., Hung, S. F., Lee, C. C., and Tang, C. P. (1998). *Child Behaviour Checklist—CBCL—Hong Kong norm*. Unpublished manuscript. The Chinese University of Hong Kong.

Manery, G. (2000). Theraplay with Asian-Canadian Families: Practical and Theoretical Considerations. *Theraplay Newsletter*.

Munns, E. (ed.) (2000). *Theraplay: Innovations in Attachment Enhancing Play Therapy*. New York: Jason Aronson Ltd.

Patrick, M. R., Synder, J., Schrepferman, L. M., and Synder, J. (2005). "The Joint Contribution of Early Parental Warmth, Communication and Tracking, and Early Childhood Conduct Problems on Monitoring in Late Childhood." *Child Development 76*, (5), 999–1014.

Siu, A. F. Y. (in press). "A Prevalence Study on Internalizing Problems among Primary School Children in Hong Kong." *Journal of Child and Family Studies*.

Smith, P. B., and Wang, Z. (1996). "Chinese Leadership and Organizational Structures." In M. H. Bond (ed.) *Chinese Psychology*, pp. 106–170. Hong Kong: Oxford University Press.

Yang, K. S. (ed.) (1988). *Chinese People's Psychology*. Taipei: Gwei Gwan Tu Shu. (In Chinese).

10

Theraplay in Germany

Ulrike Franke

INTRODUCTION: HOW THERAPLAY WAS INTRODUCED IN GERMANY

In the summer of 1983, when I began my 2-month practical work at the Rehabilitation Institute of Chicago, I had never heard of Theraplay®. I had been working as a speech and language pathologist for five years and I dreamt that I might find something new and fascinating for my profession in the "big America." I learned about Theraplay from one of my colleagues and a book called *Theraplay* by Ann Jernberg in one of the libraries in Chicago.

What I read excited me, so, after a few months, I flew back to Chicago and watched Theraplay films at the Theraplay Institute at 444 N. Michigan Ave. What I saw in the films shown by the therapist Ernestine Thomas, differed from what I had read in the books on client-centred nondirective play therapy by V. Axline (Axline, 1980). It was livelier, leading, and more cheerful in a positive atmosphere. Ernestine's procedure was familiar to me, but I lacked an explicable structure and theory. I became more and more attracted by the ideas of Theraplay.

In order to internalize the contents of the book, I decided to translate it into German and was fortunate to find my publisher having an open mind to this still unknown project. At the same time, I tested what I had seen in the films and read in the books and articles while working with children with communication disorders. To my great surprise, I was very quickly successful, and fortunately my supervisor was prepared to offer me the freedom to experiment.

After receiving training at the Theraplay Institute in Chicago and undergoing supervision from Ann Jernberg, I began to share my experiences with my colleagues and widened my practical experiences with more and very different children—and again and again I had surprising successes.

In 1987, my translation of Ann Jernberg's book was published. In 1994, the German edition of the Marschak Interaction Method—the *Heidelberger Marschak Interaktion Methode*—was published.

Between 1997 and 2006, I conducted two large Theraplay evaluation studies with Dr. Herbert Wettig: a longitudinal study with 60 children and a multi-center study with 317 children. The positive, significant results of these studies helped to further establish Theraplay as an effective, evidence-based intervention method (see www.therapieforschung.de and Wettig, Franke, and Fjordbak, 2006).

At present, in German-speaking countries, more than 30-licensed Theraplay therapists are continuing their education in a Further Education Institute and through a Theraplay Newspaper (*Schwierige Kinder*), both serving as resources to therapists in helping many emotionally and behaviorally disordered children and their parents.

WHAT IS MY WORK SITUATION? WHO ARE MY CLIENTS?

When I first came across Theraplay, I worked in the phoniatric-logopedic outpatient department of a rehabilitation center in Heidelberg. My duties were to examine patients with speech, language, voice, hearing, and swallowing disorders and to treat them, including difficult children with complex disorders. My clients were mostly children with all kinds of learning and communication disorders (including mutism and stuttering), cognitive deficits, pervasive developmental disorders, and attention deficit disorders. Now, in my own speech therapy practice, I am treating approximately 20 children with Theraplay each week. Some, mainly autistic children, receive intensive treatment—twice daily for five days a week.

ADAPTATION OF THERAPLAY TO THE GERMAN CULTURE

In order to learn more about the principles of Theraplay, I made many observations of mothers with their young children, much as Ann Jernberg did in the sixties (Jernberg, 1979). Different cultures, which are shaped by their history, environment, and social customs, produce varying parental practices. My observations, which focused more on the west European mothers (mostly German) and less on the American mothers, led me to formulate a number of distinct conceptual and practical differences between them (Franke, 1993). They are the following:

Challenge. Since our German society is very competitive and children easily get into enormous achievement stress, we value the intra-individual challenge more than the inter-individual challenge—except with small or older children toward the end of Theraplay. This means that the child does not need to compare herself/himself with another person, but only with themselves. The therapist refers to the child's internal progress and process: Hence, wow! Little Sandro does not only find the blue, but also the red super-soft mouse in his sleeve.

Sitting position. When we treat the children alone, we sit them onto a beanbag chair, since this enables better eye- and body-contact and the therapist's hands are free to move. When the parents are present they sit on a floor mat while leaning on a cushion next to the wall holding the child, who sits on a specially shaped floor cushion in their arms. Hence the child feels protected, and while she/he is held, hopefully will be less tempted to stand up and walk around the room. This could easily turn into a "catch me" game where the child "calls the shots." This is not encouraged. When the parents are actively engaged, the therapist takes the child onto his/her lap.

Generally key things to keep in mind are: a) the child has good stability in her/his body and can feel safe and protected; b) parent, child, and therapist can sit comfortably and relaxed; and c) the therapist can maintain good eye and body contact.

Use of verses, songs, and poems. Many of these are known in the German language and are used extensively by parents and in nurseries. Finger, toes, and movement verses of all kinds have proved to be very useful. They have an effect like rituals that help children to calm down and facilitate the process of language acquisition (Franke, 1999). They occur in all German Theraplay sessions and often use up to a majority of the time, especially with handicapped children.

Dealing with parents. We dispense with giving homework to parents. Many children and parents spontaneously adopt the verses and games from Theraplay. Because children and parents choose them, they are happy with their choices and incorporate them more often into their daily lives.

Focus on language. Naturally, as an SLP, I pay a great deal of attention to the children's language-speech development. German research (Amorosa, von Benda, and Wagner, 1986) has found that 48 percent of all language disturbed/delayed children show behavioral and emotional disorders. Before traditional speech-language therapy can be done, these children need a different kind of therapy—like Theraplay. Theraplay opens them up to social interaction and communication and enhances their attention, eye contact, and cooperation (Franke, 1998). Not only this, I try to engage them so intensely, that they begin to speak and improve their understanding. Research shows that this combination is effective (see below).

Scientific knowledge on language acquisition mainly based on social theories, indicates that without a relationship, language is not learned (Bruner, 1987, Papoucek, 1994). That idea influences my thinking and doing in Theraplay. Important general factors, which are helpful for language development within Theraplay, have materialized:

- The Structure, for example, a well-defined outer frame (eye contact, closeness), which gets the child's attention and calms the child.
- Children with receptive language disorder and speech development disorder need to hear simple words, short sentences, and repetitions, and need to see complementary and explanatory signs, so that they can be more attentive and understand more easily.
- Children need interactive play, so that they realize how important speech is in having fun together.
- Awareness as an input may be more valuable than speech (output).
- At times, the therapist/co-therapist or the mother may take on the child's role in speaking to enable the child to learn what one says in that situation.
- Short, simple rhyming verses can be much easier remembered than normal sentences, and promote the memory and the feel for language.
- The short, simple games (e.g., I hide a freckle under the lotion and the child rediscovers it by wiping it off) offer the developmentally challenged child a certain play-repertoire, which she/he can easily imitate and use with other individuals. The child becomes active and internalizes communication.

HOW THOMAS BEGAN TO TALK—A CASE STUDY

The following is an account about a little boy called Thomas and his Theraplay therapy (Franke, 2007).

Thomas is 27 months old when I first meet him. His mother describes him as friendly, curious, and alert. He likes music—but he utters only a few words. He communicates through gestures and noises with the family. Other people do not understand what he means. His mother is concerned. I introduce Theraplay as an intervention and she agrees.

Thomas agrees evidently as well. He is sitting in front of his mother, so that he feels very safe and the mother can assist and help when necessary. At first, he is rather reserved, but is prepared to let some of the games and activities happen to him. When I pull hard at his shoes to take them off and I don't succeed, a little smile appears on his face. He lightens up when his socks sit on his toes like a hat, and then fly off while being moved to and fro. *That gives me a first indication that he needs clear proprioceptive stim-*

uli and is open to surprises. I continue to experiment with what he likes and what pleases him." Peek-a-boo" does not engage him, but he is fascinated by the caring of bruises and a little scratch. *At the start of Theraplay, rituals are often more accepted from young children than games. They take place in a thoughtful environment and are calming and inspire confidence. Toddlers need the experience of self-efficacy. When they can pull their foot or their hand out of my large (lotion-covered) hands, they feel pride and are delighted.* Just like Thomas. "Noma" (once more), he says. I ask him, "are you saying you want to pull once more?" He nods. The second time, I hold on a little tighter and realize that Thomas himself pulls his hand out of mine. He babbles something. I answer, "you're saying you would like to pull once more?" Thomas replies "aa!" These are the beginnings of a short dialogue which in time will be internalized and be constantly extended. Here speech is integrated in a game; Thomas takes pleasure in expressing himself and notices the need to do so.

Thomas likes the song of the train which carries all the people Thomas wants to include, and which involves rhythmically stretching and bending his legs. *Naturally, he does not realize now that his brain is fed with many different sense stimuli which will be integrated eventually—a facilitation of perception, which is fun.*

Today, I offer him a game called "hide and seek mice." At the beginning, he observes how I hide a blue plush mouse in his sleeve. "Where is the mouse?" I ask him with surprise. Thomas looks at his sleeve and looks at me hesitantly in anticipation. "Do you think it is there?" I ask, while slightly lifting his sleeve, and then he understands. He tries to pull it out, but the mouse is stuck. "Mouse come out! Out mouse!" I call again and again until he has got hold of it and pulled it out. *(Through play Thomas receives new and simple ideas and learns how and when to use language).* More mice are introduced and even when his mother covers his eyes Thomas manages to find them and pull them out. *We know as well that children love guessing games in which they can succeed and this makes us resort to the use of guessing games for all senses.*

Just like all children, Thomas has to test my boundaries. After he has found the yellow mouse, he smiles impishly at me and then throws it away in a high sweep. I see that Thomas knows that he provokes others and that most adults usually get angry and reprimand him. He is surprised when I do not react at all, but get another mouse and hide it. *Thomas has new experiences with Theraplay; through new experiences he can learn and improve his development.* During the following sessions, it becomes clear that what Thomas's mother describes as "curious and alert" is actually his distractibility and his aim is to be in control.

Until now the goal was "language acquisition" but now it is expanded to increase attention, focusing, and cooperation, all of which will provide a good input to this child. The directive procedure of Theraplay offers many possibilities to reach these goals.

One of the ways of lessening a child's verbal interruptions is by ignoring them. If he averts his gaze or notices something in his surroundings, it is possible to gain his attention again through a change in voice or a physical stimulus. He should not receive any reinforcement for his distractibility. Furthermore, it is important that the therapist is a role model for him in how to stay focused.

By the tenth session, Thomas has given up on trying to be in control. This means, he does not put so much thinking into what he should say or do (output), but is more prepared to accept and receive input from the therapist. He still loves self-efficacy, being able to make an impact on others. Above all he loves the food that is offered. At the end of the session the plate is always empty.

He has problems in blowing a cotton wool ball. However, this is a play therapy session, so practicing blowing is not required, as it would be in a speech therapy session. Meanwhile, he participates actively in lotioning small hurts, during therapy and at home.

It is noticed that he reacts hesitantly to what is said to him. Delayed language processing (Franke, 2007a) is postulated, which might be one explanation for the gap in his speech development. Meanwhile, his mother reports that he is striving to express himself verbally more often.

After 30 sessions, a decision is made with the mother, to end the Theraplay therapy. He is starting Nursery school where he will receive further stimulus. For his language development, he will receive traditional speech-language therapy on site.

During the last sessions, Thomas is able to carry on a normal conversation. He reports, he notices, he asks questions—his speech pattern has reached a near enough normal state. Meanwhile, he has learned many verses, loves our Theraplay games and invites his brother and mother to play all the games at home. However, for his speech comprehension, and receptive language, he still needs some special input: slow speech, little distraction, and many repetitions.

Which factors are recognized in Theraplay with Thomas, as important components for therapeutic success?

- The structure frame in which the therapist leads.
- Short, simple games and many repetitions of verses and games with movement.
- A great deal of eye contact and physical contact, which improve attention and perception.
- Emphasis on input until he has absorbed enough speech patterns which he can repeat.

- Proposals at his linguistic level (verses, songs, simple sentences, rhymes), which he can easily assimilate.
- No pressure to perform, but to experience fun, affirmation, and admiration.

Nine months after the end of Theraplay therapy, Thomas receives Speech-Language Therapy and makes an effort in improving his phonetic and phonological abilities. The mother, who was very concerned at the beginning, tells me that she can see his enormous progress.

THERAPLAY RESEARCH IN RELATION TO CHILDREN WITH LANGUAGE ACQUISITION DISORDERS

In 1987 and 1988, Ute Ritterfeld conducted a study with preschool children whose language development was delayed or impaired (Ritterfeld, 1989). Her aim was to find out if Theraplay influences the speech-language development of children. A random sample comprised 21 children, who were diagnosed with language acquisition disorders, had no organic handicaps, and whose mother tongue was German. Her research was published in 1989.

Ritterfeld collected socio-demographic data, analyzed the state of the speech development of the children using the Heidelberger Sprachentwicklungstest (HSET) (a language development test by Grimm and Schoeler). Children, parents, and teachers were given the TOESD questionnaire (Test of Early Socio-emotional Development by Hresko and Brown, 1984). This test gives information about the child's socio-emotional behavior and his or her self-image. The tests and questionnaire were given at the beginning of the therapy and after twelve sessions or twelve weeks' waiting time. The children were graded into three groups: one group received Theraplay, another received speech-language therapy, and the control group received no intervention.

Her summary concluded: The Theraplay intervention method is significantly effective for children with language acquisition problems, even though no direct verbal training takes place. Theraplay seems to have the edge over traditional therapies as well in the area of linguistics and communication. At the beginning, the children treated with Theraplay showed definite inferior performances, but after receiving Theraplay, they significantly progressed more than those in the other two groups. Ritterfeld's hypothesis is that Theraplay does not directly train expressive and linguistic structures as with speech-language therapy, but "instead extracts the rules of language with the help of speech reception and so is able to improve language."

The self-image, according to the TOESD, only improved significantly in children who received Theraplay therapy. However, the parents didn't change their view on the behavior and the mood of the child; they stayed with their first assessment. This tendency was also found in Wettig's research (Wettig, 2002). Nevertheless, the nursery teacher's assessments show definite changes in the direction of improvement; the factor "mood" seems to be the most important factor for them. In the nursery, the child was perceived as friendlier and less sad.

In two of our own research studies, we focused on receptive language disorders. These studies were a) the controlled longitudinal study (Wettig, Franke, and Fjordbak, 2006) with a two-year follow-up, which was carried out with a sample of N=60 clinically symptomatic toddlers and preschool children aged 2 years and 6 months to 6 years and eleven months suffering dual diagnoses of social interactive and developmental language disorders and a matched sample of N=30 clinically non-symptomatic children as a control group; b) The multi-center study (Wettig, 2008) was carried out continuously within the framework of quality control of the patients treated with Theraplay. Nine different therapeutic institutions in Germany and Austria collected basic data at the beginning and after the end of treating the indicated children with Theraplay. The diagnosed symptoms were measured repeatedly by CASCAP-D, the German version of the Clinical Assessment Scale for Child and Adolescent Pathology (Doepfner et al., 1999). The presented results were based on a sample of N=319 children, who suffered dual diagnoses of social interactive and developmental language disorders. We found receptive language disorders in shy children, autistic children, and in oppositional defiant children. All three groups made significant increases in their ability to understand language during Theraplay intervention. As well, the children receiving Theraplay in both studies showed significant positive improvement in their social emotional behavior. (For more information about these results in English see www.Theraplay-Therapieforschung.de.)

The German University of Regensburg is replicating the described Wettig/Franke Theraplay Longitudinal Research project called "Regensburger Langzeitstudie 2003–2012 zur Evaluation der Wirkung von Theraplay."

In their degree dissertations Anne Kasten (2000), Evelyn Rudolph (2000), Dominique Veith (2000), Florence Reichert (2001), and Maren Nolte (2001) worked on the subject language disordered or delayed children and Theraplay inclusive case studies. All five authors agreed that Theraplay seems to be an effective intervention when children with communication disorders also suffer behavioral and emotional disorders. Veith explained that a child can put more energy and strength in his language development, suffering no behavioral disorder. But all authors stated, that there must be more extensive research to support their results.

REFERENCES

Amorosa, Hedwig, Delia von Benda and Edith Wagner (1986). "Die Häufigkeit psychiatrischer Auffälligkeiten bei 4- bis 8jährigen mit unverständlicher Spontansprache." *Zeitschrift für Kinder- und Jugendpsychiatrie* 14, 289–295.

Axline, Virginia (1980). *Spieltherapie.* München: Reinhardt Verlag.

Bruner, Jerome (1987). *Wie das Kind sprechen lernt.* Bern: Hans Huber.

Doepfner, Manfred, Walter Berner, Henning Flechtner and Gerd Lehmkuhl (1999). *Psychopathologisches Befund-System für Kinder und Jugendliche (CASCAP-D)* Göttingen: Hogrefe Verlag für Psychologie.

Franke, Ulrike (1993). "Unterschiede zwischen us-amerikanischem Theraplay und deutschem Theraplay" (Differences between US-American Theraplay and German Theraplay). *Theraplay Journal* 7, 4–8.

——, (1998). "Theraplay als Vorbereitung für die Logopädische Therapie" (Theraplay as a preparation for the speech-language therapy). *Forum Logopaedie* 6, 13–17.

——, (1999). "Inhalt und Struktur in der Theraplay-Stunde." *Schwierige Kinder—verstehen und helfen* 18, 14–18.

——, (2007). "Thomas findet zur Sprache" (Thomas finds his language). *Schwierige Kinder—verstehen und helfen* 41, 4–10.

——, (2007a). "Über das Sprachverständnis, seine Untersuchung und Behandlung—mit Theraplay" (About language comprehension, its assessment and treatment through Theraplay). *Schwierige Kinder—verstehen und helfen* 41, 17–22.

Grimm, Hannelore and Herrmann Schoeler (1991): *Heidelberger Sprachentwicklungstest.* Goettingen: Hogrefe.

Hresko, Wayne and Louis Brown (1984). *"Test of Early Socioemotional Development."* Austin: Pro-ed.

Jernberg, Ann M. (1979). *Theraplay.* San Francisco: Jossey Bass.

——, (1987). *Theraplay—eine direktive Spieltherapie.* Stuttgart: G. Fischer.

Kasten, Anne (2000). Theraplay—Spieltherapeutische Behandlung eines spracherwerbsgestörten Vorschulkindes (Theraplay—Playtherapy of a language desordered preschool child). Degree Dissertation, Aachen University.

Nolte, Maren (2001). "Sprachheilpaedagogische Intervention bei Kindern mit Spracherwerbsstörungen am Beispiel der Arbeit mit Theraplay" (Logopedic Intervention with Language Disordered Children—Working with Theraplay). Degree Dissertation, Marburg University.

Papoucek, Mechthild (1994). *Vom ersten Schrei zum ersten Wort. Anfänge der Sprachentwicklung in der vorsprachlichen Kommunikation.* (From the first cry to the first word). Bern: Hans Huber.

Reichert, Florence (2001). "Theraplay—eine direktive Spieltherapie mit sprachauffälligen Kindern" (Theraplay—a directive Playtherapy with language disordered Children). Degree Dissertation, Pädagogische Hochschule Ludwigsburg.

Ritterfeld, Ute (1989). "Evaluation einer psychotherapeutischen Interventionsmethode—Theraplay bei sprachentwicklungsgestörten Vorschulkindern" (Evaluation of a psychotherapeutic intervention approach—Theraplay—regarding language disordered preschool children). Degree Dissertation, Heidelberg University.

Ritterfeld, U. and Ulrike Franke (1994). *Die Heidelberger Marschak Interaktionsmethode.* Stuttgart: G. Fischer.

Rudolph, Evelyn (2000). "Möglichkeiten, Voraussetzungen und Grenzen für den Einsatz von Theraplay bei sprachentwicklungsverzögerten Kindern" (Possibilities, prerequisites and limits of the application of Theraplay with language delayed children). Degree Dissertation, Dortmund University.

Veith, Dominique (2000). "Spieltherapie mit Kindern mit (sprachlicher) Beeinträchtigungen mit besonderem Schwerpunkt auf der Methode Theraplay" (Play Therapy with communication disordered children—with emphasis on Theraplay). Degree Dissertation, University of Landau.

Wettig, Herbert H. G. (2002). "Veränderung der Einstellung von Eltern zu ihren verhaltensauffälligen Kindern nach Theraplay" (Changes of the parental attitude toward their behavioral disordered children). Degree Dissertation, University of Heidelberg.

——, (2008). "Die Wirkung von Theraplay. Die Wirkung von Theraplay auf Klein- und Vorschulkinder mit klinisch bedeutsamen Verhaltensstörungen, Aufmerksamkeitsdefiziten mit und ohne Hyperaktivität und mit rezeptiven Sprachstörungen." Dissertation, University of Heidelberg.

Wettig, Herbert, Ulrike Franke and Bess Sirmon Fjordbak. (2006). "Evaluating the Effectiveness of Theraplay," in: *Contemporary Play Therapy: Theory Research and Practice*, ed. Charles Schaefer and Heidi Kaduson. New York: Guilford Press. 103–135.

11

Theraplay Used in a Multi-Cultural Environment

Nancy J. Atkinson

Theraplay® was started with preschool children in Chicago in 1967 at a Head Start Preschool Program by Phyllis Booth and Dr. Ann Jernberg.

Theraplay is a lively, fun, engaging treatment method that produces changes in the lives of children, families, and preschool teachers in a relatively short time (Jernberg and Booth, 1999).

The four components of Theraplay are modeled on the normal interaction between parents and a child, or therapist and child, or teacher and children. Most importantly, a healthy relationship is developed between the child and adults based on four underlying dimensions.

- Structuring: The adult sets boundaries to ensure the child's safety and well-being, as well as making the environment predictable and organized.
- Engaging: The adult interacts with the child in a variety of enjoyable activities that engages the child's attention and participation. Sometimes surprise and paradox are used.
- Nurturing: The adult, especially the parent, is warm, tender, calming, and comforting, leading the child to feel valued, important, and loved.
- Challenging: The adult encourages the child to strive to try new activities, take appropriate risks, master new skills, and become more independent and self-confident (Jernberg and Booth, 1999).

Theraplay works very well in a multi-cultural environment. Theraplay activities can be adapted to any culture. The YWCA of Contra Costa/Sacramento uses Theraplay in a variety of settings; all of which have improved children's behavior and built children's self-esteem. Theraplay takes place in the following areas:

- Group Theraplay: Offered by all preschool teachers for ten or more weeks for children ages two to ten years old.
- Parenting Classes: Theraplay is taught once a week for seven weeks by a parent educator to parents and their children who are part of YWCA programs.
- Parent/Child Theraplay: All mental health therapists use Theraplay when working with families who have recently adopted a child or are going through reunification services with the Department of Social Services.

All YWCA staff responsible for providing Theraplay have attended an intro Theraplay course led by a certified trainer and have been trained in group Theraplay.

The YWCA serves many different cultures with the current ethnic breakdown of families being the following: 65 percent Latino, 20 percent African American, 10 percent Euro-American, and 5 percent Asian American and American Indian. The cultural diversity of the organization includes families from India who practice the Hindu religion, Jewish families, and many Middle Eastern religions. At least 50 percent of the families are bilingual, speaking Spanish or another language with many families only speaking Spanish. A small percentage of the families being served are gay and lesbian. At least 60 percent of the families have a single head of household, which is female.

The mission of the YWCA is the Elimination of Racism, meaning that all programs place an emphasis on ensuring activities are culturally diverse, including Theraplay activities.

Theraplay will be discussed when used by preschool teachers leading group Theraplay, when being taught by a parent educator working with Latino parents, and when used by a therapist using Theraplay when working with an African American client who was going through reunification services with a child through the Department of Social Services.

GROUP THERAPLAY

Group Theraplay was started at the YWCA because many children had behavioral problems and poor self-esteem. Frequently these children were unable to play with other children in the classroom without fighting. Over 80 percent of the children in preschool programs came from low income or very low income families. At least 10 percent of the children were foster children who had special mental health needs. A sample preschool class might be children aged three and four, 50 percent female and 50 percent male, 65 percent Latino, 20 percent African American, 10 percent Euro-American, and 5 percent Asian American or American Indian. In each classroom, at least 20 percent of the children were seeing a therapist, many children had a learning disability, and 25 percent of the Latino children were learning English for the first time. Behavioral problems were a challenge daily with children being aggressive by hitting others or the teacher. At least 50 percent of the children had very low self-esteem. Teachers complained about having to work with children having behavioral problems and sent the child home if the child was being aggressive toward others.

Generally, Theraplay groups are for children who have emotional needs, children who are withdrawn, aggressive or overactive, frightened, compulsive, or rigid. Theraplay groups are adult-directed, structured play groups in which all participants are actively involved together in fun activities. Activities foster self-esteem, a sense of belonging, an awareness of the needs of others, and the ability to care for others and self, and help develop increased trust in others. The group provides participants nurturing, attention, recognition, and appreciation, which many children aren't getting at home (Rubin, 1989). This was true for the children in our groups as well.

ASSESSMENT

Before Theraplay sessions are held, each child in the classroom has an assessment completed by the Head Teacher. The assessment tool used and recommended by the California Department of Education is called the DRDP (Desired Results Development Profile). This profile is completed within the first sixty days in which the child starts a preschool program. The assessment gives a profile of a child in areas such as self-concept, self-regulation, social interaction skills, language development, problem solving, awareness of health and safety, and a variety of other skills (California Department of Education, 2006).

The profile is then used by the Head Teacher to develop lesson plans for the classroom and also to provide individualized activities for each child in order for the child to improve their assessment results before the year-end assessment is completed. The initial assessment done within the first sixty days is also shared with the child's parents so the child and parent can work on areas that need improvement. At least 50 percent of the profiles done in YWCA classrooms showed that the children weren't socially competent and that children were being aggressive toward their classmates by hitting each other when they wanted a toy or the attention of the teacher.

Theraplay provided structure and taught children to wait and ask for a toy or to wait for the teacher to respond to the child. Children in the classrooms weren't challenged and didn't want to participate in classroom activities. Theraplay challenged children and increased a child's self-esteem. Appropriate touch and nurturing behavior between children was poor with children yelling and hitting each other, as mentioned before. Nurturing was a major component of Theraplay and taught children appropriate touch, along with how to communicate a need or feeling to another child or adult. Once nurturing behavior was learned, it carried over to nurturing behavior at home with their siblings and parents. Because the goals of Theraplay and the classroom teacher were compatible, Theraplay was started in each classroom for ten weeks. Each preschool classroom had 24 children and three teaching staff, with one person who was considered the Head Teacher, who led the Theraplay activities.

GOALS OF THERAPLAY

Below are Theraplay goals in a preschool classroom of three- to four-year-old children as they relate to the above assessment tool (DRDP) and to the Theraplay Model.

Structure:

- Children will learn impulse control when relating to other children and teaching staff, reducing aggressive behavior by 75 percent.
- Children will respond to a teacher's instructions on the first request, making transitions from one activity to another without showing any resistance.

Engagement:

- Children will develop positive interactions with the teaching staff by participating in a variety of enjoyable Theraplay activities.
- Children will engage in new and fun Theraplay activities with children from a different culture, sharing toys or other objects of interest.

Challenge:

- Children will learn one new Theraplay activity each session in order to build their self-esteem.
- Children will learn a new cultural activity each session in order to understand another culture.

Nurture:

- Children will learn to express feelings of concern when another child is hurt or sad. Children will receive nurturing activities in each group session.

Reviewing the DRDP assessment tool and Theraplay concepts as they relate to the above goals can be seen in the following example of a Theraplay session used during a ten-week period. The Theraplay session was conducted by a classroom Head Teacher. There were three staff with a classroom of 24 children age three or four years old with the Theraplay session being 45 minutes in length. Each staff member was assigned eight children to work with when doing small group work. Each small group had at least one or two children labeled as difficult, most likely being seen by a mental health therapist. All Theraplay activities were culturally diverse, remembering at the YWCA, 65 percent of the children being served in a preschool classroom were Latino, many who spoke very little English. Activities were done in both English and Spanish so the Latino children learned English and English-speaking children learned Spanish.

THERAPLAY SESSION

Below is a sample Theraplay session with an explanation on how to do the activities. The goal of a beginning session would be engagement since children had not experienced Theraplay before and they would need to adapt to Theraplay activities. The activities would also be challenging to keep the children engaged in Theraplay.

Hello Song

This song is sung in English and then in Spanish to let the children know Theraplay is starting. The song can be any song about friendship or sing the "Hello song." The words are, "Hello Everyone, Hello Everyone, Hello Everyone, We're glad you're here to play." This activity is done as an entire group of 24 children.

Music Movement/Follow the Leader

A CD is put on and the children participate in some form of movement. Tapes should reflect the diversity of the cultures being served. For example, an African-American singer, Linda Tillery, sings traditional African-American songs. Tony Chestnut is a CD used by many preschool teachers to teach younger children movement. Movement songs are also done in Spanish. The Head Teacher leads the class in movement and the children follow her. This activity engages the children in movement and challenges the children to follow the teacher's movements exactly the way she does them. The teacher can also appoint another child to be the leader, which the children enjoy.

Skin Color Prints

The next activity is a sit-down activity with each staff member working with a group of eight children. Different types of paper are given to each group, which represent the skin color of the children in the group. The children select the paper that matches their skin color. The group does handprints and foot prints by drawing their hand and then drawing the hand of another child. They also draw each other's foot. After the prints are completed, the children talk about the different skin colors that exist in the group. Some groups work slower than others, hence, the need for flexibility—children may draw both hands and feet. This project takes 15 minutes with groups working to ensure each child has drawn her hand and a hand of another child. This activity engages and challenges the children to work together as they make prints of each other's hands and feet. The children learn nurturing behavior because they are touching each other's hands appropriately and learning skin differences.

Fortune Cookie Feed

This activity is done in small groups with the children feeding each other a fortune cookie that has been hidden on their body. Again, the children work in pairs, hiding one fortune cookie on another child's shoulder, knee, or near a hand while the child has his or her eyes closed. This activity teaches patience, because the child who is looking for the fortune cookie must keep his or her eyes closed, which isn't easy for a young child. The child hiding the cookie must hide the item in an appropriate place, which teaches the child appropriate touch. Both Theraplay concepts of structure and nurturing are part of this activity. The children really like this activity and reading the fortune is an exciting activity which teaches the children about the Asian culture.

Duck, Duck, Goose—A Hug

This activity is now done when the entire groups gets back together. The game is played like the traditional game of Duck, Duck, Goose, except when the child chases another child and catches the child, the child is given a hug. This encourages nurturing. It is important that each child get the opportunity to participate in this activity. The activity is sometimes done in Spanish which teaches the children Spanish as well as English.

Balloon Volleyball

This activity is done by using a balloon which serves as a volleyball. The children are divided into two teams and the balloon is volleyed between the teams. The goal is to keep the balloon in the air and for it not to touch the ground. This activity is a challenging activity if you keep score, and the game teaches structure because the children have to stay behind a line and wait for the balloon to come near them. Learning the rules of the game teaches children to follow instructions.

Nurturing Each Others' Hurts

This activity is done in pairs as part of the large group. A small bottle of lotion or powder is used. Each child is paired with another child and a child is instructed to put lotion or powder on the other child's hand or arm where there is a hurt or a "boo-boo." The teacher instructs the children where to put the lotion or powder. This teaches the children to nurture each other and to be gentle when touching each other. Staff monitor the children to be sure they are gentle with each other.

Choo-Choo Train

This activity is done as an entire group and is the ending activity. The group forms a train with a staff member being the leader. The group moves through the room doing different activities such as bending, going backwards, going fast or slow, and singing "Choo-choo-choo." This is a great way to end Theraplay and the children enjoy being part of a train and doing a variety of activities. This teaches the children structure by following instructions and challenges the children to follow the leader.

The above activities are a sample of activities that can be done during a group Theraplay session, with a group of 24 children, with some of the activities being done as an entire group and some activities being done in smaller groups of eight children. Small groups should be no larger than eight children.

PARENTING CLASSES

Parenting classes are held for seven weeks. The classes are based on the Theraplay model. The entire family is invited to participate in the class providing they are a member of the YWCA and have a child enrolled in a preschool program. Children who participate in the program are usually three to eight years old. Many of the families taking part have been referred by their preschool teacher because their child has difficulty adjusting to the preschool. Usually, the child has some sort of behavioral problem like hitting another child. Many of the children have low self-esteem. Because at least 60 percent of the families are Latino, the parenting classes described below are based on activities that are from the Latino culture. The class is held in Spanish because this is the first language of the majority of the participants. English-speaking-only participants have an interpreter or attend a class where English is spoken. Understanding the Latino culture is important to the types of activities that take place during Theraplay, and parenting skills taught are based on Latino values. Research shows that permissiveness characterizes Latino parenting; however, traditional parenting by Latino parents values authoritarian structures when child-rearing with a patriarchal authoritarian structure that respects males and the elderly. Latino parents are very nurturing, affectionate, and warm with their children. Latino parents overall are more interactive and engaged with their children during play. Parents demonstrate significantly higher levels of connectedness and affiliation than either European American or mixed ethnicity child-parent pairs during play (Gil, 2005).

Latino parents and their children were very willing to participate in Theraplay and thoroughly enjoyed interacting with each other during the seven-week parenting course.

ASSESSMENT

No official assessment was done with the parents and their children before enrolling in the Parenting Class. Parents and children involved with the YWCA preschool program were told that the DRDP would be used to understand their child's needs, especially in the area of social interaction with other children and their ability to respond to instructions given by the teacher. Parents were also given the opportunity to participate in the Marschak Interaction Method (MIM), a technique developed to provide a structured way of measuring various aspects of the parent-child relationship (Munns, 2000). The majority of the parents decided not to participate in the MIM, because they were afraid they would be judged as being poor parents. However, once they became involved in Theraplay, they had no hesitation and were very willing to take part in the MIM. It was important to be sensitive to other cultures and their fears about being tested, because parents didn't want to be judged as being poor parents by a member of the dominant culture.

GOALS OF PARENTING CLASS

The parenting class lasted a total of seven weeks meeting for two hours weekly. The class started with a meal so everyone could become acquainted with each other. The YWCA provided the meal, but after the third session, the families became engaged with each other and many families brought a dish to share from their culture. Families from the Latino culture feel it is important to break bread together at an event, which means sharing food with each other that was cooked by a family member. This helped families feel closer to each other, and parents were more willing to talk about the problems they were having with their children. Meal time was a very festive event and lasted for a half-hour. After dinner, a topic for discussion was selected by the parent educator. Topics were based around Theraplay concepts. Below are goals of the parenting classes, which was based on topics that were discussed weekly.

- Understanding your birth family, how you were raised, how family values and discipline techniques carry forward from one generation to another.
- Developmental milestones your child achieves from age three to eight years old using the DRDP assessment tool to discuss what your child should achieve throughout the school year.
- Learning the importance of engaging with your child on a daily basis, spending quality time with your child daily.
- Learning the importance of providing your child with a structured environment and how to set limits for your child.
- Building your child's self-esteem by challenging your child and acknowledging his or her efforts when completing a task.
- Providing your child a nurturing environment and spending time daily nurturing your child.
- Understanding how Theraplay can be implemented in your home daily by spending quality time with your child.

The above goals were completed in a seven-week time frame. After the meal was completed, the parents and children were divided into two groups. The parent educator presented the topic for discussion to the parents and then held a group discussion answering all parent questions. The children spent time with another teacher learning different Theraplay activities that would take place later when they worked with their parents. After the parents and children were done meeting separately for 45 minutes, they met together as a group and participated in a Theraplay session for the remaining 45 minutes. Each parent interacted with their own children. If a parent had more than one child, a staff member would assist the parent.

The goal was for the parent and child to have a positive experience working on Theraplay skills through structuring, nurturing, challenging activities and being able to engage the child for 45 minutes of Theraplay activities. The majority of the parents had one child age three to eight years old. Below were some of the activities done during Theraplay sessions.

Hola (Hello Song)

The group sings the song, but each parent faces her child and sings. The parent sings the following song. "Hola (name of child), Hola (name of child), Hola (name of child), Soy feliz que usted está aquí (I am happy you are here)." This song establishes the start of the Theraplay session and allows the parent to engage the children immediately in Theraplay, providing the child with nurturing by holding the child's hand and looking into the child's eyes.

Positive Comments

Next, the parents tell the child something positive about herself. This comment is to be about the child, not something the child did today at school or at home. Comments such as, "What beautiful eyes you have," or "Your hair is really curly." A parent could say, "I love you. You are a beautiful child." The comments help build the child's self-esteem and then the child usually willingly wants to participate in the other activities that will take place.

Nurturing Hurts

The parent then spends time nurturing any hurts a child could have, a bruise, cut, anything they notice on the child's arm, face, or hand. Usually, the parent uses lotion, but they could use powder if they didn't want to use lotion. This gives the parent the opportunity to express concern for hurts the child has, nurturing the child and letting the child know that the parent really cares for her child. Again, eye contact between the parent and child is very important.

Pase la Botella (Pass the Bottle)

Next the group comes together and participates in group activities. When the music starts, you pass the bottle as you would when playing Hot Potato. When the music stops, the person enters the circle to dance with the bottle by placing it on their head as you turn the music on for a few seconds. You then repeat a dance. The plastic bottle is decorated with glued-on gems. One Spanish song used is called "Pass the Bottle," with a calypso beat.

Uno, Dos, Tres (One, Two, Three)

Place three hula hoops in a line. As the people walk around, clapping and chanting, "A la uno, a la dos, a la tres, zass, zass, zass, todo, todo, entra la circulo, rapido, rapido, ra, ra, ra." Hula hoops are then taken away one at a time until there are none left and the people must form their own circle.

Cultural Musical Chairs

Musical Chairs for two-person teams. Chairs are placed in a circle. The parent and the child must be 'glued' to each other by holding each other. When the Spanish music starts, the parent and child walk around the chairs. When the music stops, the parent and the child must sit together in one chair with the child on the parent's lap. Continue until there is one team remaining.

Dancing with the Broom

Make a large circle with one person in the middle holding the broom. When the Spanish music plays, the person holding the broom spins around with her eyes closed. At the same time, the people in the circle hold hands and walk around in a circle. When the music stops, the person holding the broom points to the person in front of her, who will then have to dance with the broom for a minute inside the circle. This person will then spin around with her eyes closed while the rest of the group walks around in a circle. Repeat. All music is Latino music sung in Spanish.

CASE STUDY: REUNIFICATION SERVICES WITH AN AFRICAN-AMERICAN PARENT AND HER DAUGHTER

The YWCA works very closely with Child Protective Services, who are responsible for protecting children who have been abused or neglected by a parent. Many of the children seen by therapists at the YWCA have been away from their parents for more than a year. In the majority of the cases, the child has been placed in a foster home and in some cases many foster homes. The parent must work toward reunification with their child or the parent risks the child being adopted or placed in long-term foster care. Most parents want reunification services to take place, but are afraid of how the child will react to coming home. They are unsure of their parenting skills and want their child to have a positive experience when returning home. The child is also afraid of going home, because she doesn't know if her parent has changed. The child is often angry with her parent, because she had to leave home and be placed in a foster home. If the child was removed because her parent had a substance abuse problem, the child is afraid the parent will have a relapse and they will have to remain in the foster care system.

Before a parent is ready for reunification services, they must accomplish the following goals with the Department of Social Services: 1) have a place to live; 2) have a job or income to support the child; 3) if they had a substance abuse problem they must be drug-free and test drug-free for several months; 4) have an individual therapist to work through issues that caused her to lose her child, and 5) take a parenting class in order to understand how to work with her child. It should be noted that each case is different. Some parents have goals that are different than the above goals. After they have accomplished the above goals, the judge usually grants supervised visits with their child and recommends the parent and child attend family therapy to work on the reunification process before the child is placed back in the home.

Theraplay fosters attachment and helps the parent develop a secure attachment relationship with the child. A secure attachment relationship is a relationship that is caring, reciprocal, and develops over time. It is a loving relationship between the parent and the child (Jernberg and Booth, 1999). This relationship is very important and must start to be developed before the child moves back in with the parent. In most of the families being seen, the mother is the person working toward reunification. The father has no contact, is in jail for domestic violence or substance abuse issues, is unknown, or the mother doesn't want the father involved. The mother is now totally responsible for the household including providing for all expenses. The mother wants the Department of Social Services to return her child, and must attend family therapy for this to occur. YWCA Therapists use Theraplay for over 75 percent of the families being seen. Families seen are from many different cultures and it is important to understand the culture and family value system when working on reunification with the family. Some cultures don't believe touch is important after a certain age, other cultures feel discipline is very important and respect is the number-one goal for the child. The therapist must understand the culture, the family value system, and how the parent was raised for Theraplay to be a positive experience. The therapist must know what structure the parent provides her child, how the parent sets limits, and what type of nurturing the parent provides the child daily. In order for Theraplay to be effective, the therapist must engage both the parent and child in the process. The parent usually has resistance to Theraplay, because of feeling forced to seek treatment, being mandated by the court system to attend family therapy before the child is returned home.

The following Theraplay concepts were considered when doing reunification work with an African-American mother who had a four year old child and wanted the court to return her child.

Legal/Ethical Issues

The mother was required to attend therapy for six months in order for her child to be returned. Theraplay was conducted for 15 sessions. The parent was concerned about having the sessions videotaped which is usually done in order to help the parent see the progress she has made during a session and help her understand areas she needs to work on with her child. She was afraid the videotape would be used against her in court. We agreed that Theraplay sessions done with her child and the therapist would be taped and any sessions done with her and her child would be erased after being reviewed. Taping sessions were done to protect the therapist in case the parent was hesitant about leaving the child with the therapist alone, especially when nurturing was taking place by the therapist. The tapes were also used to show the parent what took place in therapy and explained the four dimensions of Theraplay: structure, nurture, engagement, and challenge. Most therapy sessions were done with a two-way mirror, so the parent could observe what the therapist was doing during the session. In some cases, another therapist (an interpreting therapist) was available to explain what was taking place in therapy. However, taping sessions when the parent was involved in the court system was very scary to the parent, and many parents refused to allow taping to occur.

Marschak Assessment

Before Theraplay sessions are started with the parent, a Marschak assessment takes place. This assessment helps the therapist understand how the parent and child interact with each other and their relationship. In this case, the parent participated in seven activities, which took a half hour to complete. She did the following activities:

- She played with her daughter using two squeaky toy ducks.
- She put lotion on her child and had her child put lotion on her.
- She taught her child something she didn't know.
- She left the room for one minute.
- She taught her child a game.
- She told her child about being born and her first memories of her daughter.
- She fed her child a snack.
- She and her daughter put hats on each other.

The MIM helped to determine the type of Theraplay activities that would be planned for future Theraplay sessions. The MIM gave the following information:

Engagement: Did the mother and child engage easily in a variety of activities? In the above MIM, the child was hesitant to participate in some of the activities. The mother had a very hard time engaging her in playing with the ducks. However, as the MIM progressed, the child was more willing to participate in the activities.

Structure/Setting Limits: This was a challenge for the mother. The child wanted to control the entire session. She wanted to read the instruction cards. She would take over the activities and her mother would allow her to decide when an activity would end. The mother attempted to lead, but had very little control over her daughter when participating in an activity.

Challenging: She rarely gave her daughter any positive reinforcement. When they were drawing a picture and playing a game, the mother was more interested in completing the project than giving positive feedback to her daughter. In fact, no feedback was given to her daughter at all. The daughter told her mom that she drew a great picture, however, the daughter did not draw a picture of herself, which the mother had asked the daughter to do.

Nurturing: Mom had her daughter nurture her first by putting the lotion on her as opposed to the mother putting lotion on her daughter. Mom had a very hard time touching her daughter or giving her any nurturing or positive feedback.

The MIM showed that mom needed to work on structure and setting limits with her child in a positive way. They both needed to work on participating in Theraplay activities because in the beginning of the MIM, the daughter didn't really care if she participated in any activities with her mother. The mother needed to give her daughter more positive feedback when she completed an activity, especially an activity where she challenged her to participate. Most importantly, the mother needed to provide nurturing to her daughter. She had great difficulty with hugging her daughter or telling her daughter that she loved her. When asking the mother how she felt about the MIM session, she said her daughter needed to listen to her and show respect. Showing respect was very important to her.

A complete Theraplay assessment takes at least three sessions. During the first session the therapist meets with the parent alone and gets a history of the parent's life as a child. The greatest predictor of an infant's attachment patterns are the attachment patterns of her primary care giver. Parents need to explore their own attachment histories and associated attachment behavioral patterns. Comparisons need to be made between the parent's patterns in their families of origin and those manifested by their child (Hughes, 2007). The mother stated that when she was bad, she got whipped with a tree branch or the belt. She was told that she was to listen to her parents, no questions asked. She was also told that she was to respect her parents and all elders. Her parents weren't overly nurturing to her and they told her education was important in order to be successful. She was raised by both parents and both parents worked. Church was an important part of her upbringing and she was required to attend church three times a week and for five hours on Sundays.

During the second session of Theraplay the MIM takes place. After the MIM is completed, the therapist asks both the mother and daughter how they felt about the experience. A tape is usually done so that the therapist can review the tape the following week with the parents. The mother allowed the session to be taped, providing the tape was erased at the end of the session, which was done.

During the third session, the therapist and the mother met to talk about the MIM sessions. By reviewing the tape, the mother was able to discuss activities that she felt comfortable doing and those with which she felt uncomfortable. Again, Theraplay concepts were reviewed—engaging, challenging, structure, and nurturing. She agreed that she and her daughter were nervous in the beginning, but as the activities continued, she became more relaxed. She stated that she had a hard time teaching her daughter an activity and wasn't used to giving her daughter any type of positive feedback or encouragement to complete a task. She also stated that hugging her daughter was difficult and wasn't something she experienced as a child, which was discussed during session one. She stated that her daughter wouldn't listen to her and she wanted her daughter to show her respect. It was decided the therapist would work with her daughter for five to six sessions and the mother would join the sessions. At first she would watch the session through a see-through mirror. It was also agreed that we would have a debriefing time after each session to discuss what was taking place and for her to ask questions about the session.

Cultural Understanding

The therapist was a Euro-American woman age 55+ and the mother was an African-American single parent in her 40s who was considered low-income. Religion was important to her and raising her daughter in the church was a high priority. It was imperative to understand her value system and how she wanted to raise her daughter.

African-American parents have to overcome adversity, develop mobility paths for their families, and socialize their children for devalued positions in our society. African-American churches often serve as a major part of family life. Churches have special strengths for the family, because members of the church support one another and the church serves as a way to cope with the daily struggles in life (Webb, 2001).

Understanding that discipline was very important to mom and that her daughter needed to show respect was repeated on several different occasions. Talking back wasn't acceptable. Her mother also expected her daughter to do well in school by listening to the teacher. Attending church was also important, even though her daughter wasn't involved in church in her foster home.

This mother's values were typical of many African-American families who feel discipline is very important and put an emphasis on structure when talking about Theraplay activities and what they want to accomplish. In fact, structure is their number-one priority when doing Theraplay and Theraplay isn't considered successful if the child is not obedient to their directions. Many African-American parents have stated that they want their child to behave and they want the therapist to talk to their children about behaving. Because Theraplay has fun, engaging activities and is well-liked by the children, there is resistance from some parents to participate in Theraplay. Time must be spent explaining how Theraplay will accomplish structure and teach respect, along with providing nurturing to the child, and engaging and challenging activities.

DSM-IV Information

Both the mother and her daughter were being seen by a therapist. Contact with the mother's therapist stated she had a substance abuse issue and also suffered from depression. She had just left a six-month substance abuse center and, to date, had not experienced a relapse. At the time of Theraplay treatment, she was not taking any medication for her depression, but this option was being explored for the future.

Contact with the child's therapist stated that the child had attachment issues and was experiencing trauma from being removed from her home. Since her mother had a long history of substance abuse problems, her daughter had very little attachment to her mother. She was caught lying in school and at home, and stealing food and other items at home. She had been in several fights with other children in her foster home. She refused to talk to her therapist about her birth mom or other foster home placements. The concern her therapist had was her staying in her current foster home which was questionable, because she had been in so much trouble with her foster parents.

Both of the above clients are typical clients seen at the YWCA and it was felt that both clients would benefit from Theraplay. Theraplay was the selected model for therapy with the intent of helping both the mother and daughter develop a positive relationship with each other again, strengthening their bond and teaching mom how to develop a structured environment for her daughter that would help her daughter become more obedient. Teaching mom the importance of nurturing her daughter and giving her positive reinforcement was also stressed.

Theraplay Goals

The following are specific Theraplay goals discussed by mother and therapist for 15 weeks with an evaluation taking place after the 15th week. Week four through eight would be done with the Therapist and the daughter with mom watching the activities taking place and the therapist explaining what took place after each session. In the remaining sessions, mother would directly participate in the sessions with her daughter.

1. Mom and daughter will engage in a variety of Theraplay activities, learning to have fun with each other and to enjoy being together.
2. Mom will challenge her daughter to complete a Theraplay activity, giving her positive reinforcement, and ensuring her daughter wins at whatever activity is taking place.
3. Mom will learn to set limits with her daughter, helping her to complete an activity by following her instructions.
4. Mom will be encouraged to show affection and warmth toward her daughter, touching and nurturing her during the Theraplay session.

All the above goals were agreed upon by the mother with some resistance being shown to participating in nurturing activities, but being very enthusiastic about giving her daughter instructions and setting limits.

Sample Therapy Sessions

Three Theraplay sessions will be described. All sessions were done by the therapist first with the four-year-old daughter with mom observing what would take place when she participated in Theraplay.

Agenda for Beginning Treatment Phase

This session was one of the first sessions done with both mother and her daughter, with the therapist observing the activities taking place and assisting when needed with the activities.

- Hello Song (described earlier)
- Positive Comments (described earlier)

- Nurturing Hurts (described earlier)
- Play Dough Hand Prints (Make handprints out of play dough, both hands and foot prints if there is time, both mom and daughter)
- Cotton Ball Throw (Throw cotton balls at each other on cue, aiming for certain body parts such as the knee. This is a structured activity and throwing one cotton ball, then two, and then three at the same time are done on cue, when mom says a specific word)
- Build a Cotton Ball Snowman (Build a snowman together with cotton balls engages participants in a fun activity together and helps clean up the cotton balls)
- Hiding Potato Chips on Her Body (Explained earlier using a fortune cookie. Should only hide about three potato chips. Mom hides chips and then feeds them to her daughter)
- Mommy May I (This activity is a structured activity where her daughter asks permission to take so many steps with the goal being to get to her Mom by asking permission saying, "Mommy may I . . . take 3 steps?")
- Paper Basketball (Mom and daughter play basketball by throwing a ball or newspaper balls made from newspaper in a wastebasket and keep score, which serves as a challenging activity, which the daughter is to win)
- Back Massage/Tell a Story (Mom gives her daughter a back massage while making up a story in order to do different types of massage on her daughter's back, which serves as a beginning nurturing activity)
- Feeding a Cookie or other food (Mom feeds daughter a cookie or other form of food, which serves as a nurturing activity)
- Goodbye Song (Mom and daughter sing a goodbye song that states they will see each other next week)

This session was one of the first sessions done with mom and nurturing was kept to a minimum in order to get mom to engage in the activities. Mom stated she liked the structured activities and enjoyed the challenging activities. She needed to be reminded before the session that it was important to let her daughter win when doing challenging activities and give her lots of positive reinforcement. Mom liked the session and felt her daughter also enjoyed the activities. Mom felt uncomfortable feeding her daughter and felt her daughter could feed herself. Mom was somewhat egocentric in feeling that her daughter should give her a massage which again was explained to her that she needed to nurture her daughter first to begin the bonding process.

Agenda for Middle Treatment Phase

This was a session done in the middle of treatment with her daughter. The goal of this session was to get mom to provide more nurturing toward her daughter.

- Hello Song (described earlier)
- Positive Comments (described earlier)
- Nurturing Hurts (described earlier)
- Slip and Slide (Lotion is placed on her daughter's arms and hands. The daughter then tries to pull her hand out from the grip of her mother's hands when her mom gives her a cue by saying a word)
- Measuring Smile (Measuring her daughter's smile with a fruit roll-up and feeding it to her is always a positive experience for her daughter and is a nurturing activity)
- Tin Foil Mask (making a face mask out of tin foil, also can do hand-prints)
- Cotton Ball/Feather Paper Blow (Mom and daughter blow a feather or cotton ball from one piece of paper to another which serves as a challenging activity)
- Cotton Ball/Feather Touch (Her daughter closes her eyes and her mom touches her with a cotton ball or a feather and she guesses which object she is touched with. This activity is done with mom also closing her eyes)
- M&M Hide (This is a nurturing activity where instead of hiding a potato chip, mom hides about 5 M&Ms on her child, then finds the M&Ms and feeds them to her daughter)
- Squirt Bottle at Target (Water is placed in two squirt bottles and mom and daughter aim at a target on cue given by mom with the goal being to hit the target, which serves as a challenging activity with lots of positive reinforcement being given to her daughter)
- Red Light, Green Light (Her daughter stands at one end of the room and tries to walk to her mom who has her back turned at the other end of the room. Mom uses "red light" to stop and "green light" to go. When her daughter reaches her mom, they hug each other)
- Lollipop Feed (Mom cradles her daughter and sings a special song about her as she feeds her a lollipop giving her lots of hugs and nurturing her)
- Goodbye Song (discussed previously)

This session had a lot of nurturing with mom actually holding and cradling her daughter at the end of the session for at least five minutes. Mom was feeling more comfortable with Theraplay activities now, but was still showing some resistance to feeding her daughter the lollipop. However, she was beginning to see that her daughter loved the nurturing given to her by her mom and really enjoyed the Theraplay activities. Mom had made significant progress with nurturing activities and was showing less resistance to feeding her daughter. She continued to like the structured activities and saw how her daughter was now responding to her when she set limits and provided structure.

Agenda for Ending Treatment Phase

This was one of the last sessions done with mom with the majority of the session being based around nurturing activities and bonding.

- Hello Song (described earlier)
- Positive Comments (described earlier)
- Nurturing Hurts (described earlier)
- Slip and Slide (described earlier)
- Measuring Smile with fruit roll-up and feeding (described earlier with the understanding that other parts of her body can be measured with the goal being that mom feeds her daughter and nurtures her as she is measuring her hands, ears, or other body parts)
- Powder Prints (Mom and daughter do powder prints together which is done by putting lotion on her hands and then putting powder over the lotion and making a print on black paper. Prints were done with hands and also feet. Mom also washed her daughter's hands and feet to get the powder and lotion off, which was very nurturing)
- Cotton Ball/Feather Paper Massage (Mom gives daughter a massage using a feather and then the cotton ball. She can also have her daughter guess which item is being used which is a challenging activity along with a nurturing activity)
- Licorice Pull and Eating (Two very long pieces of licorice are put together and mom and daughter start eating from their end of the licorice to the middle, where they end up giving each other a hug and kiss)
- Karate Paper Chop (Mom holds newspaper, and her daughter attempts to use her hand like a karate master to chop the paper in half. This is a challenging activity because the paper gets smaller. Her daughter does the karate chop when given the cue by her mom, which teaches her daughter structure and also expressing aggression in a safe, controlled way.
- Candy Bottle Pop Feed (Mom feeds her daughter a candy bottle pop which is shaped like a bottle and holds her in her arms while singing a song to her about how wonderful she is which is a very nurturing activity. This activity took place for about ten minutes)
- Goodbye Song (discussed previously)

This session included almost all nurturing activities with some structured activities taking place, but the goal was for mom to nurture her daughter as much as possible. Mom had finally accepted that nurturing her daughter was important and that her daughter really enjoyed being held. Because her mother was spending time nurturing her daughter and being more attuned to her needs, her daughter became more receptive to listening to her and following her instructions when asked to do a task.

Mom was successful in finishing fifteen sessions of Theraplay and finally understood the importance of nurturing her daughter and being more responsive to her needs. Theraplay brought mom and her daughter back together again and they became much more attached to each other. Eventually, mom finished the reunification process and her daughter was returned to her by the court system.

It has been our experience that Theraplay is a very successful form of therapy to use when working on the reunification of family members.

Note

A special thank-you for Theraplay activities included in the Parenting section which were planned by Monica Garcia, the parent educator who has been very successful in providing Theraplay for Latino families at the YWCA.

REFERENCES

California Department of Education. (2008) *Desired Results Developmental Profile-Revised User's Guide*. 45.

Jernberg, A. and Booth, P. (1999) *Theraplay.* San Francisco: Jossey-Bass.

Gil, E. (2005) *Cultural Issues in Play Therapy*. New York: The Guilford Press.

Hughes, D. (2007) *Attachment-focused Family Therapy*. New York: W. W. Norton and Company.

Marschak, M. (1960) A method for evaluating child-parent interaction under controlled conditions. *Journal of Genetic Psychology*. 97:3–22.

Munns, E. (2000) *Theraplay: Innovations in Attachment-Enhancing Play Therapy*. Northvale: Jason Aronson, Inc.

N.A. (2006) *Infant/Toddler Learning and Development Program Guidelines*. Sacramento: California Department of Education.

Rubin, R. (1989) *Play with Them: Theraplay Groups in the Classroom*. Springfield: Charles C. Thomas.

Webb, N. (2001) *Culturally Diverse Parent—Child and Family Relationships*. New York: Columbia University Press Publishers.

IV

THERAPLAY INTEGRATED WITH OTHER THERAPIES

12

In Sync

Gail Smillie

In Sync is a program designed with the fundamentals of Theraplay® in mind: a multi-sensory program for parents and children age birth to six with a focus on building, enhancing, and strengthening parent-child attachment. The program uses the Marschak Interaction Method (MIM), a video assisted family assessment approach, followed by Theraplay and parent counseling. The program is informed by attachment theory, interpersonal neurobiology, child development research, as well as concepts from Circle of Security (Marvin, Cooper, Hoffman, and Powell, 2002, pp. 1–17). The program's goal is to weave together pleasure and human connection. Bruce Perry explains that "the association of pleasure and human interaction is the important neurobiological "glue" that bonds and creates healthy relationships" (Perry and Szalavitz, 2006, p. 85).

Formal Theraplay training begins an adventure, but the art of Theraplay is learned later from the children and parents who join with us in the search for greater comfort and joy in their lives. Often moving frantically, clinging and pinching, head butting and laughing, tantruming and bolting, collapsing and hiding, Haley was the little girl who taught me how Theraplay helps. Comforting Haley was like trying to grasp water or corral the wind. Living with Haley left the adults responsible for her care emotionally drained and remarkably insecure. Remembering that Daniel Siegel said, "Negative emotions can be seen as an opportunity to deepen a child's capacity for self-regulation and self-understanding" (Solomon and Siegel, 2003, p. 39), I knew why, but not exactly how. Haley had learned how to survive, but not how to trust adults—to care and nurture, sooth and warm, provide and protect. Haley was living out her nightmare and we were a witness to her history as I stepped into her life and began the process of engagement.

Through many difficult sessions, I recall reminding myself of how Bruce Perry describes the process: "These children need patterned, repetitive experiences appropriate to their developmental needs, needs that reflect the age at which they'd missed important stimuli or had been traumatized, not their current chronological age" (Perry and Szalavitz, 2006, p. 138). Haley gradually learned to rely on adults, accept love and caring touch, and to play with joy. Although Haley did "not speak the language of love without an accent" (Perry and Szalavitz, 2006, p. 98), as Bruce Perry describes children who are traumatized during critical periods of development, it was evident that some repair had taken place, as Haley was connected to safe others who could care for her.

Early in 2002, a remarkable movement spread across Canada. Brain research and attachment theory hammered its way into the hearts and minds of Government funding, which shed light on the importance of the early years. Money was being directed into programs that worked with parents and children ages zero to three years old. In Sync's proposal followed simple guidelines: the first is that traveling with babies/toddlers is hard and the program must go to the client, and the second is that we must always remember that the parent-child dyad is the customer, not one or the other. We had learned that approaches that inherently separate the parent and child must be replaced with approaches that promote connection; approaches that promote parenting as a "learn-in-the-classroom" subject must be replaced by experiential learn-by-doing—emotionally reciprocal, play-filled approaches. Theraplay fits this framework. The parent-child-dyadic work of Theraplay viewed the mind and body as working together, followed by parent coaching where the pull for self-reflection and empathy was assisted.

During the 5 years of operation, while more attachment informed therapeutic parenting has been assisted by neurobiological research (Siegel and Hartzell, 2003), and while science has taken a more prominent role in the art of parenting (Sunderland, 2006), In Sync has been enriched, but the foundation remains "Theraplay-in-action."

What helped in gaining acceptance in a traditionally informed agency? It was decided to cast a wide net. Psychologists, social workers, counselors and early childhood specialists, working in all aspects of the helping profession, joined together in an Introductory Theraplay course. This created a synergy around the new program and provided the program with a large, well-informed referral source. Bringing together the latest information on child development, attachment literature, play, interpersonal neurobiology, and parenting was interesting to all.

Play is a serious strategy in the program—a platform on which emotional reciprocity, the give and take of relationships, and the natural hierarchy in the parent-child relationship can unfold. Counselors are often heard repeating to parents, "All the toys get in the way," or "You're the biggest toy in the room!" as the concept of play is introduced to a generation of parents who have been heavily exposed to the kidnapping of play by computerization and big business. As Jaak Pansepp (Third International Theraplay Conference, July 2007, Chicago, Keynote Address) the neuroscience of play researcher, describes, play is safe medicine. Play accesses the most wonderful pharmacy in the world—the one inside the human brain. To release "joy juice"(Sunderland, 2006, p. 90), to turn on "the big light switch" (Sunderland, 2006 p. 95), to activate the seeking system (Sunderland, 2006, p. 101), or to prevent "hormonal hell" (Sunderland, 2006, p. 187), we need to know how to access the right chemistry, and play is a wonderful mechanism to do this. (For a more detailed description of this playful way of explaining the brain and the chemical dance in the brain read Margo Sunderland's, *The Science of Parenting* 2006.)

Theraplay looks for open, uncluttered spaces. Although almost any natural medium can be incorporated into Theraplay, everything selected has the purpose of promoting the interaction at a deeper level and pulling for increased parental ability to engage, structure, and nurture the child, while the child learns to trust, rely, and explore with confidence.

At the beginning of treatment, the parents in the program had the opportunity to complete an Adult Attachment Interview. Daniel Siegel and Mary Hartzell in their book *Parenting from the Inside out* state, "coherent narratives are the best predictor of a child's having a secure attachment to us" (Siegel and Hartzell, 2003, p. 48). Changing parental perceptions, body sensations, and emotions, what Daniel Siegel calls implicit memory (Siegel, 1999, p. 22–23), is an enormous task—one that the In Sync program knew required an experiential approach aided by the parent's review of and reflection on their own narrative. Introducing the concept of earned secure attachment (Siegel, 1999, p. 123–124) to parents and providing the opportunity for the parent to experience the Adult Attachment Interview opened new possibilities to promote parental understanding, insight, and empathy for themselves and subsequently for their child.

CASE STUDIES

Case 1

Before coming to In Sync, Marlene, a family worker, had worked with children diagnosed with autism. The approach in which Marlene was trained was patient, planned, practical—one which required "on the spot" imagination and creativity. "You learn to take risks and not to take surprises personally," said Marlene, "Everything a child does, everything a parent does is rich data—important information—and that's where you start." Marlene was well versed in teaching parent's to do start-up requests rather than stop-requests and in re-phrasing, working with tactile sensitivities, and breaking down activities into tiny steps. Working with children with autism taught Marlene to see the world the way the child sees it. The step into Theraplay was a natural one for Marlene.

An energetic, organized, insightful, and diminutive therapist, Marlene arrives early each morning at a shared office packed with Theraplay supplies, where she starts her day by checking her case supply lists. The supply list is created quickly at the end of each previous session. Most of the day is spent in homes. "Doing in-home Theraplay is the best," she explains, "because families build it into their lives easily—but staying organized is important!" Each In Sync therapist is provided with an over the shoulder, large monogrammed bag in which plastic containers hold lotion, powder, scarves, balloons, and bubbles. In addition, a camcorder, and portable DVD player allow for easy feedback; while videos, such as: *The Simple Gift* (Wolpert and Benoit, 2005) and books on Theraplay and parenting (Jernberg and Booth 1999) are always on hand.

Marlene's Theraplay-in-the-van case revealed the philosophy of starting with whatever the parent presents. After viewing the MIM and having an introductory Theraplay session, the mother described during the parent counseling time, that her main complaint was the explosion, anger, tears, and power struggles that resulted whenever she and her husband attempted to take the children in the family vehicle. Because the father had suffered a life-changing stroke the previous year, the family had many on-going adjustments and certainly very real losses. Of the two young children in the family, the eldest seemed to be coping while the three year old, Sara, was in constant distress as the mother had returned to work and the father's presentation to the children had changed dramatically.

To assist with putting the father's stroke in context for the child, Marlene started by writing a social story. "A little story to help Sara understand her daddy's slow and awkward movements and to help dampen Sara's over arousal pattern," she explained. The book was all about Jocelyn and incorporated one message that Marlene wanted Sara to understand. "Sometimes his brain is really busy and it takes a long time for him to smile." "Sometimes I wave at Daddy and it takes a long time for him to wave back . . . because it takes a long time for his brain to figure out how to wave." This laid the ground work for the following Theraplay session—Theraplay in a van!

Little Sara protested vehemently at Dad putting her in her car seat; Dad, then, became more determined; Sara resisted and it went from mess to disaster. While en route Sara screamed for hugs and kisses, "right now!" "It's not safe and it's definitely not bringing out my hug-and-kisses-side," protested her mother. "We've become so discouraged that we just avoid going anywhere."

To tackle the power struggles and dampen Sara's fears, Marlene designed a van Theraplay session and co-opted the parent's involvement. The "hello song," "lotioning of hurts" and "inventory" (see appendix) took place in the yard on a colorful quilt. A trail of chalk footprints led the way to the van, where Dad was challenged to put on Sara's seat belt without opening his eyes. "Watch that he doesn't peek, Sara," said Marlene in an upbeat voice. As they drove around the neighborhood, Marlene led the family in "the peanut butter jelly game," "guess the sound game," and "the wheels on the bus hand motions," which kept Sara engaged. A special handshake occurred during all stops. Kisses that could be blown and magically caught were a big hit. "We only had to do it once," Marlene said in amazement, "it switched the dad's way of thinking" (that he should automatically be obeyed) "and the mom's way of responding" (that she felt she needed to intervene between her daughter and husband). It strengthened the bond and they had fun. Marlene explained, "I wasn't sure if I could make it strong enough to spill over into the van, so I decided to do it in the van."

In Theraplay, there are activities that we think of as down-activities and ones that we think of as up-activities; then we choose combinations of alternating up and down in an effort to co-regulate, using the relationship as the vehicle for the delivery of the experience. We also think of activities as sensory activities and combine these in interesting ways. "Sound effects go so far with young children—almost like the effect music has on gaining cooperation." Marlene has incorporated sound effects into almost everything she does. In helping gain cooperation she simply adds "boom, boom, boom" to putting objects in a basket or "swoosh, swoosh" to rolling up sleeves to get ready for a game.

At the final In Sync session, each child is left with a goodie bag, filled with the materials needed to carry on with the Theraplay activities. Simple brown bags with their names written on them make the goodbye ceremony a special one.

Case 2

Leanne joined the program after working in an intensive day program for "at risk children with behavioural difficulties." Leanne's first In Sync family gave her insight into the Theraplay process: In Angelica's short two years of life she had lived in three different homes. Born to parents who were described as somewhat lower functioning and who used alcohol to excess, Angelica was removed from her parents care at 11 months of age. The young parents had been following through on attending mandated programs identified by the courts. When In Sync became involved the Permanent Guardianship Order trial was imminent and the social worker indicated that her recommendation was that little Angelica be permanently removed from her parent's care. The parents were hostile, suspicious, and untrusting upon Leanne's first encounter. Although they had stopped drinking, the parent education courses were virtually useless as they could not apply the parenting strategies when Angelica was in their care. The MIM revealed that they were afraid of making mistakes and completely unsure of how to engage or structure activities. There were periods of disrupted communication, but there was also appropriate nurturing and underutilized strengths noticed by Leanne. During the MIM feedback session, Leanne focused on their strengths and the delightful nature of little Angelica. Hoping to begin the process of creating high intensity moments, Leanne watched the parents' eyes fill with joy and loving intention. The decision was made to have the parents watch part of each session and be involved in replicating immediately after. It worked: their gaze softened and both parents became more intentional; they were more purposeful and confident in their engagement; they learned to follow and lead; they became aware of themselves in the parenting of their child. Keeping in mind that "The child does not experience the parent directly—the child experiences the parenting" (Mate, 1999, p. 56), Theraplay allowed little Angelica to have an experience of her parent's parenting immediately. "By the third session, they had found their wings," said Leanne. "Highlighting strengths is so important—it is the building block for all skills." Being with their child in planned ways was immediately followed by parent counseling, which helped these parents to be active and appropriate with their child.

"This was my first introduction to Theraplay and I could really see the difference between Theraplay and the parent education courses that I was familiar with—it is the deep emotional connection created, it is the turning on of the right chemicals, it is the nurturing of the parents" said Leanne with a smile.

Case 3

The following describes one of the saddest cases encountered by the program. The referral call arrived from a grief counseling agency, asking for "that play based therapy that helps attachment." A family, decimated by the murder suicide of the mother and father, left two-year-old Loreen and 6-year-old Karen, yearning for their mother and confused about what had happened. The anger, guilt, and sadness were palpable when I first met the aunt and these two extraordinarily quiet little girls. A history of domestic violence had put the family in a shelter once; and the extended family was aware of the father's excessive drinking and gambling, but no one would have imagined this outcome. The maternal aunt, who had been looking after the children when the father killed the mother and then himself three days later, had stepped into being the caregiver for the children. Along with the deceased mother's parents and a recent immigrant nanny, Auntie Anna was doing her best. During the history taking and current functioning assessment, it was revealed that the pregnancies were healthy, the children wanted; earlier happy times may have provided some degree of pre-trauma health—how much was unclear.

Karen's reaction to the loss was to become the replacement mommy for little Loreen: an exhausting and virtually impossible task. Between the extended family support and a good response to grief counseling and trauma therapy, Karen was able to continue with school and have friends. All of the health markers of sleeping, eating, eliminating, and playing indicated that her recovery was underway. Loreen, on the other hand, was frozen. Large dark eyes stared ahead as she clung to her auntie. The aunt described how Loreen was passed around at the funeral and subsequent gatherings, passively without making a sound. Any words she had previously spoken had vanished. Most skills, like feeding herself and playing with toys, had stopped. The family grimaced as they told me how Loreen cried without making a sound. English was a second language for the family and using an interpreter was not wanted by the family, as they felt shamed and exposed in their cultural community. Loreen's symptoms were largely ones that were observed, as her internal world was unexpressed and her personal story untold. A diagnosis of PTSD was complicated due to the predisposition of less well-developed verbal capacity, lack of parental report, and an ESL caregiver. It was evident, however, that there had been a significant loss, exposure to domestic violence, behavioral indicators of regression, and an overdeveloped startle reflex. Loreen smiled at nothing and showed fear toward many things (toys, taking her arms from her side, holding hands in a circle, and especially at having food put in her mouth). Loreen was in a perpetual state of protection or defense; this would compromise her development as emotional growth and protection are thought to be somewhat mutually exclusive (Lipton, 2000, Videotape). Various relatives requested to care for Loreen and indeed competed for her attendance at public functions. A guilt-driven family was trying to sooth and comfort, but was having an unintended destabilizing effect. A number of structural interventions were put into place: no overnight visits, consistency in bedtime routine, and consistency in daytime child orientated activities. Grief counseling was prescribed for all adults. With this, some of Loreen's symptoms began to subside. Now trauma recovery and attachment based interventions were required. Because Loreen had lost all capacity to explore her world or show interest in toys or objects of any kind, traditional play therapy, usually a good option for trauma recovery, was unsuccessful and taking too long. Theraplay was selected to establish and strengthen the secure base (Marvin, Cooper, Hoffman, and Powell, 2002) to re-introduce nurturing, to engage and provide challenge in gentle ways, and to hopefully put play back into Loreen's heart.

The MIM was difficult: Loreen clung to her auntie; no activities were completed. The modifications to Theraplay involved breaking all activities into smaller steps. Loreen was not separated from the caregiver for any sessions. During the first session, the "hello song" took place with Loreen sitting on her aunt's lap, while the adults held hands, smiled, and sang softly. Her hands recoiled when the lotion was introduced. "That's not what you want," I said softly, "maybe you want to put lotion on us?" That was a hit and Loreen worked hard at getting the lotion onto each of the adult's hands. (Guessing at the child's inter-subjective experience was a Daniel Hughes [Hughes and Booth, 2007] concept that blended well with Theraplay and helped pull for greater reflective capacity in the parent while increasing attunement in the relationship.) At the end of the session, we sang the "goodbye song" while I cradled Loreen in my arms—she fell asleep immediately. As Gordon Neufelt explains the orientation instinct: "getting our bearings will command all of our attention and consume most of our energy" (Neufelt and Mate, 2004, p. 18). That first session was hard work for little Loreen and we all knew how well she had done: small steps in the right direction.

Theraplay continued for twelve sessions; during four of the sessions we welcomed the participation of older sister, Karen. Both of the sister's loved it. Little Loreen showed her sister all of the games and Karen relaxed as the adults naturally assumed the parental role. Near the end of treatment, an Introductory Theraplay course was being offered locally and I was asked if I had a family who could participate. Because the progress had been so remarkable, and because the family wanted to "give back," the family agreed to participate. At an agreed upon time and place, the newly constituted family arrived. Tears welled in many eyes as little Loreen entered the room, looked around, excitedly ran ahead, then stopped to see if her secure base (Marvin, Cooper, Hoffman, and Powell, 2002) was following. A MIM was completed with all activities, including feeding, accomplished. The auntie and nanny laughed and smiled frequently and some hints of trust appeared in Loreen's large dark eyes.

Joseph LeDoux, neuroscientist and author of *The Synaptic Self*, explains, "People don't come preassembled, but are glued together by life" (LeDoux, 2002). Helping parents understand the building blocks that promote attachment, and explaining interpersonal neurobiology is an excellent goal, but one that can be "hit or miss." Having parents learn to understand themselves and their child through Theraplay is an easier, more practical way to build the most important relationship of all—that of child and caregiver.

Theraplay activities (see appendix) included in some of the sessions:

Case 1 Theraplay in the Van: hello song, baby oil hand prints, care for hurt and lotion, chalk footprints to the van, seatbelt do up with eyes closed, peanut butter jelly, guess the song, blow kisses, special hand shake, feeding pretzels off the fingers, goodbye song.

Case 2 Theraplay to reunify family: Mirror special inventory, lotion caring for hurts, band aids, slippery slippery slip, bubbles, blocks, pat-a-cake, ring-around-the-rosie, story time, feeding cheerios, cotton ball feather, row-row-row-your-boat, peek-a-boo, piggy-back ride, hide-and-seek, freeze dance, paint toenails, hand trace, bean bag toss, tunnel, blanket wrap and cuddle.

Case 3 Theraplay following parental death: soft hello song, lotion caring for hurts, powder puff, bubbles-break with various parts of the body supported by caregiver, two feeding activities in each session, cotton ball feather, peek-a-boo, piggy-back ride, climbing onto pillows and falling into waiting arms, hand prints, blanket swing, blanket wrap-surprise, rocking and singing, tunnel crawl, smartie hide, paper punch and snowball toss, good bye song.

REFERENCES

Jernberg, A. M. and Booth, P. (1999). *Theraplay: Helping Parents Build Better Relationships through Attachment-Based Play.* San Francisco: Jossey Bass.

Hughes, D. and Booth, P. (2007). *In Pursuit of Regulation and Attunement: Examples from Theraplay and DDP.* Paper presented at the 3rd International Theraplay Conference. Chicago, Ill. July 2007.

Les Doux, J. (2002). *The Synaptic Self: How Our Brains Become Who We Are.* New York: Viking.

Lipton, B. (2000). *The Biology of Belief.* Murfreesboro, TN: Spirit 2000 Inc.

Marvin, R., Cooper, G., Hoffman, K. and Powell, B. "Circle of Security Project: Attachment-based Intervention with Caregiver–pre-school Child Dyads," in *Attachment and Human Development*, vol. 4, no. 1, 107–124.

Mate, G. (1999). *Scattered Minds: A New Look at the Origins and Healing of Attention Deficit Disorder.* Toronto, Canada: Random House.

Neufeld, G., and Mate, G. (2005). *Hold on to Your Kids: Why Parents Need to Matter More Than Peers.* Toronto: Vintage Canada.

Perry, B. and Szalavitz, M. (2006). *The Boy Who Was Raised as a Dog.* New York: Basic Books.

Siegel, D. (1999). *The Developing Mind.* New York: The Guilford Press.

Siegel, D. and Hartzell, M. (2003). *Parenting from the Inside Out: How a Deeper Self-Understanding Can Help Raise Children Who Thrive.* New York: Penguin Group Inc.

Solomon, M. and Siegel, D. (2003). *Healing Trauma: Attachment, Mind, Body and Brain.* New York: W.W. Norton and Company, Inc.

Sunderland, M. (2006). *The Science of Parenting: How Today's Brain Research Can Help You Raise Happy, Emotionally Balanced Children.* New York: Penguin Group.

Wolpert, R. and Benoit, D. (2005). *A Simple Gift: Ending the Cycle of Hurt.* Infant Mental Health Promotion, Department of Psychiatry, Hospital for Sick Children, Toronto, Ontario: Dreams & Realities.

13

Theraplay and Dyadic Developmental Psychotherapy

Phyllis B. Rubin, Dafna Lender, and Jessica Mroz

When we three Theraplay® therapists began working with adopted children with challenging histories, we became faced with what we felt were Theraplay's limitations with this population. Theraplay was highly effective in helping clients to emotionally connect with parents, to learn to trust them, and for the family to learn to have fun together. Once that was accomplished, however, some of these children were still troubled by past experiences. Family relationships were better and life had settled down, but other problems remained. Theraplay could not help these children understand what had happened to them, nor could it adequately heal their pasts that were filled with neglect, rejection, and intense emotional pain. Dyadic Developmental Psychotherapy (DDP) seemed to offer a way to connect with children in the same highly interpersonal and highly attuned way that Theraplay does, yet it goes deeper to help the child verbally and affectively process past trauma. As Dafna Lender has stated, we have found Theraplay and DDP to be like twins separated at birth, now reunited (Lender, Mroz, and Rubin, 2005), offering us compatible models with which to address more fully the needs of our children and families that would not exist with Theraplay alone.

DYADIC DEVELOPMENTAL PSYCHOTHERAPY

DDP is an integrative, humanistic, highly interpersonal, and affective form of therapy. Rather than focusing on a child's compliance and getting a child to "behave," DDP focuses on what is underneath the problematic behavior—within the child's inner life—that is providing the motivation for its persistence. These children come to us feeling worthless, unwanted, undeserving, and unlovable. As in Theraplay, the DDP therapist strives to change the child's inner working model so that the child takes on a self that is positive and worthy and comes to interact with others in ways that reflect this more positive inner perspective. We also help parents understand that the negative way the child feels about himself colors how he feels about others and drives the problematic behavior. For this behavior, however undesirable, the DDP therapist and parent give the child acceptance and empathy. The essence of DDP is found in the attitude of PLACE that both therapist and parents use, and also in DDP's form of exploratory dialogue, termed *Affective/Reflective (A/R) Dialogue*.

"The Attitude" of PLACE

Playfulness: Familiar to the Theraplay community, this is the quality that draws a client into relationship and into the therapeutic process. By expanding positive affect, play reduces anxiety and can help increase comfort level. In DDP, the therapist jokes, is silly, gently teases the child and maybe even the parent, or laughs at herself to lighten the mood at the beginning, during, or at the end of a session. As in Theraplay, playfulness strengthens the therapeutic and parent-child bond.

Love: The therapist encourages spontaneous demonstrations of love between parent and child and facilitates it when necessary.

Acceptance: The therapist accepts a client's behavior, thoughts, and emotions, whether positive or negative, and treats these as communication, something from which to make meaning.

Curiosity: The therapist enters into explorations of painful topics without an agenda or preconceived right answer, but with a curious attitude demonstrated by adopting a curious facial expression and vocal tone. In so doing, the shame that might be triggered when discussion becomes difficult is reduced. Shame feels threatening, halts therapy, and causes the child to defensively self-protect. The DDP therapist is highly attuned to the shame reaction in children so that she can quickly repair it with a healing, empathic response.

Empathy: The therapist is always ready to communicate that *the therapist* knows how hard it is for the child to remember, feel, and talk about past and current pain.

Affective-Reflective Dialogue

DDP focuses on the in-the-moment connections between child, parent, and therapist, the *inter-subjective* moments that generate change (Hughes, 2007). By accepting what the child is feeling and experiencing, and by reflecting—and helping the child reflect—upon the positive and negative aspects of his inner life, the DDP therapist aims to help the child make sense of his own experiences. Through this process, therapist, parent, and child *co-create* new and potentially healthier meanings.

A/R dialogue contains several crucial characteristics that make DDP a unique therapeutic approach. *Connection-break-repair* refers to the ebb and flow of emotional connectedness we feel with others. Replicating this pattern, the DDP therapist makes a positive connection with the child at the start of a session. Then, the therapist brings up a difficult subject (i.e., the child's behavior at home; the child's past traumas). This usually causes the child to experience uncomfortable feelings such as disapproval, self-doubt, or self-hate, which breaks the attuned connection he had been feeling with his adults. The DDP therapist does not avoid these breaks, but rather accepts them, is curious about them, and initiates attempts to repair the relationship. A break in connection and the repair that follows are used as opportunities for personal growth and the development of new meanings. *Follow-lead-follow* refers to the pattern of interaction that is similar to the rhythm of the parent-infant relationship. The DDP therapist sometimes follows the child's lead, and at other times leads him into discussions that he may be avoiding. As in Theraplay, *non-verbal communication* is a vital part of DDP. The therapist uses her whole self and communicates clearly through tone of voice, eye contact, facial expressions, touch, gesture, and body posture. *Affective/reflective balance and integration* means that the dialogue should contain both affect as well as cognitive reflection. We can see here the striking similarities and also the differences between Theraplay and DDP.

Typical Sequence of A/R Dialogue

When the DDP therapist begins to discuss an event that elicits shame or other negative intense emotions in the child, she does not change her tone, but rather uses the same tone of acceptance and curiosity as used for discussing more positive content. The therapist begins to explore with the child how he feels and thinks about the particular event, and works to discover the motives the child attributes to himself and others regarding the event. As the child and therapist uncover together the child's inner life experience of the event, the therapist allows this to have an emotional impact on her and responds with genuine empathy for the child's experience. The therapist's response, in turn, has an impact on the child and enhances his ability to consider new meanings about his experience. The DDP therapist normalizes the child's actions based on his underlying beliefs, communicating that, given how the child was thinking and feeling, his actions certainly make sense. The DDP therapist helps the child communicate these underlying beliefs to his parent. By sharing this new meaning with his parent, the child is more likely to integrate the experience. The parent then expresses her understanding and empathy for the child's experience. You will see this sequence in the vignettes that follow.

How Theraplay and DDP Are Integrated

Theraplay and DDP can be integrated in a variety of ways based on the specific needs of each child and family. With young children, with children who have not built an attachment with their parents, or with families who do not play very well, we will start with some Theraplay sessions. Sessions are planned in the typical way with a check-up, relevant activities, and a song and feeding at the end (Jernberg and Booth, 1999). When we are successful in increasing playfulness, structure, and nurturing in the parent-child relationship, we are likely to begin to talk with the child about behaviors and the past. We tend to find that children need the foundation of being emotionally connected with and nurtured by parents in order to engage in DDP's exploration of current problem behaviors and the painful past. In the following examples, Susie is such a case. In other cases, we start with DDP, particularly with older children who are more familiar with talking about problems and less familiar with play. With these children, we are likely to interweave playful Theraplay activities into sessions to lighten or calm the atmosphere and help the child maintain a positive sense of self and other. Another time we use Theraplay is when a situation occurs in a session that increases the child's anxiety. In the following vignettes, Tommy is such an example. In Grace's case, Theraplay was being used, but her negative reaction to having fun prompted some DDP processing of why she had this feeling. Sometimes the switch from one therapy to the other within one session is planned, but often it occurs spontaneously. The advantage of being able to switch from one modality that involves processing experiences and thoughts to an experiential modality is invaluable.

INTEGRATIVE CASE EXAMPLE: TOMMY

Tommy was a very anxious and insecure four year old, adopted from Romania at age three after having lived in an orphanage since one week of age. Tommy's parents brought him for treatment because they were concerned about his anger and oppositional behavior in the home as well as his sadness and fearfulness. Tommy would often demand angrily that his parents meet his needs and would say "no" to most of their directions. He would wake during the night crying out and would often be inconsolable, convinced that his parents were going to die or that he would be taken from them by a stranger. This session describes how the use of PLACE and A/R dialogue helped Tommy with a frightening experience.

This was Tommy's fifth Theraplay session with the therapist. The session was planned in the typical format, beginning with a check up, then focusing on Theraplay activities that address separation and reunion, as well as fun and nurturing activities for Tommy and his mother. The session was planned to end with Tommy's father joining in to sing the "Twinkle song" and for a sock and shoe race. Tommy arrived for the session with his father, and his mother was to meet them there. Just before the session was to start, Mom called Dad to say she would be late. Since, at that time, the therapy was focused primarily on the mother-child relationship and Dad was observing for most of the session, Dad and the therapist decided to wait the anticipated ten minutes for Mom to arrive to start the session. Not only did it take much longer than ten minutes, but phone contact with Mom was lost. In the waiting room Tommy became highly dysregulated, flopping his body around, smashing toys into one another and throwing them around, laughing frantically, and making loud demands of Dad. He became hypervigilant, startling when doors opened and when sirens and sounds of traffic were heard from the street below. When Mom arrived 30 minutes late, the therapist attempted to get the family quickly engaged in the Theraplay session in the treatment room. The therapist began gently piling large pillows on Tommy, which had calmed him in past sessions, and, this time, helped him relax a bit. When Tommy appeared more regulated, the therapist then helped Tommy move to Mom's lap (the way sessions normally began). Tommy wrapped his arms and legs around his mother and began squeezing her tightly and arching his back. He repeatedly called "Mommy, Mommy," twisting his body and flailing his limbs. To help Tommy get more physically regulated and have a more organized way to express deep feelings, the therapist helped him lean back on pillows so that he was facing Mom with his legs gently over her legs and with a pillow over his torso to avoid his tactile sensitivities. The dialogue proceeds:

> Therapist: (accepts Tommy's behavior and speaks in a tone that matches Tommy's intensity) It seems you have SO much you want to say to Mommy . . . Your fists are so tight, you probably feel so tight inside . . .
>
> Tommy: Mommy, Mommy (speaking more softly now.)
>
> Therapist: (joins Tommy speaking softly) Mommy, Mommy . . . I bet it's hard to find the words to say all those feelings to Mommy.
>
> Tommy: Yes! (teeth clenched) . . . Mommy, Mommy!
>
> Therapist: How about I help you find some words to say to Mommy?
>
> Tommy: Yes!

Therapist: Okay, I'll do the talking you can relax.

Tommy: (making an exaggerated sigh and visibly relaxing his body)

Therapist: Okay. You can hold hands with Mommy and just look at her and I will talk. I'll pretend I'm you when I talk. Is that okay?

Tommy: Uh huh. (nodding emphatically)

Therapist: (leans down so her head is even with Tommy's so therapist and child are facing up toward mother) Mommy, that was kinda scary waiting for you. I was worried. Daddy said you were going to be here in a little while, and I thought it was going to be ten minutes, but it was forever. I was worried and scared.

Mom: (in a soft empathic tone) You were scared, Tommy?

Tommy: (nods while quietly watching his mother.)

Mom: I'm sorry you were scared. I don't want you to feel scared.

Tommy: I was scared like seeing a big monster!

Therapist: (looking at Tommy) It was that kind of scary? Like the seeing a big monster scary? Oh that's really scary!

Mother: Wow, Tommy that is really scary. That must have been hard.

There is a quiet moment. Mom and Tommy are gazing at each other and holding hands. Mom's face expresses her empathy for Tommy's experience and they both begin to look sad.

Therapist: I'm going to say some more. (as Tommy continues to gaze at his mother, the therapist speaks again in Tommy's voice, this time using a sad tone) Mommy it's hard for me sometimes when I'm away from you . . . I haven't always had you in my life . . . I didn't have you when I was a little baby. Sometimes I worry I will lose you.

Tommy: (makes an exaggerated baby cry, points to therapist, and then speaks in an age appropriate voice) Mom, I'm saying that.

Mom: (soft and empathic) You're saying that? You get worried?

Tommy: (grabs mother's finger) I got your finger. I'm gonna bend it and hurt you.

Therapist: (gently moves Tommy's hand away from Mom's hand) Sometimes I get so scared, I think I could hurt you.

Tommy: Yeah! (exaggerated cries, banging hands on the pillows)

Therapist: (following Tommy's affect, the therapist matches his intensity and expresses the anger he only knows how to express through aggression toward his mother) Mommy, when you go away I get scared, and when you come back I get mad at you for leaving me. I don't like to be scared.

Tommy: (on his own moves to mother's lap, nuzzling into her)

Mom: (cradles Tommy and feeds him juice and some crackers, and gently strokes Tommy's face) I wish you had always been with me since you were a baby so you would know that I will always come back. I want to help you learn that I will always come back when I'm away from you . . . I know it's hard . . . I know . . . I will always come back.

After several minutes of nurturing, the therapist then transitions to leading Tommy and Mom through some engaging Theraplay activities that focus on separation and reunion (Peekaboo, Cotton Ball Hide) and nurturing and engaging activities (Lotion-Powder Hand-Print, Swinging, Feeding, and the Twinkle song). With his feelings articulated and validated by the therapist and his mother, Tommy was now able to engage in Theraplay activities.

INTEGRATIVE CASE EXAMPLE: SUSIE

Susie's adoptive mother brought her to therapy when she was 4 years old. Before coming to this home, her life had been marked repeatedly by tragedy, disruption, and loss. She was moved from family member to family member from very early on and never had a chance to experience stability. Susie's school had given her enough time at home to adjust, so they thought, and she soon was to start preschool for special education services. Mom asked for help with the separation issues that were clearly evident to her. This session shows how the interweaving of Theraplay and DDP helped Mom understand what upsets Susie and both verbally and non-verbally facilitated the process of healing her fears of abandonment and loss.

The therapist first focuses on a problematic behavior that Mom saw the day before the session. Mom tells the therapist that Susie had been upset at the playground when Mom went home and left her with Dad and her siblings. The therapist starts the session assuming that to be the triggering event—that she still cannot tolerate Mom leaving her. Mom also says that at home, they do not have one-on-one time to play together in a Theraplay way. This is hypothesized to be contributing to Susie's clinging behavior with Mom. More emotionally connected and intense play would help Susie have a stronger internal sense of her mom and, eventually, allow her to separate more easily.

With this hypothesis, the therapist starts the session with Theraplay. The first game is for Susie to somersault from therapist to her mom and back again. She would experience getting close to Mom and also leaving her to somersault to the therapist, paralleling the experiences of reunion with Mom and separating for school. As we begin, Susie protests by not somersaulting to Mom, but standing by the therapist and wiggling with eyes lowered. As typical in Theraplay, the therapist says, "Mom, don't say 'go' until you see Susie's eyes." Susie actually is at quite a young emotional age and is not ready for separation. Instead, she wants to be found by Mom.

Susie starts to look around the room instead of at Mom. Again, as in standard Theraplay practice, the therapist says, "Is she hiding herself?" and renames what Susie is doing as "The Look Away Game." Susie just does not want to somersault to Mom, and continues to avoid this more advanced interaction. At this point, the therapist notices that Susie's jeans are slipping. The therapist uses a DDP intervention, based on Susie's past loss and recent playground experience, to verbalize Susie's concerns to Mom. While Mom helps with the jeans, the therapist speaks for Susie in a more childlike tone of voice: "You never know when you're going to need your mommy." This comment evokes Susie's experience of needing her Mom to be present and available to assuage any feeling of abandonment or loss.

But Susie stays mad. The therapist has not yet hit the mark. Continuing with DDP and the exploration of the child's inner life, the therapist verbalizes for her, using a lot of empathy and emotion: "See, Mommy, I may need you. And when you go away, I just feel a little bit alone. What would I do if I needed my mommy? I really, really miss you. Even though I'm 5, I still miss you a lot." Susie begins to wiggle. Mom is facing Susie and holding her arms, but Susie averts her face, trying to avoid the intense feeling that comes with needing her mom. The therapist continues with DDP to help figure out and express what Susie is showing by her anxious and somewhat avoidant behavior. The therapist says how hard it is for Susie to talk about missing and needing Mommy and that it's hard to look at Mom when she talks about it.

The therapist says for her: "It's hard for me." (Susie repeats exactly.) Therapist: "I'm trying . . ." and Susie adds, "my best. I'm trying my best." She has heard this apparently, and seems angry about having to try her best. The therapist helps her say: "It's hard for me to feel safe."

Then the therapist gives her to Mommy to comfort her because of how unsafe she feels. At this point, Susie becomes more baby-like. Spontaneously, she says, "Never let go" and "Don't let me go." She is stating her intense need on her own, signaling that the "mark" has been hit.

While therapist and Mom continue to explore Susie's feelings, Mom cuddles her, strokes her hair, and looks into her eyes. The therapist gives time for comforting and non-verbal repairing. With the feeling they now have had a good amount of nurturing, the therapist decides to return to the initial Theraplay activity: somersaults. Now Susie is able to look at Mom and somersault to her knowing, for now, that Mom understands how much Susie needs her to hold on and stay close. This suggests that the words the therapist gave Susie and the opportunity she had to tell Mom "Don't let me go!" was, indeed, just what she needed.

After the somersault, the therapist responds to Susie's need to be found by setting up a "Find me" game so that Susie can look away from and come back to Mom and get nurtured no matter what. Therapist: "Mom, when Susie looks at you, give her a smile and a squeeze. When she looks away, give her kisses!" They begin to engage in a highly reciprocal, intensely positive interaction. And Susie laughs. Not like a five-year-old, but like a little baby, delighted at the novelty of highly charged and pleasurable engagement with another that is meeting her deep need for the security that comes with intense emotional attunement and engagement.

Then the therapist asks Mom if they can play this game at home. Mom says that a good time is the morning when Susie comes into Mommy's bed. Very observant, Mom notices that Susie's face clouds over. Here is another opportunity for some DDP-style exploring. Quickly, Mom responds, stating what Susie is feeling and showing empathy for and curiosity about it:

> Mom (to Susie): "Are you mad all of a sudden? Are you mad that I said that you like to come into our bed in the morning?"
>
> Susie: "NO."
>
> Mom: "Then why are you upset?"
>
> Susie: "Because you leave me all alone! And I thought I'd never see you ever again!"
>
> Susie is verbalizing the motive and fears behind her anger. To explore Susie's feelings more deeply before "fixing" them, the therapist stops Mom from reassuring Susie that she always comes back, and helps Susie to elaborate on her thoughts and feelings.
>
> Therapist: "That's scary, Mom."
>
> Taking the therapist's lead, Mom (with curiosity) asks Susie: "Were you afraid for a long time?" Susie nods her head.
>
> Then Susie angrily says that Mommy went shopping for a gift for her teacher. So the therapist guesses about what is bothering her—that she's mad that Mom's not keeping her in her mind while Susie is feeling scared and alone. In formal terms, the experience of inter-subjectivity has been lost. Again Susie says, "And she left me all alone."
>
> Mom: "Do you think I wanted you to feel alone and scared?" Mom is accepting Susie's thoughts and feelings and verbalizing Susie's negative experience of her.
>
> Susie: "Yes."
>
> Mom: "Oh no, Susie! I didn't want you to feel alone or scared. I thought I could go shop before you woke up. But you woke up!"
>
> Susie: "And you were GONE!"
>
> Mom: "I'm sorry you were scared." (Using empathy, Mom is healing Susie's experience of an abandoning and scary mom.)

Therapist: (Speaking for Susie) "Mommy, it's hard for me when you're not there. It may be hard for a while. Just stay close." And Susie gets into Mom's lap for a cuddle, which provides more healing and a repair of the relationship. Sometimes, Theraplay cannot proceed until a child's inner experience and fears are known, expressed, and accepted.

INTEGRATIVE CASE EXAMPLE: GRACE

Grace, a three-year-old girl adopted from Guatemala at age two, was becoming increasingly more of a behavior problem at home. When her mother, Beth, came into Grace's room to wake her in the morning, Grace would scream, "Go away! Leave me alone!" and this angry, belligerent attitude continued throughout the day. She would vacillate between being unhappy and dissatisfied to being superficially cheery, and would always ruin any fun that the other family members were having. She would walk by one of her siblings and smack them or knock down their blocks. Her seemingly calculated aggressiveness angered Grace's parents and brought them to seek treatment. Beth and Mark were at their wits' end because in their home, treating people unkindly was simply unacceptable. Beth prided herself on being even-keeled and not losing her cool with her children, but Grace's victimization of the other children caused Beth to feel incompetent as a protector and also to feel hateful toward Grace, which were horrible feelings for Beth.

Theraplay sessions were planned to include games such as Caring for Hurts, Popcorn Toes, Beep Honk, Peekaboo, Cotton Ball Hockey, Beanie Drop, Lotion-Powder Handprints, Swinging, Special Delivery, Feeding, Twinkle, and Sock/Shoe Race. But as Grace began to experience the fun of Theraplay, it was clear that she felt bad about herself. Within the first few sessions, Grace stated that she was "sad" and that the activities were hard, despite the fact that the level of challenge was minimal. The therapist was able to use DDP to help her to expand upon and understand these feelings that were triggered simply by the fun of Theraplay.

In one example, Grace and her mom were playing "Cotton Ball Hockey." They blew the cotton ball back and forth a few times on a pillow between them, and Grace seemed to be engaged. Mom, upbeat and lively, had a big smile on her face, and both Mom and the therapist said, "This is fun!" Suddenly, a look of sadness or anger clouded Grace's face, and she crossed her arms and pouted. Mom stopped and asked "Why are you mad? Did I hurt your feelings?" Grace folded her hands even tighter across her chest, frowned more, and threw the cotton ball aside. The therapist hypothesized that Mom's level of happiness and excitement did not match Grace's. Rather than agreeing that Grace was mad, the therapist asked a more open-ended, curious question.

Therapist: I wonder what made Grace upset?

Grace kept pouting, but was looking at the therapist.

Therapist: I wonder if it's hard to have fun?

Now, Grace looked more curious, and the furrow in her brow unknotted a bit. (This is a sign that the therapist is on the right path).

Therapist: (speaking to Mom for Grace) Mom, it's hard to have fun sometimes,

Mom: That's too bad Grace, because I want you to enjoy yourself and be happy.

Therapist: (to Mom) I know you do, Mom, but sometimes it's hard for Grace to feel happy, and maybe when she sees you and me having fun, maybe she just feels bad that she can't have fun and be happy like every one else.

Grace: Yeah!

Therapist: Wow, thank you for telling us that! You feel bad when everybody's having fun and you can't do it!

Grace: Yeah! (then immediately) Can we blow the cotton ball or something?

With Grace looking visibly lighter and eager to move on, Mom and Grace played a few more rounds of Hockey before going to the next activity. Acknowledging Grace's difficulty feeling happy allowed her to be happy and re-engage in Theraplay.

Later, the therapist explained to Beth her guesses about why Grace got uneasy when everyone around her was having a good time. Grace did not have a lot of happy feelings to draw or expand upon, so both observing others feeling joyful, as well as sensing that she too was supposed to behave that way, may have made her feel lonely and deficient. Knowing this, Mom was able to have more empathy for Grace when she "ruined" the other family members' happy moments. She also toned down enthusiasm when she interacted with Grace. When Mom wished Grace to be happy, she was inadvertently telling her that something was wrong with her. In subsequent sessions, the therapist coached Mom to accept Grace's negative feelings rather than try to wish them away. As Theraplay therapists, we, like Beth, may inadvertently wish to intensify positive affect during our activities. This example alerts us to the need to be sensitive to the meanings under the child's behaviors and to modify our focus to resonate with the child's needs.

ENDING THOUGHTS

The more challenging the child's history, the more need there is for therapy to articulate and help to discover the inner feelings, fears, needs, and wishes that motivate problematic behaviors. There is also a pressing need to help parents accept and feel empathy toward their confused and distressed child. Without acceptance and empathy, attachment may continue stunted, distorted, or absent. These examples show how Dyadic Developmental Psychotherapy can facilitate our Theraplay work as well as touch the child's inner world in ways that Theraplay's here-and-now emphasis, alone, cannot. Using DDP allows the child's past to inform us about the reasons underlying the "resistance" to structure, nurture, engagement, or challenge. DDP is an asset to the Theraplay therapist and, we feel, an added gift to our families.

REFERENCES

Hughes, Daniel A. (2007). *Attachment-Focused Family Therapy.* New York: W. W. Norton & Company.

Jernberg A. and Booth, P. (1999). *Theraplay: Helping Parents and Children Build Better Relationships through Attachment-Based Play.* San Francisco: Jossey-Bass.

Lender, D., Mroz, J., and Rubin, P. (2005). *Integrating Theraplay and Dyadic Developmental Psychotherapy.* Paper presented at the Second International Theraplay Conference, Chicago, IL.

14

Parent Session in Theraplay: A Way to Consolidate Therapeutic Alliance and Joint Focus

Minna Laakso

In the past few years, the incorporation of a parent session in Theraplay®, before the beginning of the child's sessions, has been tested in Finland. During the session, the parent is given an opportunity to realize how the child will experience the therapy as he or she can reflect on their own childhood events and anticipate their child's experiences. The session often evokes memories of the parent's own childhood, which facilitates reflective work during the therapeutic process. Therapists' experiences from the parent's own session have been positive. The aim of this article is to discuss the therapeutic work done together with parents and to handle the session's potential to facilitate changes. My object is also to describe the course of a parent session and delineate what kind of roles therapists can have in it. This article has originated from the experiences and discussions of Theraplay therapists who work in Finland.

THERAPEUTIC ALLIANCE

Studies have revealed that the therapeutic alliance is a crucial factor in the success of a therapy. In child-parent therapies, the therapeutic alliance should be developed not only with the child, but also with the parent. The establishment of a therapeutic alliance presumes that clients feel safe in a relationship that provides for the examination of their acts, thoughts, and feelings on both verbal and emotional levels. In his introduction about early preventive interventions, Daniel Stern (2006) points out two essential factors that affect the relationship between a therapist and a client: the client's need for safe attachment and the significance of Winnicott's holding environment. Also Mitchell stresses the importance of attachment by writing, "secure attachment provides the safety to explore not just the external world, but the internal world of personal preferences, desires, and impulses" (Mitchell, 2000). Thus, the therapist's role could, at its best, be described as a role of a good-enough grandparent that fulfills the client's need for safe attachment and offers a holding environment. The image of a grandparent refers to safety, wisdom, and attitudes that imply respect for other people and trust in their capabilities. A wise grandparent has time to focus on another person and can put things in perspective with the help of life experience. A wise grandparent also knows that change can happen by creating a feeling of safety and by promoting non-intrusive attitudes. The process of change requires safe interaction, which consists of shared exploration instead of a situation where the therapist gives pat answers. In fact, a wise grandparent utilizes Theraplay elements by signaling: "I can see you; I am interested in you; I will take care of you; the world is a safe place; I will help you through the change; you are skillful and adept." A wise grandparent also wants to share experiences with you on both informational and emotional levels. When working with parents, their session is a feasible instrument to enable them to experience Theraplay elements and start to develop a therapeutic alliance. During the session, the therapist enters into a playful and empathetic state of mind together with a parent, in order to create a shared experience. The experience binds them both to a shared process and the session can be a way to create moments of shared awareness that promote change. As Sander (1998) writes about the importance of shared moments of awareness, "these shifts in consciousness are brought about through moments of shared awareness between patient and therapist as they experience 'moments of meeting' within their 'intersubjective environment.'"

PARENT'S REFLECTIVE WORK

It has been noted in several studies that the parents' ability to reflect is related to the quality of attachment and the sensitivity of caregiving (Slade, Grienenberger, Bernbach, and Locker, 2005a; Grienenberger, Kelly, and Slade 2005; Slade, 2002). Therapy research and child-parent therapies have increasingly emphasized the development of parents' mentalization and reflection abilities as a catalyst for change. "An important aim of psychotherapy, then, if not its central aim, is the extension of mentalisation" (Fonagy et al., 2002). Studies have shown that a therapeutic intervention can be used to improve a mother's reflective capabilities (Slade, Sadler, DeDios-Kenn, Webb, Currier-Ezepchick, and Mayes 2005; Schechter, Kaminer, Grienenberger, and Amat, 2003). Parents, who observe themselves and others in a reflective manner, observe also their own and their child's actions, so that they think over the feelings, thoughts, and intentions that underlie the actions. As Fonagy et al. (2002) put it, "Reflective function, or mentalization, enables one to 'read' other peoples minds." The ability to read other people's behavior helps to realize the purposes of their actions and to predict them. In Theraplay, the reflective work also helps parents to think about how their own experiences of attachment are manifested through the child-parent interaction. An adequate ability to reflect enables parents to create more versatile and flexible images of their own child that take into account the child's individuality. The ability to reflect also gives parents an opportunity to form a more realistic picture of their parenthood. Furthermore, the ability to reflect assists them to make choices in real life. Thus, in relation to the child, parents can act instead of react; respond to the child as a whole instead of its external behavior. Child-parent interactional problems often bewilder parents. A child's reactions cause them to easily react only to external actions, e.g., to scold a child that is throwing a tantrum. Thus, parents often are unable to understand the underlying causes, such as the child's need for attention. In Theraplay, the reflective work has already begun during the planning of treatment. At an MIM (Marschak, 1960) feedback discussion, the parent can reflect together with the therapist on the hopes, wishes, needs, and emotions that are behind the child's, as well as the parent's, behavior. Reflective work continues as the parent watches the child from behind the one-way mirror. The parents' therapists' purpose is to create a secure base for them to practice reflection. The parents' pre-treatment session gives them referential information on which to found the reflection of their child's actions. The theraplay session evokes emotional experiences in parents, which makes it easier for them to think over their child's experiences and feelings during Theraplay. In the course of the session, parents may take a break to think about the different meanings of Theraplay elements with the help of the therapists. Through their own experiences, parents become acquainted with the underlying messages of activities. The parent session can also be used to model the forthcoming work done behind the one-way mirror and to derive implications for their child's behavior, as well as to think about the emotions that are related to it. According to Fonagy, "the caregiver's capacity to observe the moment-to-moment changes in the child's mental state is critical in the development of mentalizing capacity The caregiver's perception of the child as an intentional being lies at the root of sensitive caregiving, which attachment theorists view as the cornerstone of secure attachment" (Fonagy et al., 2002). The ability to reflect can develop only in interaction with other people. During the session, parents are encouraged to interact, because it enables safe exploration of their own experiences and feelings in immediate interaction. The session can also consolidate the parents' ability to be emotionally present during therapy sessions, both behind the one-way mirror and with the child. "After all, life is lived in the present moment, which, in turn, is the temporal stage on which memories and future anticipations play" (Stern, 1985).

FAILED PARENTHOOD

Many of our clients feel that they have failed as parents and feel themselves inept and helpless in terms of the possibility for change. It has been noted that a parent's feeling of ability is related to child-parent interaction and the sensitivity of caregiving (Coleman and Karraker, 2003). Parental sense of failure hurts and may affect a parent's self-image. The feeling of failure may prove to be so hurtful that it causes some parents to build up defenses by pushing disappointment and painful feelings away from themselves by, for example, laying the blame of difficult feelings on the child. It may be hard to change feelings and thoughts only by an effort of will, because change requires new experiences that can compensate for the old ones. The parent session is one way to provide these compensatory experiences. During a session, the therapist signals to parents, his or her willingness to make eye contact and stop for a shared experience, which in itself can be a nurturing event for the parents. Basic human needs include the need to be seen, and this applies also to parents, even if their child's problems are the primary reason for therapy. In child-parent therapies that strive for an interactional change, it is equally important to pay attention to both the child and the parents. Parents need to feel indispensable to the treatment in order to be able to commit to it. In the parent session, the therapist uses playfulness to help parents to believe in the possibility of change. By taking charge of the situation, the therapist signals to the parents that he or she is willing to contain the parents' difficult thoughts and feelings as well. As John Bowlby states: "The first is to provide the patient with a secure base from which he can explore the various unhappy and painful aspects of his life, past and present . . . impossible to think about and reconsider without a trusted companion, to provide support, encouragement, sympathy, and, on occasion, guidance" (Bowlby, 1988). To touch a parent during the session implies a willingness to establish shared therapy sessions with the parent as a whole other.

The parents' own session can give the parents a sense of being active participants in the therapy process from the very beginning and help them to feel that their thoughts and feelings are important. "Interpersonal interaction that permits the registration of perceptions, thoughts, and emotions as causes and consequences of action and the contemplation of these mental states without fear must constitute an important part of the foundation of self-agency" (Fonagy et al., 2002). During the session, the therapist can show trust in the parent's role as a co-therapist, and the parent has an opportunity to feel respected and be seen as the one and only parent of this child in particular. The parent should have a feeling of being an active participant in the therapy process, because the treatment's target is, after all, interaction. To experience oneself as active and capable encourages the parent to launch into the process of change. The session can be helpful also when therapists try to create a therapeutic and soothing atmosphere, where the parent can be sure of being seen as a person with individual needs. This makes it easier for the parent to concede to the child all the positive things that result from Theraplay sessions.

BUILDING A NEW NARRATIVE OF INTERACTION

In his book *The Interpersonal World of the Infant,* Daniel Stern asks, "How might a therapist and a patient reconstruct a therapeutically effective narrative about the past?" Often the essential focus in working with parents is in the building of a more coherent narrative about the parents' and the child's joint past or history of interaction. The narrative may give one explanation as to why the interaction is not working well between the child and the parents. The new narrative may include parents' own problems and/or problems that stem from the child's actions. It is important that therapists and parents can build a narrative of interaction that includes both the child and the parents as intentional human beings, who are trying to build a good relationship with each other with their weaknesses and strengths. The therapist should listen to the parents' stories carefully, give space, and respect the parents' pace. The therapist should show empathetic curiosity and "make the task of reconstruction more of a true adventure for both patient and therapist" (Stern, 1985). Having a coherent narrative of interaction gives agency to parenthood, which facilitates the change. When you have a "narrative point of origin" of problems, you can reflect about it and make decisions about the actions you want to make. The building of a narrative of the child-parent history and their present interaction is related with the parents' own attachment history. The present interactions are influenced by our experiences of other significant people in the past. The parent session often evokes memories of the parent's own childhood experiences, for example, if the parent received little physical nurturing. The parent may then realize how significant physical nurture is and how important it is. During the session, the parent can reflect on his/her own childhood events and visualize what kinds of experiences to give to the child. The parent session can contribute to the composition of a story that covers problems and includes the parents' narratives of their own childhood and parenthood. The session can help them to see and remember things: it is a means to awaken parents on an emotional level that is based on experience, but also on a cognitive level. The session's aim is to make parents reflect on parenthood and its basic tasks. The parents' session can be useful in the beginning of the formulation of a new, more realistic and positive interactional story that could make change possible.

PARENT SESSION

Secure Base

Parent sessions can evoke difficult memories and emotions, in which case the protection from the therapist becomes an important safety element. If a parent feels that the therapist does not see, appreciate, or support his or her feelings, the parent may have to strongly defend him/herself from feelings that have been evoked during the session. Prior to the session, the therapist should examine which level the parent is ready to work on, at that moment. Parents should not be forced to work in such a manner that ignores the level of readiness. Before the session, we have used assessments such as the Adult Attachment Interview, AAI (Main, Kaplan, and Cassidy, 1985) and The Working Model of the Child Interview, WMCI (Zeanah, Benoit, Hirshberg, Barton, and Regan, 1994) to investigate parents' own attachment backgrounds and interactional representations. During sessions and when working with parents, the therapist should ensure that the therapy is focused on the child-parent interaction instead of encouraging a parent to participate too much in his/her own therapy process if the therapist cannot follow through with individual therapy for the parent. It is advisable to talk with each parent separately, immediately after the session, because it enables discussions about the thoughts and emotions he or she has had during the session. Afterwards, Finnish therapists have also performed an attachment interview developed by Dan Hughes (The Theraplay Institute) in which the parent is asked about interactional experiences with significant others in both his/her own childhood family and the current family. After their own session, parents often begin to think about their childhood events in a new, more experiential way. A mother of a 7-year-old boy answered as follows when we asked about her childhood family:

"Before the session I would've said that my childhood was normal and secure, but now I can remember that my mother probably didn't have much time to hold me in her arms. I have many siblings, and I don't really recall that either of my parents would ever have held me in their arms. I guess that situation hasn't changed much, since I have too little time to be with my own kids and hold them. It feels good that I can now think about this more, even though it also makes me sad. Anyhow, I might be able decide that I want to give more care to my children than what I got from my parents. You just don't always realize its importance in everyday life."

Helping Reflection

Reflective work with a parent presumes that the therapist interrogates rather than claims to know. Empathetic questioning is important because too much knowledge by the therapist can deprive the parent of the ability to share his or her thoughts. An empathetic attitude toward questioning leaves room for interaction that can develop reflective capabilities. As Winnicott (1965) says, talking about the good enough mother, "It could be said that if now she knows too well what the infant needs, this is magic and forms no basis for an object relationship." During the session, therapists ponder together with parents about how the child presumably will experience the therapy process. Together they can think over thoughts, emotions, and intentions that can be deduced from the child's behavior. Relating them to the child-parent interaction and child's everyday behavior can further process answers. It is important to maintain a secure and ruminative approach, so that parents feel they are in such a state of mind that they can go through with the session and play with ideas. "If too much certainty is employed by the therapist, this offers a patient what appears to be a shortcut to 'knowing'" (Casement, 1985), intellectualized without insight.

A mother whose 4-year-old daughter suffered from ambivalent attachment said, in the beginning of a session, that her child will probably start to cry and bawl for mom. We discussed what feelings and thoughts might be the source of the child's behavior, and the mother stated that she also was bewildered and even scared sometimes, because she did not know what was going to happen next. She reflected that the child must feel likewise and continued by saying that the everyday tantrums might be the result of a sense of insecurity. Together we came to a conclusion that Theraplay signals to the child that she is not alone with difficult emotions. The mother thought about her childhood experiences with a depressed mother, but also about her own post-natal depression after she had given birth to her daughter. After this, therapists told her that they were going to be sensitive toward both of their fears about being left alone in an excessively difficult situation.

Levels of Working and the Choice of "Language"

During a session, therapists should "speak the same language" as the parents do. Parents' abilities to reflect and express themselves can be evaluated before the session by, for instance, interviewing and especially during the MIM feedback, which can be used to establish a joint language and pace. With some parents, therapy work begins with activities, with others from the handling of feelings or cognitive factors. Parents get to define the level on which they want work, but the therapist can lead or encourage parents to pass to new ones, to next levels of the therapy process. This must not, however, happen by force. Using force to speak a language that is not familiar to the parent is intrusive treatment and may result in increasing the parent's defenses. The session should take into account the rhythm and use of the language of both parents. For example, the parents of a restless and defiant 6-year-old boy reflected, both in their own ways, on how the child would probably show resistance in the sessions. The mother began from the child's sense of insecurity and thought that her son might be afraid of a new and strange situation, because she felt the same way in new situations. She hoped that her son would gain courage and believe in himself. Afterwards, the mother stated she had been exhausted before the session, but she now had new faith and strength in her own abilities as the child's supporter. Meanwhile, the father started to challenge therapists by, for example, mischievously blowing cotton balls (see appendix) away from them over and over again. The father stated that this was exactly what he thought his son would do. He recognized the same feature also in himself, a difficulty in cooperating without challenging others to compete. The father and therapists began to reflect together on the situations where challenging could be a source of shared joy and where it was inappropriate to challenge. The father was able to recognize situations when he would start challenging the child, but instead of having a good time together, the boy would end up crying or behaving aggressively. The cotton ball task was repeated after the discussion, and as the father blew the ball to the therapist, he said: "Well, this does feel different now."

Joint Focus

It is important to find a joint focus for the treatment together with parents, because it strengthens their commitment and enhances therapy. When the therapist tells parents about their own session, they can be told that the purpose of the session is to better understand their child's problems, which helps parents and therapists to plan the treatment together. Parents' difficulties are usually related to the child's behavior, and the therapists' task is to help them to understand how a child's behavior is linked to their common interactional history, as well as to their own past. The therapist can use questions and discussion to handle the problem by linking it to the parents' experiences of the on-going therapy session. A parent may in his or her own session identify with the child. However, the session must also encourage the parent to take over an adult's role. A shared therapy focus comprises also a support of parenthood.

The parents of an 8-year-old boy had doubts about the usefulness of Theraplay in helping their ill-mannered son. They found it hard to believe that praises and unconditional acceptance could actually help. In an activity where parents dropped down small beanbags from their heads to the hands of their therapists, (see appendix) each successful drop was met with cheers and the parent was told how skillful he or she was. During discussion, the parents realized how important it was to engage with others and that they often tended to order the child to do or act without any connection to him. They could understand through their own experiences how good it felt to have common activities if one could be sure of getting attention. Parents also began to think about why it was so hard to give positive feedback about small things in everyday life. The mother said during discussion: "As a mother I should pay more attention to positive things so that my son would not have to act so aggressively in order to be seen."

Rhythm and Structure

Activities and discussions alternate during the parent session. The therapist should remain sensitive toward parents' experiences and allow them to keep their distance if, for example, closeness feels too intimate. Therapist's questions and explanations about treatment methods create natural pauses between intensive periods of interaction. Parents need pauses during which they can reflect on the new experiences. The number of activities and discussion breaks depend on the parents' progress. The therapist must be sensitive to the parents' needs and notice if either of them wants to return to the role of an adult after an intensive experience. On the other hand, the therapist can also encourage experimentation. With some parents, the therapist may want to increase the amount of experiential activities, with others it may be essential to emphasize discussion. For example, a mother of a 3-year-old girl found it difficult to launch into a shared experience with a cheerful attitude with her own daughter. In the session, her task was to burst soap bubbles (see appendix). At first, she was unsure, as if she was ashamed of something and looked confused when she was met with delight and positive feedback. She needed to digest this for a moment, but then she began to reflect on how it was difficult for her to receive positive feedback from others and to believe in what was said to her. She stated how confusing it was to be together in such an intensive manner and to receive praise when she succeeded in small things. The soap bubble task was repeated, now at a slower pace, which made the shared experience more intensive. Mother responded to praises by saying: "I might actually participate in this therapy. It is good for me to learn how to be more playful and how to enjoy the little moments of shared happiness. And of course, I like it when people compliment me."

Building a Session

Both parents participate in the session at the same time. Parents' and child's therapists take part in the session so that the therapists can perform activities simultaneously with both parents. Therapists can change places during the session so that parents can work with both of them. The parent's session is built similarly to the child's session and begins much in the same way. The session includes activities from each Theraplay dimension and the atmosphere is positive. The therapist is in charge of the course of the session and leads parents to their beanbag chairs. Parents can now be told about the adult-led nature of the session and how it affects the therapy. The session advances through activities, and parents get an opportunity to learn what surprises and positive feedback really mean. Therapists and parents also reflect on the understanding of different Theraplay elements. In general, the functions of activities are not explained to parents before the session. Instead, therapists first create an experience and then give parents time to stop and think about the emotions that the experience has evoked. Discussion revolves around these experiences, if possible. Calm and nurturing moments alternate during the session, and finally, everybody plays together. After the session, parents often state that they find it easier to grasp what Theraplay actually means. As one mother said: "I found it a bit difficult to understand how the blowing of soap bubbles could help us. Now I realize that this is all about accepting other people as they are; you don't always have to perform. You just need to be yourself and have the courage to spend time with someone else."

CASE STUDY: WORKING WITH LEENA'S MOTHER

Leena was a 4-year-old girl living with her mother. Leena's mother had been depressed and lonely long after Leena´s birth. In the MIM assessment, Leena paid hardly any attention to her mother at first. Then she protested loudly when her mother was to leave the room. The mother felt disappointed about herself as a parent and said she felt timid with her own child. She also described how she had difficulties in trusting other people.

Below is a description of how we began the work with Leena´s mother by trying to build up trust, security, and respectfulness in a surprising and emphatic way and by inviting the mother to start a joint journey to new ways of being together.

We led the mother to a beanbag chair and invited her to sit down at the same time with us.

Mother: "Oh no, there is a video camera. I hate to see myself on videotape."

Mother's therapist: "Yes, I know, one looks and sounds so different, but we use the video because it helps us all to see better how to help Leena. Is it ok?"

Mother: "Yes. Should I take my shoes off?"

Child's therapist: "I'll take them off. (Therapist takes shoes off, making contact with the mother and counting to three. Mother looks surprised, and a little embarrassed). We will do the same with Leena. We will show her that adults take care of children in sessions and in everyday life. What do you think? How will Leena react?"

Mother: "She will start shouting at me."

Child's therapist: "That's good to know. You know your child best. Why do you think she does that? What does she feel and think? What do you feel?"

Mother: "Maybe she is afraid. I suppose she won't trust you. Maybe it is something like that . . . I feel a little embarrassed about being so near . . . I am not used to do this."

Mothers' therapist: "Yes, this may be a totally new situation and you have to think about how you experience it."

Child's therapist: "We hope that we could offer Leena these new situations and ways of being together. It is good if you, as a mother, can help us to know what is too much for Leena when it comes to new things. Do you think that this, to be so near now, will be too much for her?"

Mother: "No, I think this is good for her. Now, it is OK for me, too. I was just so surprised at first."

Mother's therapist: "Yes, it is something new. We don't want to do anything that you feel is not OK."

Child's therapist: "If Leena is too afraid, I can try to help her with soap bubbles . . . Look at these bubbles. I am sure you can burst them with your finger. (Mother bursts the bubble and smiles.) Wow, you are good at this! Do you think Leena will do the same?"

Mother: "No, I think she will refuse to do it."

Child's therapist: "I'll show you what I might do then. (Therapist blows a bubble and takes it to the mother's toe.) You really are special; you know how to burst bubbles with you toes. What special toes you have."(Mother starts to laugh.)

Mother: "I see. It is strange to hear how good you are even if you have decided not to co-operate. I don't know why, but for a second, I really felt I am good."

Child's therapist: "You are good, and we also want Leena to think that she is good and special and can do many wonderful things and have fun with you and others. Let's try once again." (Mother bursts bubbles with fingers.)

Child's therapist: "You have really skilled fingers. How many of them do you have? Let's count them. (Therapist counts the fingers and finds a little wound while doing it.) You have a little wound here. Let's take care of it and put some lotion on it."

Child's therapist: "In Theraplay, we want Leena to know that we are interested in her and that we want to know her well. We will also take care of hurts. How do you feel about it?"

Mother: "I noticed that I was looking at my fingers when you were counting them, and I saw the little wound you found."

Child's therapist: "Yes, this is exactly what we hope that Leena also would notice. There are so many interesting and wonderful things about her, and we wish to know her well, take care of her, and enjoy being with her."

The following are three typical Theraplay agendas used in this case. Note that after the first session with the mother, the child's session begins with only the child and therapist present in the room while the mother observes. Later, the mother enters the room to interact with her child under the guidance of the therapists.

FIRST AGENDA, MOTHERS' SESSION

Sitting together after counting 1-2-3, taking mothers shoes off playfully, popping the bubbles with fingers and toes, counting fingers, lotioning mothers hands, caring for hurts, blowing cotton balls to each other, Newspaper punch, putting mothers shoes on playfully

MIDDLE AGENDA, SIXTH SESSION, MOTHER IN SESSION 10 MINUTES

Leena hides with the therapist under a blanket and mother finds Leena, mother counts and admires Leena fingers and toes, mother gives special kisses; butterfly and elephant kisses, mother lotions Leena's feet, mother and Leena press each other's noses and supply different noises, mother feeds Leena holding her in her arms

END AGENDA, LAST SESSION BEFORE PARTY AND FOLLOW UPS, MOTHER IN SESSION 20 MINUTES

Mother finds Leena under a blanket, mother feeds Leena and admires the sounds, mother lotions Leena's hands and feet and takes care of hurts, mother gives special kisses, mother blows bubbles and Leena pops them, mother asks Leena to come to her in different ways while therapist helps Leena, Mother and Leena and therapists throw balloons to each other, Leena flies to mother's arms in blanket swing, mother touches different parts of Leena's body with a cotton ball and Leena indicates where mother touches her, mother and Leena press each other's noses and supply different noises, mother feeds Leena in her arms, mother and Leena leave the room holding each others hands and watching each others eyes.

REFERENCES

Bowlby, J. (1988) *A Secure Base: Clinical Applications of Attachment Theory*. Hove and New York: Brunner-Routledge.

Casement, P. (1985) *On Learning from the Patient*. London and New York: Routledge.

Coleman, P. K., and Karraker, K. H. (2003) Maternal self-efficacy beliefs, competence in parenting, and toddlers' behaviour and developmental status. *Infant Mental Health Journal* 24(2), 126–148.

Fonagy, P., Gergely, G., Jurist, E., Target, M. (2002) *Affect Regulation, Mentalization, and the Development of the Self*. New York: Other Press.

Grienenberger, J., Kelly, K., and Slade, A. (2005) Maternal reflective functioning, mother-infant affective communication, and infant attachment: Exploring the link between mental states and observed care giving behaviour in the intergenerational transmission of attachment. *Attachment & Human Development*, September 7(3): 299–311.

Jernberg, A., and Booth P. (1999) *Theraplay: Helping Parents and Children Build Better Relationships Through Attachment-based Play*. San Francisco: Jossey Bass.

Main M., Kaplan N., and Cassidy J. (1985) Security in infancy, childhood and adulthood: A move to the level of representation. In Bretherton I. and Waters E. (eds.) *Growing Points of Attachment: Theory and Research, Monographs of the Society for Research in Child Development*, 50, Serial No. 209, 66–106.

Marschak, M. (1960) A method for evaluating child-parent interaction under controlled conditions. *Journal of Genetic Psychology*, 97, 3–22.

Mitchell, S. A. (2000) *Relationality from Attachment to Intersubjectivity*. London: The Analytic Press.

Sander, L. (1998) Interventions that effect change in psychotherapy: A model based on infant research. *Infant Mental Health Journal*. 19(3), 280–281.

Schechter, D. S., Kaminer, T., Grienenberger, J. F., and Amat, J. (2003) Fits and starts: A mother-infant case-study involving intergenerational violent trauma and pseudoseizures across three generations. *Infant Mental Health Journal* 24(5): 510–528.

Slade, A. (2002) Keeping the baby in mind: Critical factor in perinatal mental health. *Zero to Three* 22: 10–16.

Slade, A., Grienenberger, J., Bernbach, D. L., and Locker, A. (2005) Maternal reflective functioning, attachment and the transmission gap: A preliminary study. *Attachment & Human Development*, September 7(3): 283–298.

Slade A., Sadler L., DeDios-Kenn C., Webb, D., Currier-Ezepchick J., and Mayes L. (2005) Minding the baby: A reflective parenting program. *Psychoanalytic Study of the Child* 60: 74–100.

Stern, D. (2006) Introduction to the special issue on early preventive intervention and home visiting. *Infant Mental Health Journal* 27(1): 1–4.

Stern, D. (1985) *The Interpersonal World of the Infant: A View from Psychoanalysis and Developmental Psychology.* New York: Basic Books.

The Theraplay Institute (2006) Introductory Workshop; Theraplay and Marschak Interaction Method (MIM). Umeå, Sweden.

Winnicott, D. W. (1965) *Maturational Processes and Facilitating Environment.* London: Hogarth Press.

Zeanah, C., Benoit, D., Hirshberg, L., Barton, M., and Regan, C. (1994) Mothers' representations of their infants are concordant with infant attachment classifications. *Developmental Issues in Psychiatry and Psychology,* 1: 9–18.

15

Theraplay in Combination with Sensory and Handling Techniques: The Body/Mind Connection in Pediatrics

Anita Johanson Maddox and Carol R. Bettendorf

INTRODUCTION

It has long been known that there is a connection between our physical bodies and our emotional states. For instance, a massage can alleviate tension in the body and improve the person's overall feelings of pleasure and comfort (Field, 2001). Infant massage, the receiving of touch in a loving manner, can be very important to the well-being of an infant (McClure, 2000). Tension held in the tissues is often secondary to stress, either physical or emotional (Upledger, 1987). During an unexpected fall or accident you tighten your body for protection and in emotional alarm. This tightness in your tissue may stay in your tissue until released with assistance. Infants and young children often carry stress and tension in their bodies that has been gained during the birthing process (Upledger, 1987). The body of knowledge concerned with releasing held tissue tension available to therapists and the public in general is growing rapidly (Oz, 1999; Hunt, 1989; Smith, 1986; Upledger and Vredevoogd, 1983; Feldenkrais, 1981). Combining physical handling techniques with Theraplay® can be a very effective way of treating the young child.

THERAPLAY IN CO-TREATMENT

The co-treatment used was an interweaving of two different types of therapies with significant improvements in the child's overall development. The co-treatment concept began in an effort to address and enhance the body's ability to calm, organize, and receive structure from hands-on therapy given as the Theraplay session unfolded.

The physical therapist sat either behind the child or at the child's side. Often seated activities were used as initial activities since they lent themselves well to this method of co-treatment. During the Theraplay session the therapist, who was directing and providing the Theraplay activities, was facing the child and was usually the person most aware of the child's eye contact as well as facial and body expression. The Theraplay therapist might have occasionally commented on the child's facial feedback or asked the physical therapist providing the sensory and handling techniques about the timing for beginning gross motor activities.

Co-treatment did not compromise the integrity of either the Theraplay work or the sensory and handling protocols used. Theraplay was carried out as it was designed to be administered. Sensory Processing, Feldenkreis Method®, and Craniosacral Therapy were also given using accepted procedures. These methods will be discussed further.

SENSORY INTEGRATION/PROCESSING THERAPY

The theory of Sensory Integration and Sensory Integration Dysfunction was first presented by Dr. A. Jean Ayres (Ayres, 1979). Dr. Ayres conducted extensive research of literature for studies of sensory function. She used these studies, along with her clinical observations to formulate the Theory of Sensory Integration. In 1972 she defined the sensory integration process as "the ability to organize sensory information for use." Sensory integration or processing is a neurological process occurring in the brain. The person receives sensory input from the environment through sensory nerve receptors. Environmental sensory input is received through touch, joint (proprioceptive), vestibular (the sense of movement and balance), hearing, vision, taste, and smell nerve receptors. The information from sensory nerve receptors is conducted to the brain for processing. After the brain processes or integrates the sensory information, a course of action or behavior is decided on (Fisher et al., 1991). The sensory input results usually in appropriate behaviors. For instance, if touch is unpleasant, we move away from it. If a radio is too loud, we turn it down. If movement on a swing is making us uneasy, we stop swinging. We are taking appropriate actions to keep ourselves comfortable.

Sensory Processing Disorder occurs when the brain is not interpreting sensory input correctly. The brain is either too sensitive to sensory input or it is not sensitive enough to sensory input. If it is too sensitive to the sensory input, we can get a stressed or a fight or flight response. If the brain is not sensitive enough to the input, the individual does not react (Wilbarger and Wilbarger, 1991; Kranowitz, 1998; Frick and Hacker, 2001; Miller, 2006).

For example, an adult with sensory processing difficulties might comment that her skin felt like she had sunburn. She needed to avoid being touched unexpectedly. A young adult with vestibular dysfunction felt like the ground moved under her feet as she walked. She needed to walk slowly and carefully. A child who is underresponsive to sensory input might not cry when she fell down.

Therapies are available which can be effective in improving Sensory Integration/Processing Dysfunction. There are times when a therapy technique can make changes in the behavior of a child in a short length of time such as four weeks (Frick and Hacker, 2001). Other changes in behavior can take longer, but, in general, Sensory Processing treatment techniques produce relatively rapid results (Wilbarger and Wilbarger, 1991).

Deep pressure can help the brain integrate sensory input (Fisher et al., 1991, Wilbarger and Wilbarger, 1991; Miller, 2006). Deep pressure can be given by making a sandwich with the child between two cushions and the therapist giving pressure through the top cushion or by having the child lie down and rolling a large ball over him with deep pressure. Deep pressure can also be given using a brushing program taught by a physical or occupational therapist (Wilbarger and Wilbarger, 1991).

Therapeutic Listening can have a profound effect on a child's sensory processing. It has been based on the ideas and technology created by Alfred Tomatis (Tomatis, 1991), Guy Bernard (Stehli, 1991), and Ingo Steinbach (Steinbach, 1998). Shiela Frick, OTR (Frick and Hacker, 2001), is the primary author of the course on Therapeutic Listening in the United States. Therapists must take a five-day course before they can access the head phones and compact discs for Therapeutic Listening. Therapeutic listening impacts the vestibular and the auditory portions of the inner ear. It is not uncommon to see immediate changes in components of movement such as righting reactions, equilibrium, and stability. Changes are typically observed in attention; organization of behavior; self-regulation; development; refinement and mastery of postural and motor skills; bilateral motor patterns; articulation; emergence of praxis; and fine motor skills (Frick and Hacker, 2001).

There can be chemical imbalances, diet intolerances, and/or allergies which are impacting the function of the brain (Bock and Stauth, 2007; Pangborn and Baker, 2005) and may be impacting sensory processing in the brain. Common diet intolerances are the inability to process gluten and casein products correctly. Improvements in behaviors have been observed when these foods have been taken out of the child's diet (Lewis, 1998). Also, there may be enzyme imbalances that affect the child's ability to digest food and get the necessary nutrients to the brain (DeFelice, 2006; DeFelice, 2002). Some children, especially after using antibiotics, develop yeast infections which can move into the blood stream and subsequently into the brain, impacting the brain's ability to process sensory input (Bock and Stauth, 2007; Pangborn and Baker, 2005).

Feldenkrais Method®

Moshe Feldenkrais, D.Sc. (1904–1984), was an engineer, physicist, and martial arts expert. Drawing on his extensive knowledge of these fields as well as linguistics, biology, perinatal development, and athletics, Dr. Feldenkrais avoided surgery and taught himself to walk without pain after a severe knee injury. This event resulted in the development of the Feldenkrais Method®.

The Feldenkrais Method is a form of somatic education that uses gentle movement and directed attention to improve movement and enhance human functioning. With this Method, range of motion, flexibility, coordination, and graceful, efficient movement can be increased. By expanding the self-image through movement, the Method enables adults and children to become aware of their habitual neuromuscular patterns and rigidities and learn to move in new ways (Feldenkrais, 1990) with less effort and less muscle tension. Dr. Feldenkrais considered his treatments to be lessons for the body and nervous system and his clients to be his students.

There are two forms of Feldenkrais Method. One is called Awareness Through Movement (ATM). ATM's are often done in a class, like yoga, with the students lying on the floor or in other positions, following verbal directions of the instructor. The movements are very gentle and comfortable and are in non-habitual patterns. ATM lessons result in relaxation, relief of pain, improved movement patterns, and organization of movement, sensory, and cognitive functions. The other form of Feldenkrais Method is called Functional Integration (FI). This form is given in one-on-one situations, with the therapist handling the client or "student," the term used by Moshe Feldenkrais. FI has therapeutic effects similar to ATM. More specific individual issues can be addressed in FI lessons.

The form of Feldenkrais Method used in this case study was Functional Integration. FI is a hands-on therapy that uses touch on the skeleton or bones of the person receiving the therapy or "lesson." The touch is gentle and explores movement of the skeleton in a nondirective way. The Feldenkrais practitioner shows the client, in this case study a child, how he can move easily and effortlessly. The practitioner's intent is to explore just how and where the child can move without causing any discomfort or effort. When touched and moved in this manner, the child can relax deeply and in this relaxed state, his nervous system registers the movement.

We all have habitual ways of moving, including children. These habitual ways of moving can contain tension patterns. When the nervous system learns that there are new ways of moving that are easier and do not contain stress or tension, it seeks these preferred movement patterns. The child then learns to move and function with less tension in his movements.

Tension, or tightness, in the tissues is often secondary to stress, either physical or emotional. For example, during an unexpected fall or accident, it is common to tighten the body for protection and in emotional alarm. This tightness in the tissue may stay in the tissue until released with assistance. It can become part of the child's movement patterns (Upledger, 1990; Feldenkrais, 1981). The Feldenkrais Method is one way of helping the body release this trapped tension or tightness and the accompanying physical or emotional stress.

FI lessons are given over clothing and can be provided in lying down, sitting, or standing positions. Working over clothing provides an environment which is comfortable for the child. When combining Feldenkrais Method with Theraplay, the ability to work in many different positions of the child's body, enables the Feldenkrais therapist to provide lessons during most of the Theraplay session.

CRANIOSACRAL THERAPY

Craniosacral Therapy as we know it today has been developed by Dr. John Upledger, DO, FAAO, founder and medical director of The Upledger Institute, Inc.® Dr. Upledger has published numerous articles in journals and has written many books including: *Cell Talk, A Brain Is Born (Exploring the Birth and Development of the Central Nervous System)*, and *Craniosacral Therapy.*

Dr. Upledger first came in contact with the Craniosacral System when he was assisting in surgery to remove a calcium plaque from the posterior aspect of the Dura Mater at the third cervical vertebra level. His job was to retract tissue so the other surgeon could remove the plaque. He noticed a rhythm of pulsing under the Dura Mater as he held the retractor. The rhythm was about seven pulses per minute and was not synchronous with either the heart beat or respiration. He asked other physicians what the rhythm was and no one knew. He began his study and research of the Craniosacral System (Upledger, 2003).

The Craniosacral System is a semi-closed hydraulic system contained within a tough waterproof membrane (the Dura Mater) which envelops the brain and the spinal cord. An important function of this system is the production, circulation, and reabsorption of the Cerebrospinal Fluid. Cerebrospinal Fluid is produced in the Arachnoid Granulatons, primarily in the Sagital Suture of the brain and reabsorbed in the Choroid Plexus primarily in the ventricles of the brain. Cerebrospinal Fluid maintains the physiological environment in which the brain and nervous system develop, live, and function. As Cerebrospinal Fluid is produced and reabsorbed, the Craniosacral Rhythm is produced. The rhythm is the change in pressure in the Dura Mater as the Cerebral Spinal fluid increases with production until it reaches a pressure where it begins to be reabsorbed. Then pressure decreases until more production is triggered. This rhythm is about six or seven cycles per minute and is independent of pulse or respiration. The rhythm can be palpated through the skin and connective tissue (Upledger and Vredevoogd, 1983).

Craniosacral Therapy is accomplished using very light touch (about the weight of a nickel). Light touch is required in order to palpate the Craniosacral System and follow it to where it needs assistance. When there is a restriction in the Craniosacral System, caused by physical or emotional trauma, the restriction can be relieved using Craniosacral Therapy. The therapist learns to detect a restriction and to stop the rhythm until enough pressure builds up behind the restriction to cause it to release. Physical or emotional traumas, which have become stored in the tissues as restrictions, can be released. When the restrictions are released, function can improve, in both physical and emotional areas (Upledger, 1987).

CASE STUDY OF WILLIAM

William, a three year old, was referred for Theraplay (Jernberg, 1979; Jernberg and Booth, 1999) in co-treatment with handling techniques by his occupational therapist. He had characteristics of a child with autism in the severe range (American Psychiatric Association, 2000). He was unable to accept adult, directed structure, had a very high activity level, and was unable to relate to others using typical social interactions (Sameroff et al., 2004). He had a sweet disposition as long as he could control his environment. He was not speaking and did not appear to understand what was said to him. He seemed to be in his own world and not relating to his environment.

History

William was the three-year-old middle child of three boys. Neither of his siblings had characteristics of autism. William's birth history was uneventful. His health in general had been good. William had occupational therapy and speech therapy for one year before beginning Theraplay. Mother/child interactions were first assessed using the Marschak Interaction Method (Jernberg, 1991a) (Marschak,1960) a method for evaluating child-parent interactions under controlled conditions.

Pretreatment Marschak Interaction Method with William and His Mother

It was clear during the Marschak Interaction Method (MIM) (Jernberg, 1991a) that William's mother worked hard to engage him, but William became overwhelmed, frustrated, and upset when he couldn't communicate his desires. He spent most of the MIM either standing by the door or laying down on the floor. During the feeding task his mother made a few "yummy!" sounds, asking him how many pretzels were in her hand, because she believed counting might be of interest to him. However, William continued to scream during this task and mother chose to move on to the next activity.

When William accidentally bumped his head on a doorknob his mother attempted to console him by talking to him and rubbing his head. However, he eventually appeared to stop crying, because he became interested in the next task item she brought out. The task with the doll interested William enough to do some of the actions himself. He didn't repeat the actions that his mother showed him or respond to her instructions, but when she asked, "Should we give the dolly a bath?" He said, "ba," and she responded, "Bath. Good."

The MIM that was conducted appeared to verify mother's description of William as a sweet-natured, smart boy who had a bond with his family members. During the MIM he became upset when his brother needed to leave the room. While he was crying he called out sounds that resembled his brother's name as well as "Let me out!"

William showed contentment when he built a block structure by himself. But, after his mother praised him regarding the structure, he scattered the blocks, shrieked and didn't build again. It appeared as if William was content to play on his own, but had difficulty when he felt intruded upon. When mother played Peek-a-Boo with William he shrieked, and when she sang to him he attempted to scratch at her face in an effort to make her stop.

It was pleasing to see mother's non-judgmental perseverance throughout the MIM. She calmly attempted to help William move along at his developmental and emotional level as the tasks were performed.

Treatment: Sessions 1 to 6, Involving One Therapist

William's first six sessions were Theraplay sessions with one therapist. For the first session, the room was small and empty of toys except for a closed Theraplay box. However, there were a few videos on a high shelf with a TV set. William entered the room and immediately spotted the TV and the videos, went to them and refused to be directed to the bean chair. His mother had no control over him at the time and he was very fast and very strong. The session consisted of unsuccessfully trying to structure William. For William's next two or three sessions, the therapist removed the heavy TV and stand. The room was empty except for a couch, a beanbag chair, and a Theraplay box. William was able to sit in the beanbag chair or on his mother's lap for Theraplay. As long as he had no distractions and his mother and therapist structured him physically, William was happy and able to attend to the Theraplay activities. If the therapist presented objects of special interest to him, such as crayons, he would group them and refuse to transition to another activity. Transitioning from a favorite activity was extremely difficult for William. By session four, William was enjoying Theraplay, participating in activities with smiles, and especially enjoying lotion and the lotion song. His mother expressed how pleased she was to be in sessions with William and be able to participate in his enjoyment. In sessions five and six, William began to talk in therapy, repeating the name of an object after the therapist had named it.

Activities in these first sessions were selected because they were simple and easy for the child to understand. The child could experience success and enjoyment in a directive learning experience. Activities used were popping bubbles with a specific finger while verbally and physically assisted by the therapist, placing beanbags in a tube as a game, putting lotion on specific body parts by verbally and physically indicating the body part first, nurturing by feeding the child, and using the child's hands and feet to squeeze play dough.

Initially activities were presented in the same order so that the child became familiar and comfortable with the routine, the playful intrusion, and the adult-directed structure. Words were kept simple and physical prompts were used to improve William's comprehension of the activities.

Treatment Sessions 7 plus, Involving Two Therapists

The decision to combine Theraplay and Sensory and Handling Techniques was precipitated by availability of both therapists and our belief that this could provide optimal opportunities for William's developmental and emotional needs. Therapy sessions were conducted with the Licensed Clinical Professional Counselor (LCPC) presenting and directing the Theraplay activities and the physical therapist sitting either behind or to William's side using handling techniques (described above) to help him organize, increase body awareness, and decrease tissue tightness resulting from either physical or emotional causes. The physical therapist was also a certified Theraplay therapist and participated in Theraplay when appropriate. Occasionally including another person he was familiar with allowed William to expand his ability to interact with others and to accept changes in the dynamics of the session.

The room set-up consisted of the TV on a stand, a beanbag chair, Theraplay box, and a couch. The therapists brought William and his mother into the room and he went to the couch or beanbag chair and sat with smiles, showing his enjoyment, and anticipating activities. His mother commented that all she had to say was, "We're going to see Carol and Anita" and he immediately stopped what he was doing and got ready to go.

Activities were now varied in content and in order of presentation during each session. It was no longer necessary to keep the routine the same in order to maintain William's comfort level. Activities included play dough activities, feeding, Ring Around the Rosy, directive ball game with an accompanying interactive song, catch with a ball, squeeze game between cushions with deep pressure, and recognizing self in mirror. While she presented activities, the LCPC verbalized what was happening in the moment and labeled possible emotions involved for William.

Using Theraplay and sensory and handling techniques, William made significant progress in his ability to enjoy social interactions and his ability to transition easily both at home and in session. He could easily shift his attention from a highly desired object to one presented by the therapist. In the past, letting go of a highly desired object was impossible without temper tantrums and strong resistance. He was able to attend to adult-structured activities for extended periods of time. He displayed empathy for others, for example, when his brother was crying he said, "I love." His self-esteem and sense of himself as a person had emerged. He demonstrated pride in his accomplishments with smiles and pleasure. When William displayed emotions the LCPC verbalized possible emotions or feeling states and William was able to show recognition when she correctly defined the emotion he was feeling. Speech and language progressed from about five words to approximately two hundred words.

Following these significant improvements, William began to take supplements prescribed by a naturopath to enhance his body's biochemical balance. Subsequent to taking the supplements, his mother and therapists noticed significant improvements in his expressive language, and in his overall ability to organize and calm himself. William was speaking in sentences and was answering questions in a nearly age appropriate manner. It can be noted that these improvements probably would not have occurred without the base of social interactions and language learned during Theraplay with sensory and handling techniques.

ACTIVITIES

Artful pacing and an animated voice should always be considered essential elements in Theraplay activities. Where therapist is written, parent can also be inserted after the parent had been instructed and/or had seen a demonstration.

Deep Pressure with Cushions: The child was laid down on a cushion or pillow. Another pillow was placed on him to hide his tummy, arms, and legs. Care was taken to have a cushion or pillow be placed not higher than the child's collarbone so that the child's face was carefully observed for an indication of discomfort as well as the establishment of eye contact. The therapist then played a game of "Squeeze," and firm, even pressure was applied to the top pillow. The pressure could be varied by applying pressure from top to bottom or bottom to top of the cushion. This activity is an engaging activity, but the child may perceive this as challenging as it involves the risk of being partially hidden. This activity also involves sensory play when deep pressure is applied. The child was "hidden" between the two pillows which could be placed on the floor or propped up against the wall. The child could also be "hidden" for a parent to happily discover. The goal of this activity is the establishing and maintaining of eye contact, calming and organizing of the body, as well as offering the child to trust the therapist's ability to keep the child safe. A variation of squeezing deep pressure was to have the child made into a pizza, sandwich, or hot dog. The therapist and parent put imaginary toppings such as cheese, mustard, ketchup, tomato sauce, etc., on the cushion. Different speeds and amounts of pressure were applied as the imaginary toppings were added.

Stretchy Tube: This activity used a plastic accordion like tube that made noise when pulled or pushed back together. This is an engaging activity with structure. The goal of this activity is maintaining eye contact, enjoyable teamwork, and following of directives on the part of the child. The tube was placed in both of the child's hands, with therapist assist if necessary. The therapist exaggerated the stretching of the tube by leaning back as far as possible. While the tube was stretched the therapist commented with an animated tone of voice about the length of the tube and the child's strength and skill. Variations on this game included signaling the child (either with words or facial signals such as blinking) when the tube should be stretched. The child and the therapist also pushed the tube together as a joint activity. The tube was made into a circle and played with as a hat.

Lotion with Dots: The lotion bottle is held by the adult and the lotion is put on the child. One of the most successful activities can be applying lotion. Often lotion is the activity that seems to become central in the treatment and becomes the "ice breaker" when the child maintains some eye contact and is delighted and relaxed. Smiles and laughter are elicited. The lotion is often tolerated and the activity can be sustained because of the deep, firm pressure applied. For some children the lotion is enjoyed if it is dotted on the hands, arm, and legs. The dots can be counted as each dot of lotion is applied. The routine and familiarity of counting is pleasing to the child. Younger children or those who appear more sensitive to big movement have relished having the lotion applied in dots on each finger while the therapist expressed delight in the child's fingers, arms, toes, and legs. Older children or children of a higher developmental level also enjoy the application of stripes or their names written in lotion. Once trust is established with the child, lotion putting dots of lotion on the face with gentle circles can be very nurturing.

Zip with Lotion: After lotion is applied, the therapist (or parent after learning the activity) held one hand on the top of the child's arm and one hand on the underside of the child's arm. With firm pressure, the therapist's hands glided over the child's arm while counting, "1-2-3-Zip!." The 1-2-3 was done only after eye contact was established and "zip" was said while the therapist's hands quickly glided over the child's arm. This activity can also be done on a child's leg in the same way.

Ball with Holes: Using approximately five multi-colored chiffon scarves: Balls with holes that are designed to be caught easily became a unique and fun activity when scarves were used. The ball was held by both the child and the therapist so this became an engaging activity that afforded eye contact between the child and therapist or parent. Scarves were presented to the child one by one with the therapist showing the child how the scarf could be inserted in the holes in the ball. Each time the scarf was presented to the child, the therapist was playful in the presentation of the scarf. Options included playing peek-a-boo with the scarf, putting the scarf on the therapist's head so that it could be taken off while maintaining eye contact, or bringing the scarf up to the therapist's face. These placements on the part of the therapist ensured that the child didn't simply take the scarf from the therapist, but instead played an engaging game with another person. The scarves were put in the holes by the child or therapist and child together. The therapist commented on the beauty of the child's hands and fingers while doing the activity and also on the beauty of the ball with the scarves clearly visible inside. The action of pulling the scarves out of the ball became a fun activity as well as they were drawn out of the holes.

Scarves on the Head Become a Hat: The scarves used in the above activity were placed on the child's head. The child often commented that this is a hat. He enjoyed feeling the scarves on his heads as scarves were placed there by the therapist. The child also liked the feeling of the scarf on his face while the therapist directed a peek-a-boo game. The scarves were placed by one person or together on the head. A variation included the therapist assisting the child with placing the scarves on the therapist's and parent's head. A group activity developed as each person felt the scarf on their head and face and looked at and commented on the other person's scarf.

Tube with Beanbags: The tube was made of poster board thickness paper rolled and taped into a tube. The therapist held the tube and put the child's hands on the bottom of the tube to receive the beanbags inserted one by one. The therapist held the beanbags at eye level, and eye contact was established with the child as the beanbag was put in the tube. The element was often surprising to the child, as the beanbag was felt by the child as it dropped in his hands.

REFERENCES

American Psychiatric Association (2000). *Diagnostic and Statistical Manual of Mental Disorders DSM-TR Fourth Edition (Text Revision)*. Washington D.C. pp. 70–75.

Ayres, J. (1979). *Sensory Integration and the Child.* Los Angeles: Western Psychological Services.

Bock, K., and Stauth, C. (2007). *Healing the New Childhood Epidemics: Autism, ADHD, Asthma, and Allergies: The Groundbreaking Program for the 4-A Disorders.* New York: Ballantine Books.

DeFelice, K. (2006). *Enzymes: Go with Your Gut: More Practical Guidelines for Digestive Enzymes.* Johnston, Iowa: Thundersnow Interactive.

——. (2002). *Enzymes for Autism and Other Neurological Conditions: Practical Guide to Bio-Medical Therapy.* Philadelphia: Jessica Kingsley Publishers.

Feldenkrais, M. (1990). *Awareness Through Movement.* New York: HarperCollins, Publishers.

——. (1981). *The Elusive Obvious.* Capitola, Calif.: Meta Publications.

Field, T. (2001). *Touch.* Cambridge, Mass.: MIT Press.

Fisher, A., Murray, E., and Bundy, A. (1991). *Sensory Integration: Theory and Practice.* Philadelphia: F.A. Davis Company.

Frick, S., and Hacker, C. (2001). *Listening with the Whole Body.* Madison, Wisc.: Vital Links.

Hunt, V. (1989). *The Infinite Mind: Science of the Human Vibrations of Consciousness.* Malibu, Calif.: Malibu Publishing Co.

Jernberg A. M., and Booth, P. B., (1999). *Theraplay: Helping Parents and Children Build Better Relationships Through Attachment Based Play.* San Francisco: Jossey-Bass.

Jernberg, A. M. (1991a). "Assessing parent child interaction with the Marschak Interaction Method" (MIM). In C. E. Shaefer, K. Gitlin, and A. Sandgrund (eds.) *Play Diagnoses and Assessment.* New York: John Wiley & Sons.

Jernberg, A. M., et al. (1991b). *Reciprocity in Parent-Infant Relationships.* Wilmette, Ill.: The Theraplay Institute.

Jernberg, A. M. (1979). *Theraplay.* San Francisco: Jossey-Bass.

Kranowitz, C. (1998). *The Out-of-Sync Child: Recognizing and Coping with Sensory Integration Dysfunction.* New York: Penguin Putnam Inc.

Lewis, L. (1998). *Special Diets for Special Kids.* Arlington, Texas: Future Horizons.

McClure, V. (2000). *Infant Massage: A Handbook for Loving Parents (3rd revised edition).* New York: Bantam.

Marschak, M. (1960). "A method for evaluation of child-parent interactions under controlled conditions." *Journal of Genetic Psychology.* (97): 3–22.

Miller, L. J. (2006). *Sensational Kids: Hope and Help for Children with Sensory Processing Disorder (SPD).* New York: Penguin Group.

Oz, M. (1999). *Healing from the Heart.* New York: Penguin Group.

Pangborn, J., and Baker, M. (2005). *Autism: Effective Biomedical Treatments.* Boston: DAN!

Sameroff, A. J., McDonough, S. C., and Rosenblum, K. L. (2004). *Treating Parent-Infant Relationship Problems: Strategies for Intervention.* New York: The Guilford Press.

Smith, F. (1986). *Inner Bridges: A Guide to Energy Movement and Body Structure.* Atlanta: Humanics Limited.

Stehli, A. (1991). *The Sound of a Miracle.* New York: Avon.

Steinbach, I. (1998). 3rd Ed., revised. *SAMONAS Sound Therapy: The Way to Health Through Sound.* Kellinghusen, Germany: Techau Verlag. (Original work published in German, 1994).

Tomatis, A. A. (1991). *The Conscious Ear: My Life of Transformation Through Listening.* Barrytown, New York. Station Hill Press.

Upledger, J., and Vredevoogd, J. (1983). *Craniosacral Therapy.* Seattle: Eastland Press.

Upledger, J. (1987). *Craniosacral Therapy II: Beyond the Dura.* Seattle: Eastland Press.

———. (2003). *Cell Talk: Talking to Your Cells.* Berkeley: North Atlantic Books.

Wilbarger, P. and Wilbarger, J. (1991). *Sensory Defensiveness in Children Aged 2–12.* Denver: Avanti Educational Programs.

16

Relinquishment Visits: Saying Goodbye Is an Unnatural Process

Terra Bovingdon and Karen Fabian

A sobbing child, confused, anxious, scared; an angry, grief-stricken parent coming together in a sterile environment, under the watchful eyes of the same system that has deemed their relationship unhealthy, a risk to the welfare of the child. The "final visit" is memorable for its finality, tension, and stoicism. All too often this is the scene that plays itself out for children in foster care, when parental rights are terminated and they are court-ordered to have a final visit with their biological parents. Rather than providing a springboard for future thinking, this final visit has the "stickiness" of a negative memory that endures through time (Perry, 2006).

No process may ever exist that makes the "final visit" healthy and "okay." However, by using a more therapeutic approach the scars may be less damaging, resulting in fewer barriers as the child moves forward to adoption. At Calgary Family Services, an approach has been designed to help all parties through these unnatural visits, and to move children along the path of permanence. It is not a process that mitigates the sadness, loss, and grief that accompanies such a significant loss, but it is a process that guides birth parents toward success during this important moment with their children. This process has seen powerful outcomes as birth parents have stated, "I didn't think I could do it, but I did a good job for [my child]."

Seven years ago, the Adoption Counselling Program at Calgary Family Services was asked to undertake a "relinquishment visit" in an active case in the program. Knowing the typical scenario of how these visits go and the lingering fallout, the Child Welfare worker succinctly stated, "You can do the visit or clean up the mess after we do it." Thus began the process of developing an approach which would combine the learning from several fields, and be underpinned by the program's mainstay of Theraplay® (Jernberg and Booth, 1999).

By combining the current research on child development, Dyadic Developmental Psychotherapy, attachment, trauma, neuroscience, grief, and loss, the "Therapeutic Relinquishment Visit" was born. The framework empowers the parents to play a positive role in moving children forward and allows parents to walk away with a sense of having "done a good job" at the difficult and extraordinary task of saying a final goodbye to their child.

In keeping with the parameters of Theraplay, all parties are prepared for the final visit and are brought together through the use of anxiety-reducing play. It is through the positive aspects of structured play that anxiety is reduced, allowing children to ask their toughest questions and adults to answer these questions in a health-promoting manner, one final gift to their children. The play-based visit gives the children an opportunity to relax and receive the goodness to which they are entitled and which the adult provides without expecting anything in return (Jernberg and Booth, 1999).

TIMELINE

When a request comes in for a relinquishment visit, a therapeutic team is assembled. One counselor will undertake the preparation of the biological parent(s), one will prepare the child, and a third team member is identified to support the foster/adoptive family. Whenever possible, the workload is based on who already has a working relationship with the child, as this is the relationship that will carry forward, supporting the child in their placement following the relinquishment visit.

The initial work begins with the biological family identified for the visit. Making contact and getting the parent(s) engaged is often the first hurdle—this process will be discussed in length later in the chapter. Once the family is engaged in the process, three to four sessions are scheduled with their identified counselor to begin preparations.

The parents' level of commitment, stability, and focus are assessed in these initial sessions and a date is established for the actual visit, usually two weeks following the initial parent session. In scheduling the date of the final visit several things need to be considered: visits typically occur near the end of the week to allow all parties some time before returning to their regular routine and they are never scheduled close to important holidays; or near the child's birthday.

The child is not prepared for the visit until there is a strong sense of parental engagement and "child-focused" follow through. Even then, the child is only informed of the impending visit a few days prior to the established date. This is to allow the information to resonate for the child, but not to linger for a lengthy period unresolved and heightening their anxiety.

The child's counselor meets with the child at least twice prior to the final visit, with the focus being on informing the child, explaining the structure of the visit, helping the child to create a gift to give during the visit, discussing questions they may want to ask, and answering questions the child has about the process. Foster and/or adoptive parents are included in this preparation as they will be the individuals supporting the child emotionally on a more constant basis, following the final encounter with birth parents.

PREPARATION FOR BIRTH PARENT(S)

The work with the birth parents initially focuses on getting them into the counselor's office. Frequently, these parents are angry, hurt, and defensive. They usually come to the first session angry at the system that has removed their children, suspicious that the counselor is "part of the system," and presenting as non-compliant. The most important part of this stage for the counselor is to validate the individual's emotions and experiences, as well as joining in an inter-subjective process characterized by non-verbal attunement, reflective dialogue, acceptance, curiosity, and empathy without the presence of judgment or criticism (Hughes, 2006). Through the use of validation and a focus on being child-centered, many parents have been able to successfully engage in the process and leave their anger "at the door." It is made very clear to families that the visit must stay child-focused or it will be canceled or stopped if deemed necessary by any member of the therapeutic team.

During the initial 3 to 4 sessions with the parents, they are encouraged to bring in pictures and meaningful gifts to present to the child. Parents are informed that any gifts, pictures, or cards they intend to bring into the room for the child, must be in the counselor's possession prior to the visit. Parents are aware that this is to ensure that there are no messages, addresses, or identifying information being passed on to the child that will place the child in dual loyalties, conflict, or at risk.

Parents are also prepared in the initial phase to plan a snack to share during the visit. This is a nurturing act in which the birth parent can bring the child's favorite treats to share. In one case, the mother insisted on bringing sushi for her four year-old daughter. Initially the team was skeptical, but when asked, the little girl stated that it was exactly what she wanted to share with her Mom.

A crucial part of the preparation stage for parents is helping them to identify the "tough questions" they may be asked by the child during the visit. One mother made it very clear that she would not give the reasons as laid out by "the system" as she deemed these "lies." She was encouraged to stay truth-based and at a developmentally appropriate age level for the child, and always to remain child-focused. This mother was able to answer her daughter's question about why she could not parent her with "I was unable to protect you in the way you needed."

System bashing is discussed with parents in order to help them to understand that such a stance could have negative implications for their child who will be still part of the system. Parents are guided to refrain from using such language as "I'm fighting to get you back," "I'll find you," "You know where to find me," as these messages do not support the moving forward process of the child.

Parents are supported in assuming personal responsibility for the circumstances that have resulted in the apprehension of their child. Parents understand that children will hold themselves responsible, especially if no one else assumes responsibility. We have witnessed parents, who are drug addicted, explain to their children that they have problems that need professional help. One mother explained that she was wrong to burn her children's hands on the stove, adding that it was not their fault and she did not know how to be a "day to day" mom.

Preparation also includes helping parents verbalize three messages that seem to be universal, into their own words. The messages include: they will love their children forever, nothing that has happened is the child's fault, and that they want the child to grow up to be happy and healthy. The third message is often expanded by parents encouraging their child to let others into their heart and reminding them that they can hold everyone (birth, foster, and adoptive families) in their hearts simultaneously.

Parents often want the children to know that they will be working hard to get themselves healthy for when they may meet in the future. Dr. Gordon Neufeld (2007) speaks to the importance of bridging children to the reunion. Thus in relinquishments it is openly discussed that in Alberta at the age of 18, individuals can put their names on an adoption registry to be reconnected with birth family. Research indicates that the vast majority of foster and adoptive children will seek out their birth family. Many answers to the "tough questions" focus on the drive to reconnect.

PREPARATION FOR CHILDREN

In the preparation stage, the child has fewer sessions. Theraplay is a key component to engaging with the children. Often a session of Theraplay is planned to engage with the child, bolster the connection to the foster/adoptive parents, and reduce the child's anxiety. Part of the preparation session is used to explain the structure of the visit and what to expect of the visit. Time is also spent helping the child prepare a gift to give to their parent. Often this gift is a very simple, but meaningful handprint of the child. Usually children will bring a current photo of themselves to give as well. Both may be placed in a frame by the child's therapist or foster parent.

In planning the final visit, the children are asked which of the Theraplay activities they enjoyed and would like to share with their parents. These activities are used in the room on the final visit to re-anchor all parties. Keeping balloons aloft and other activities that are arousing, have been utilized to re-engage the dyad at the beginning of the visit and are then followed with a settling activity, such as "trace a message" or "caring for hurts." (See appendix for activities.)

An important piece in preparing the child for the court-ordered visit, is the opportunity to ask the "why" questions. While these questions stimulate the drive to reconnect, they also play a powerful role in the development of the child's future narrative and their future relationship to their own children. As Dr. Daniel Siegel (1999) states, "A profound finding from attachment research is that the most robust predictor of a child's attachment to parents is the way in which the parents narrate their own recollections of their childhood experiences" (p. 6).

Often hearing the questions other kids have asked can be helpful in aiding the child to generate their list of questions. Some of the "tough questions" children will ask include: "Why is this happening?," "Will I see you again?," "What about my siblings?," "Will you remember me?," "How will you remember me?," and specific questions about abuse or selecting a partner over the kids.

Children are encouraged to think about and ask their "tough questions" so they can begin to make sense of events and feel the futility associated with the loss. As Dr. Neufeld and Dr. Gabor Mate (2005) state, "Registering futility is the essence of adaptive learning. When our emotions are too hardened to permit sadness or disappointment about something that didn't succeed, we respond not by learning from our mistake, but by venting frustration" (p.170).

PREPARATION FOR FOSTER/ADOPTIVE PARENTS

Preparation with foster and adoptive parents initially involves discussing logistical concerns. If they are driving, where to park, bringing a camera for pictures, bringing a current photo, and what to expect leading up to and following the visit. By including these caregivers in the preparation stage with the child, they can become familiar with the affect modulation of Theraplay and specific activities that they may employ with the child to help with self-soothing and regulation during this emotionally stressful time.

On the day of the final visit, a third counselor will sit behind the one-way mirror supporting the foster/adoptive parent and helping them to understand their role in emotionally supporting the child. Families are encouraged to observe from behind the one-way mirror, as they are the ones that carry forward with the child and are in the best position to stay present with their child's pain and offer comfort. Consistent with Dr. Neufeld's view of futility, Dr. Alan Wolfelt (2005) wisely notes, "Companioning is about being present to another person's pain; it is not about taking away the pain" (p. 33). When caregivers experience the pain and suffering of their child, they instinctively want to take the pain away. Yet, to truly companion another human being through grief requires that we sit with the pain and overcome the instinct to "fix." This requires caregivers to be the agents of futility as well as the angels of comfort (Neufeld and Mate, 2005).

We have seen foster/adoptive parents brought to tears behind the mirror, but it has offered them a deeper understanding of the child's inner subjectivity, and the bond between the parent and child. One adoptive father stated through tears that the process "made me love her more."

STRUCTURE OF THE VISIT

The structure of the visit is important in anchoring all parties in the unnatural process of saying a final goodbye to family. The visit is structured in a manner that is child-focused. The child enters and leaves the room first. This is to reduce the feeling of "being left" or abandoned by the parent leaving first. The parent is asked to arrive at least a half-hour before the visit, to review the process with their therapist and to reduce the chance of a crossover with the child and foster/adoptive family arriving. Once the child has arrived and claimed the room for the visit, and the foster/adoptive parents are set up behind the observation mirror, the interpreting therapist behind the mirror alerts the therapist and parent. The biological parents are aware that foster/adoptive parents are viewing from the observation room.

The room for the visit is colorful and child-friendly with very little furniture and no toys to cause distraction. The intent is for engagement to occur in the context of the relationship. Several therapist-directed activities are available if necessary. A blanket is usually set out on the floor to anchor the dyad in space and to provide a place for sharing the snack.

One therapist will remain connected to the child in the room, in an unobtrusive way, flowing in and out of interaction based on need. For safety reasons, usually the therapist that is present to support the parent will remain close to the door. Although relinquishment visits do not go ahead if the therapist does not feel the parent can remain child-focused, these are emotionally laden visits, and precautions are taken to ensure the child's safety. These precautions include: alerting reception staff of the visit occurring, keeping one therapist close to the door, having foster/adoptive family leave immediately following the visit, and having the biological parent remain until the family has left the vicinity. In one particular case, the grandfather had a restraining order against him for previous incidents of "stalking" the foster family. As the visit was ending he attempted to leave the building simultaneously, adding that he needed to get "some air." This was averted by the therapist stating he would have to wait.

The visits often begin with an emotional reunion of hugs, kisses, and an informal inventory similar to Theraplay. The inventory usually consists of exclamations over physical changes, and talking about how the foster/adoptive family is doing a good job looking after the child. It has also been a time where parents will collect their child, sitting down to rock them, even with older children.

Dr. Neufeld stresses the importance of emphasizing "sameness" between children and their estranged parents, highlighting that what the two share, connects them. When one six year-old boy asked his mother how she would remember him, the dyad each created a paper heart and wrote down things they shared in common with one another. This activity lead to great moments of meeting, as they both ended up laughing about their hair, printing, noses, and laugh being the same. During relinquishments laughter and tears are welcome, as they both have an integrative capacity in the brain (Neufeld, 2007).

Following the reunion, the flow of the visit naturally moves toward the sharing of gifts and looking through the photo album parents have prepared for the child. This is an intense time of engagement; usually children sit on their parent's laps to go through the album. Several parents have included blank pages at the end of the album for the child to add their future pictures. This time of connection naturally leads into playful activities, as a release for the emotionality of the engagement.

Theraplay activities such as "catching bubbles" or "keeping a balloon aloft," are often among the favorite activities chosen for the final visit. With the "nervous energy" released, the flow proceeds to the sharing of the snack. It is often during this intimate, nurturing activity that the children will begin to broach the "tough questions." The children, with encouragement from their therapist, will often have their questions written down, which offers support during this highly anxious time.

The parents are prepared in their individual sessions to answer the tough questions. Responses have included, "I am not able to be your growing up mom," "I need to get myself healthy" and "I shouldn't have hurt you, that was wrong of Mommy." If a question is asked that stumps the parent, they are encouraged to say "That's a mystery" or "I'm not sure," rather than feel obligated to give a quick answer. Occasionally the therapist will help field such questions.

Once the tough questions have been answered, the visit starts to draw to a close. Typically visits will last no more than about an hour, due to the amount of emotional energy needed by both parties to remain in a healthy interaction. By sensing the tone of the room and the emotionality, a therapist will usually structure the last few minutes of the visit by announcing that it is time to say goodbye, getting the dyad together for a final photo and goodbye hugs. In this moment a Theraplay activity such as "blanket wrap/drag" has been extremely useful in transitioning the child without fueling their anxiety.

In anecdotal experience following the visit, birth parents have expressed pride in themselves for "the gift" they just gave their child in moving forward. Parents express their amazement at doing "a good job" in an unnatural process. One father stated that he appreciated the "process" and wished he had a similar opportunity with his three older children.

LEARNING

From experience we have honed and improved the process with the focus always being on the child and the relationship with the birth parent, even though this relationship is ending. We have learned to keep the numbers in the room down, so that the child and parent can be the focus. This has meant doing separate visits with grandparents.

On occasion we have had requests for Child Protection Workers to observe from behind the one-way mirror. Generally speaking this has not been feasible, as the parents' association with the investigative nature of the "system" can act as a barrier to the therapeutic stance that is necessary during the visit.

Most importantly, we have learned that the emotionality of the preparation work and the actual visit take a toll on staff. Thus, we ensure a team approach and team support to discuss and debrief the visit when it is complete.

With limited time frames available to work within and an exceeding amount of pressure being placed on staff to provide these visits for children, we have established program parameters to reduce the strain. For example, we will provide relinquishment visits for children that are already in our programs in our center. Furthermore, we will spend no more than two weeks in preparing for and completing the visit, and we will not accept too many referrals for this specific service in a short time period.

Staff has also learned that working either or both sides of the dyad can be difficult work. Some team members are more comfortable working with the parents, while others prefer to prepare the children. It is important to support these preferences and play to the individual team member's strengths in facilitating the process.

The staff at Calgary Family Services is privileged to be involved with families during this significant time of loss and new beginnings. We would like to thank all of the participants who work hard to give children the experience of a healthy goodbye. As Dr. Wolfelt (2005) advises:

> The essence of finding meaning in the future is not to forget the past, as I have been told, but instead to embrace my past. For it is in listening to the music of the past that I can sing in the present and dance into the future. (p. 44)

CASE STUDY: RELINQUISHMENT

Background information: Susan's two children were taken into custody of Child Protection Services due to issues of neglect, maternal drug use, and failure to protect. The children were both toddlers at the time of relinquishment visits that were court-ordered when the children became permanent wards of the court.

Date: November 14, 2007
Telephone contact with Susan

Susan agreed to come in for an initial session to discuss the court-ordered relinquishment visits with her children. Susan was sad and resigned in her presentation, but did not become angry or hostile toward the therapist. (It is not uncommon for the parents to target their anger at the therapist initiating discussion about the relinquishment visit.)

Date: November 21, 2007
Session with Susan

Susan brought her cousin, who had also experienced the loss of her children to Child Protection Services to the initial visit. The cousin was assessed for whether or not she would be supportive and helpful to the process, or if she would be a detriment to the process by not supporting Susan or the process. The cousin was very supportive, and able to manage her own loss while being present for Susan.

In the initial session, Susan was receptive to the plan for the relinquishment visits with her children. Susan reported having recently left a physically abusive relationship and acknowledged that she was unable to be the day-to-day parent her children needed. Susan readily assumed responsibility and was focused on using the visit, as outlined by the therapist, to move her children forward under the difficult circumstances. Susan and her cousin, were guided in ensuring a strong support system was in place for Susan during the emotional process. Thus, when the visit was over, Susan would not return to work for the day, and would have someone supportive to be with her.

Susan expressed concern for her two-and-a-half-year-old daughter's reaction and being able to manage her daughter's anger in the visit, as previous visits had been characterized by her daughter's explosive anger vented at Susan, and avoidance. It was determined that separate visits for each of the children would be best to keep the anxiety low, and enable Susan to focus her complete attention on the child present in the room. Due to Susan's own anxiety around her daughter's potential reaction, she decided that it would be best to do the visit with her daughter first. Susan was made aware that the foster mother would be behind a two-way mirror to support the children in the home following the difficult and emotional process.

A discussion was held in detail about how the visit would be structured around playful games that were selected to enable the dyad to interact playfully, keeping their anxiety and emotionality in check during the relinquishment visit. It was explained to Susan that she could bring a snack to share in each of the visits, a photo album to give each of the children, and a gift that would not be distracting from the dyadic interactions of the visit. It was stressed with Susan that any gifts and photos had to be brought to the next preparation session for the therapist to review. She was also encouraged to have an idea of what the snack would be in advance, to enable this to be shared with the foster parent to ensure the children would like such a snack. Susan was encouraged to bring in a camera, which the therapists would use to capture pictures of the dyad.

In the first session, it was stressed to Susan the importance of staying child-focused in the visit, and the need for adults to assume responsibility for what is happening to the child. Susan was directed to think of what "tough questions" her daughter might ask regarding the circumstances and her final visit with her mother. A tentative schedule for further parent preparation sessions and the two relinquishment visits was established at the end of the first session.

Date: November 23, 2007
Parent Preparation Session #2
Susan and her cousin in attendance

Susan brought in a letter she had written and the pictures she wanted to give to the children in each of their visits. The letter was well written and child-focused, Susan agreed to remove one statement that told her daughter to come looking for her when she was older. It was discussed that this could cause her daughter to feel pressured and increase her sense of conflicted loyalties. Susan was in agreement to taking it out and staying child-focused.

Susan shared the pictures she wanted to leave with each of the children. They were reviewed to ensure the appropriateness of the pictures, and that no identifying information existed in the photos or was written on the back of the photo. Susan was awaiting her paycheck to buy a gift for each of the children. She agreed to bringing the gifts to the relinquishment unwrapped or in a gift bag that would allow them to be checked before going into the room. Susan shared her plan of support for after each of the visits, and verified that she would not be alone. There was a concern about being able to get money to purchase a gift and snacks for each child. A plan was made to inform the therapist the day before the visits if this was going to be a problem.

Susan identified several possible "tough questions" her daughter would ask in the visit. Given the age of her son (1 year old) and his developing language skills that would not permit him to ask questions, Susan covered several of the issues in the letter. Susan acknowledged that her daughter would want to know why she is not able to live with Susan any longer. To which Susan verbalized her response that she had made mistakes and was unable to care for the children properly. She was going to follow up the statement with the three things mothers want their children to know: that they love their children, nothing that has happened is the child's fault, and that she wants the children to grow up happy and healthy, and that means letting a day to day mommy into their hearts. She also wanted to inform her daughter that she was going to look after herself and get herself help.

Date: November 27, 2007
Child Preparation Session #1

The purpose of the preparation visit with Susan's two children was to provide them with the opportunity to get familiar with not only the sights and sounds of the room in which they would be having their final goodbye with their birth mother, but also to build a relationship with the therapist who would be the support person for them during this experience. The children were accompanied by their foster mother, Linda, who also participated in the preparation session.

The session consisted of a number of Theraplay activities. These activities were used in order to communicate safety and trust within the relationship, but also to diffuse the presence of anxiety and insecurity that might surface for the children. On the way to the playroom, a simple scavenger hunt, consisting of finding puzzle pieces to put together, was set up for the children. Once in the room, the children engaged in several games, which included: powder clouds, balloons aloft, popcorn blanket, bean bag balance, bubble catch, smooth ride, blanket swing and blanket drag ride (see appendix). Within the session, using pictures of homes and people ("tummy mommies," "growing up mommies"), it was explained by the therapist that the children were going to be having a "goodbye celebration" with their birth mother. Neither of the children had any specific questions for their birthmother. However, the therapist did tell a story to the older child about how most children are curious about why their moms can't be their growing up moms, and that it is ok to ask those questions. Toward the end of the session, each child had one of their hands painted and then pressed onto a piece of paper, to give to their birth mother as a parting gift.

Following the session, a meeting with the foster parent took place in order to review the underlying philosophy of relinquishment visits and provide an opportunity for any questions or concerns to be raised. During this meeting, Linda expressed her reluctance in observing this visit, as she felt it would be very hard to see a mother saying goodbye to her children. This reluctance was validated and the importance of Linda's role in this process was highlighted. Linda understood that by observing she would be better able to respond to naturally occurring reactions from the children, following the visit. She also came to understand that the children would experience a loss, however, we were hoping that by having a goodbye time and having caring adults to support them, they would "make sense" of this and integrate it into their life in a way that was not self-harming. It was explained that a counselor would be with Linda during the observation and that ongoing supports were available for her and the children following this process.

Date: November 29, 2007
Relinquishment visit with Susan and her daughter (foster mother observing behind the mirror)

Susan and the therapist met for half an hour before her daughter arrived for the relinquishment visit. This time was used to ensure the snack was ready, the gift was appropriate, and to review the "tough questions" that Susan may have to answer in the session. Susan and her daughter engaged in several activities led by the child's therapist. The activities were Theraplay based and included: powder clouds, bubble catch, popcorn blanket, blanket swing and blanket drag ride. During the activities, Susan delighted in her daughter's developing speech and mobility. Susan was visibly sad at the end of the visit and saying goodbye to her daughter, however, she did a good job in helping her daughter move forward at the time. Susan remained in the play room as her daughter left and was reconnected to her foster mother. Susan thanked the therapist for the process and support she received during such an emotional time. Susan asked to see her daughter's therapist to extend her gratitude to her as well.

Date: November 30, 2007
Relinquishment visit between Susan and her son

Susan brought a beautiful letter of appreciation for the foster mother, the letter thanked the foster mother for looking after the children so well and spoke to their health and happiness. Susan was expecting the visit with her son to be less of an unknown given the young age of her son. She was more skeptical of the first visit with her daughter and how she might be angry and rejecting of Susan. However, the final visit proved to be very hard for Susan as her son was apprehensive, wary in his interactions, and not readily engaged with Susan. Susan had been prepared for possible rejection and was able to take this initial response in stride, not pushing him and letting him approach at his own pace. The child's therapist was able to engage the dyad in playful interactions. The Theraplay activities included: powder clouds, smooth ride, bubble catch, and blanket swing.

Susan did a commendable job in the final visit and stayed child-focused in moving her son forward on his current journey. Susan expressed appreciation for the process that guided her in such a difficult task. Susan's cousin, who had lost three children from her care, stated that she wished the process had been available to her and her children when they had a final visit.

REFERENCES

Hughes, D. (2006) "The Double-Helix: Attachment and Intersubjectivity." Paper presented at the annual meeting of ATTACH Network, St. Louis, Mo., October.

——. (2007) "Dyadic Developmental Psychotherapy." Paper presented at the annual meeting of the International Theraplay Institute. Chicago, Ill., July.

Jernberg, A. M., and Booth, P. (1999) *Theraplay: Helping Parents Build Better Relationships through Attachment-Based Play*. San Francisco: Jossey Bass.

Neufeld, G. (2007) "Working with Aggressive and Violent Children and Youth." Paper presented at the conference on Aggressive Children and Youth. Calgary, Alb. April.

Neufeld, G., and Mate, G. (2005) *Hold On to Your Kids: Why Parents Need to Matter More Than Peers*. Toronto: Vintage Canada.

Perry, B. (2006) "Attachment Issues in Daycare Centres." Discussion presented at the workshop on Childcare Issues. Calgary, Alb. December.

Siegel, D. (1999) *The Developing Mind*. New York; The Guilford Press.

Wolfelt, A. (2005) *Companioning the Bereaved: A Soulful Guide for Counselors and Caregivers*. Laguna Hills, California: Companion Press.

17

Equine Assisted Therapy and Theraplay

Deborah Weiss

Four horses were led into the arena one by one. The horses did not know each other and they had never been together. These four horses had one thing in common; their owners and handlers had brought them here as a last-ditch attempt to cure them of the pains of their upbringings and to help them learn how to interact comfortably with other horses and with humans. This was to be accomplished by the horse trainer who was running the weekend clinic, and if the horses could not be helped by this trainer, the owners were likely to give up on what they considered to be dangerous horses, and send them to their death.

The dynamics were dramatic as the horses bucked and reared and made lots of noise. Their personalities emerged in the drama of the arena. One horse was clearly the bully and was chasing and snapping at the others relentlessly. One of the horses moved wherever the bully moved, staying close enough to mimic the bully, but far enough away to avoid getting kicked herself. One horse in the arena was repeatedly being kicked by the bully and seemed to come back for more. One horse remained disengaged from the drama, moving away from the noisy display throughout the entire performance. I didn't know these horses, but I knew the characters well. I grew up with these characters; the bully, the bully's sidekick, the perpetual victim, and the observer. Watching these horses now, the arena became a stage for the equine drama, as well as a stage for a metaphorical group of individuals trying to learn how to coexist. I knew that the role of spectator was a way to keep out of the direct line of fire whenever possible, and that this safe observational position provided the opportunity to develop a keen sense of awareness. I noticed that the "observer horse" was taking in every detail of the others with what seemed like hypervigilance. This heightened state of awareness is important for the horses' survival, just as it is for a hypervigilant child. In both cases, extreme attention to environment is necessary for survival. In the way that an abused child knows that a particular look on a perpetrator's face, or a nuance in the sound of the perpetrator's approaching footsteps is an indication of whether there is imminent danger, the horse also knows the nuances of its environment so that it can move itself away from harm. Chris Irwin, the Canadian horse trainer who was running the clinic that weekend, describes horses as "constantly aware of everything that goes on; the rustling of the trees, the movement of a nearby animal, an unfamiliar sound. They're evaluating and interpreting all 360 degrees of the environment around them all the time. Because they know, their DNA tells them that a predator can come hurtling toward them out of those bushes or from behind that rock at any time" (Irwin, 1998).

I had begun to study Theraplay® (Jernberg and Booth, 1999) around the same time as this clinic took place, and as I watched the trainer working with the horses to help them learn how to have trust and respect for a human, I could see the therapeutic possibilities for people. I went into my next Theraplay session as an extern, and noticed that the structure we set at the beginning of the session had the same importance as the boundaries the trainer set with the horses at the beginning of his session. The way we engaged the child in the Theraplay session reminded me of the way the trainer was engaged and present with the horses every moment. And the way he challenged the steeds and they rose to the challenge, as well as the honor and reward he gave them at the appropriate times, closely paralleled the activities we were doing in the Theraplay session in our challenge and nurturing activities. I knew there was a way to integrate the two, and I began to delve into the world of Animal Assisted Therapy.

People who enjoy being with animals know the healing bond which can develop between humans and their pets. And though humans have innately known the therapeutic qualities of animals for centuries, it is only recently that Animal Assisted Therapy has been developed as a viable therapeutic method with its own theories, practices and research. Because the very presence of animals is considered to be therapeutic, they are being brought into a variety of settings including schools, hospitals, nursing homes, treatment centers, private practice, and business corporations. Even when animals are brought in simply as visitors, positive results have been documented. The integration of animal-assisted therapy into clinical psychology was first credited to child psychologist Boris Levinson, who published a paper titled "The Dog as a Co-Therapist" (Levinson and Mallon, 1969). Levinson accidentally discovered he could make significant progress with a child with whom he was working, when his dog "Jingles" attended the therapy sessions. He went on to find that many children who were withdrawn and uncommunicative would interact positively with the dog, and his results from those sessions were noticeably different from the ones where the dog was not present.

In the 70s, horses began to take the role of "co-therapist" and the horses' special talents are now being written about. New methods are developing all over North America and Europe. "Equine Assisted Therapy" has become a viable subgroup of Animal Assisted Therapy. Horses provide a powerful paradox. They are large, strong, fast animals that can quickly become dangerous and they are also vulnerable prey animals. Being carried on the back of a 1,200 pound vulnerable giant can certainly provide access to core personal issues.

Partnering Theraplay with Irwin's horse training methods creates a powerful therapeutic tool. I developed the program "Horse Friends" to encompass these two modalities and it has since expanded to include activities from a number of equine trainers. With the encouragement of Dr. Evangeline Munns, who was director of Play Therapy Services at Blue Hills Child and Family Centre in Aurora at the time, I contacted the Ontario Trillium Foundation to see if they would be interested in funding such a venture. They were—and two years later the provincial funding agency had supported 35 children to participate in this pilot project. They continue to support our work and research to this day. The original program still exists under the name "Horse Play" and it is run by Horses At Heart Equestrian Adventures Inc. in conjunction with a number of regional child and family health service agencies.

The program consists of 12 sessions, all taking place at a horse farm with a charming farmhouse for therapy sessions. The first session consists of intake consultation and goal setting. In the second session, we conduct the Marschak Interaction Method (Marschak, 1960) for assessing family relationships, and then the family is invited over to the barn to meet the horses.

In order to evoke all the senses, and to gain rapport with the child in this initial orientation session, I ask the children what smells they expect to experience before they enter the barn. This always leads to an early opportunity for engagement, because nearly each and every child takes great pleasure in looking me square in the eye and answering "Poo!" "Yes! You are definitely going to smell horse poo in there—let's go in and see what other smells we find." And the game is on; the children know at this point that things are different here from their schoolroom or the therapy experiences they might have had to date and even the most oppositional children are eager to go in to the barn and discover this new world.

Our third to eleventh sessions consist of an equine session in the barn followed by a traditional Theraplay session in the farmhouse. The work with the horses always has clues and messages about what is really going on for the child and parent and we pay attention to what themes emerge while working with the horses. We can then tailor the Theraplay activities to address those themes. Monty Roberts, who was the inspiration for the title role of the movie *The Horse Whisperer,* says that "The biggest difference between horses and humans is that horses live honestly within an order based on mutual concern" (Roberts, 1996). Linda Kohanov, a pioneer in the field of Equine Assisted Therapy, says that horses have "an extraordinary ability to awaken intuition in humans, while mirroring the authentic feelings people try to hide" (Kohanov, 2001). Chris Irwin's first book is entitled *Horses Don't Lie*. Horseman Mark Rashid's first book is entitled "Horses Never Lie." The blatant honesty that is part of the horses' world is the most evident part of working with horses as "co-therapists." They are able to mirror behaviors and emotions without judgment or hidden agenda.

The sessions that take place at the barn start with lessons on body language of the horse in order to ensure that the participants are interacting respectfully each time they come to be with the horse. Along with traditional barn safety rules, the respectful body language also ensures that the horse does not feel threatened or imposed on, and this ensures an additional level of safety for all the participants. Always maintaining a high level of awareness is intrinsic to this program. When the participants practice this enhanced awareness with the horses, it gives them the experience of how their own actions and reactions affect the world around them. The participants are encouraged to always be aware of what the horses' posture and body language are saying to them as well as what their own body language is saying to the horse. This new awareness usually offers surprise, sometimes delight, and sometimes dismay as the participants discover that if they are feeling nervous, the horse becomes nervous too. If they are feeling frightened, the horse in turn will display signs of anxiety. However, if they are feeling frightened and are willing to admit it, either by saying out loud that they are frightened or consciously thinking about their fear while standing by the horse, the horse does not display these signs of anxiety. To the horse, a predator (as humans innately are) who is nervous or frightened around them is a dangerous thing. Physiologically, our nervous state results in a release of adrenaline, and to a prey animal, a predator with an elevated level of adrenaline is likely to be a predator that is about to attack. Once we as humans own our emotions, whatever they might be, the adrenaline level reduces, and we cease being as great of a threat to our friend the non-predator horse. When the participants begin to see this pattern, whether they be adults or children, they have 1,200 pounds of proof standing beside them in the barn that shows them that aligning oneself with an honest state of being is a safe option.

All the sessions include grooming the horses. The participants learn that grooming is a way to take care of the horse and to "check for hurts" (similar to what is done in Theraplay). The children will always let us know when they find a wound on the horse and they participate in caring for the wound. The parents are guided to use a hand-over-hand motion with the children when the child takes the grooming brush. This complements the nurturing element of Theraplay and in this case, the child and parent are together nurturing the horse.

Even grooming a horse can access deep-rooted issues. One of our participants was a mother who allowed the horse to fuss and move about while being groomed. The safety rules and one of our horsemanship lessons dictate that the horse must stand still during grooming. A fussing horse is an anxious horse, and it is our responsibility to bring the horse into a relaxed posture while grooming, which in turn becomes a safer horse for us to be near. Recognizing the discomfort of the horse, tailoring our actions in such a way that alleviates any discomfort, and taking the leadership role in setting boundaries during grooming, are all important. Exasperated by working with a "difficult" horse, this mother finally admitted that it was easier for her to work with all the fussing than to figure out how to set the boundaries. It wasn't a leap for her to realize that this was a perfect mirror for her relationship with her teenage child. The teenager disrupted the household and had a difficult time with boundaries around the home, and the mother found it easier to reactively fix the problems that arose from this, than to proactively take charge, calm the child, and create a safer emotional environment for all. This was a cathartic moment for this familial relationship. The paradigm shift the mother made that day changed the way she worked with the horse while grooming as well as hand-walking the horse. She became more assertive and began to demand more respect from the horse. This shift in her self-awareness allowed the horse to respect her more and also allowed the horse to relax in her presence, as her new-found strength was reassuring to the horse, not threatening. The mother-child relationship improved subsequently, which reduced the tension in the household as the child came to respect her mother as well.

As the participants become comfortable around the horses, they begin to focus on walking the horse and understanding the horses' body language while moving the horse on a lead line. The Irwin method for hand walking a horse involves connecting with the horse in a very specific way. The horse is not pulled by the head and no chains are wrapped around the horse's nose to intimidate or inflict pain in order to gain control. Instead, the person leading the horse is taught to walk alongside the horse, and to move the horse forward into contact with the leaders' hand. The method imitates the way horses move each other in a herd. The alpha, or leader horse is at the side or back of the herd, propelling the herd forward. This is quite different from a human "herd" where the leader is in front and the followers follow. It's easy to demonstrate to a child which of these ways feels better. Most children have experienced a leader or authority figure taking hold of their hand and pulling them forward as a way of leading. However, when the leader stands behind the child, puts their hand on the child's back and moves forward together, the leader can gently guide forward movement. There is no concurrence in the first way, and when leading the horse in the Horse Play program, even the youngest child is taught to gain concurrence with the horse so that horse and child can willingly move forward together.

By the twelfth session, the child will attempt to experience "join up." This is a term coined by Monty Roberts to mean the point where a horse will willingly follow a human without being led or coerced by any lead line, rope, or halters. The horse has to have trust and respect in the human to do this. All of the children and parents in the Horse Play program are taught to do this. It takes several weeks of hand-walking the horse, learning how to read the horses' body language, becoming aware of our own body language, and developing a mutually respectful relationship with the horse, before it will follow based on its own free will. This activity demonstrates to both parent and child that it is understanding, trust, and awareness that causes the horse to follow, not force or coercion.

CASE STUDY

A ten-year-old boy came to our program with his mother, who had identified the boy as a troubled child on medication for ADD, who had consistently disruptive behavior at school. The boy indeed was a handful in the barn and in the Theraplay sessions as he raced around and had to be constantly encouraged to stay focused. Nonetheless, over the weeks he learned that his ability to stay calm and focused was necessary to keep the horses calm and focused on him. The mother however, was less attentive as she preferred to chat and find distractions throughout all the grooming activities. We found that we constantly had to refocus her back on her son throughout the session. When it came time to teach them how to hand-walk the horse and work toward "join up," we decided to have just the boy working on these activities and that the interpreting therapist would stay with the mother to explain the process of how her son was integrating the lessons. The boy discovered that when he lost focus while walking the horse, the horse lost focus as well, and when he moved forward purposefully, eyes fixed on his goal, the horse relaxed in his hand and moved with him. Still, mom spent a lot of time chatting and diverting attention from her son. When it came time for "join up," the boy did beautifully. The little black horse he had been working with followed him along like a puppy dog. There was great satisfaction for this boy as the horse chose him as the leader and stayed close beside him with no lead lines or implements to keep him there. In one moment however, the boy lost focus and the horse began to wander off. Surprisingly, this was when mom decided to bring her attention fully to the boy and the activity. She pointed and laughed at the horse and boy and joked about how it was all falling apart. Instantly I began to talk the boy through the steps he needed to take in order to regain the horses attention and to resume the "join up." The boy listened and reacted quickly to follow the instructions and the horse did indeed move back toward the boy and continued to follow. The boy was able to experience that he could move past external ridicule to find his own success. He was able to stay present with the horse despite what must have been a hurtful moment as his mother laughed at him from the side of the corral. The experience also helped provide the mother with a larger-than-life example of some of the dynamics of her relationship with her son.

The mother did a lot of work after that point to try to understand how her support and encouragement of that boy could make a difference, and when we followed the barn session with a Theraplay session, we made sure to include activities that would reinforce her positive engagement with her son. We made sure that she "took care of his hurts" through hand and foot lotioning sessions. We included long and leisurely "inventory" sessions where she could verbalize to her son all the wonderful things he brought with him that day; his shining eyes, his wide grin and dimples, and the cute and lively cowlick in his hair. The boy was delighted to lay down on a giant piece of Kraft paper and have his mother carefully trace his outline on the page. Then mom would sit behind her son and comb his hair while telling him stories about when he was a baby. Because mom had the opportunity to watch the Theraplay externs do these activities with her son before she began participating directly in the sessions, she had a clear model of engaging without spiking the session with verbal "ouches" and insensitivities. The work with the horses helped her to understand that body language could communicate support or disinterest just as loudly as verbal language.

The barn has become the new clinic. "For a lot of people who come from a clinical setting, when you get into a barn, it's very normalizing," says Michael Kaufmann, director of education for the North American Riding for the Handicapped Association (NARHA) and founding board member of the Equine Facilitated Mental Health Association (EFMHA). "That can be a mental shift that allows you to feel differently, act differently, think differently" (www.greatstrides.org). When a person observes "The horse is difficult" or "The horse doesn't listen to me," they discover that when they change their own beliefs and behaviors, the horse's response changes.

The final Marschak tests that end the twelve sessions show great improvement in most of the families who go through the Horse Play program. There is generally greater comfort in the nurturing activities, with both children and parents who resisted nurturing in the initial Marschak. Many of the parents report that their children have greater ability to stay focused and to follow through with projects. Many of the families report that dinner-time talk often revolves around what the horse or pony did that day, or how the

Theraplay Agendas

First Theraplay Session Mother Observing Session	*Fifth Theraplay Session Mother Entering for the First Time*	*Twelfth Theraplay Session Mother Leading Activities*
Choo Choo Train Entrance	Funny Walk Entrance	Follow the Leader
Hello Song	Hello Song	Hello Song
Inventory	Inventory	Inventory
Lotion Hands	Lotion Hands and Feet	Lotion Hands and Feet
Powder Prints	Cotton Ball Guess	Paper Outlines
Peanut Butter	Motor Boat, Motor Boat	Mirroring
Tower of Hands	Tower of Hands	Hair Combing
Blanket Rock	Blanket Rock	Blanket Rock
Feeding	Feeding	Feeding
Goodbye Song	Goodbye Song	Goodbye Song

child and parent worked with the horse. The common language they now share becomes a tool for engagement at home.

The pairing of Equine Assisted Therapy with Theraplay allows us to interact with the family in an arena that provides hard to ignore metaphors that can help bring core issues to the forefront quickly. The Theraplay sessions become enriched with the information gleaned from the barn and the ability to reference some of the lessons learned from the horses, is valuable to the parents. In many cases, the work with the horses is so positive that the family continues to come visit the horses, or the children take up horse-back riding lessons. One of our teenage clients is pursuing a college Equine Science diploma.

The families are encouraged to continue the Theraplay activities at home. In 6-month follow-up sessions, families have often reported that some of these activities have become family favorites. The pairing of Theraplay with Equine Assisted Therapy offers a full sensory experience, and the families leave the farm each week with the sounds, the sights, the smell, and the feel of what an attached, mutually respectful relationship can feel like.

REFERENCES

Irwin, C. (1998). *Horses Don't Lie: What Horses Teach Us about Our Natural Capacity for Awareness, Confidence, Courage and Trust*, Winnipeg, Manitoba: Marlowe and Company.

Jernberg, A., and Booth, P. (1999). *Theraplay: Helping Parents and Children Build Better Relationships Through Attachment-based Play*, 2nd ed., San Francisco: Jossey-Bass.

Kaufmann, M. (2005). www.greatstrides.org. (April) retrieved December 2006.

Kohanov, L. (2001). *The Tao of Equus: A Woman's Journey of Healing and Transformation Through the Way of the Horse*, Novro, California: New World Library.

Levinson, B. M., and Mallon, G. P. (1969). The Dog as Co-therapist. *Mental Hygiene, 46*, 59–65.

Marschak, M. (1960). A Method for Evaluating Child-Parent Interactions Under Controlled Conditions. *Journal of Genetic Psychology* 97: 3–22.

Roberts, M. (1996). *The Man Who Listens to Horses*, New York: Random House.

V

GROUP THERAPLAY

18

Father-Son Group Theraplay

Jamie Sherman

Theraplay® is embedded in attachment theory and object-relations theory as characterized by the works of John Bowlby and Anna Freud, respectively. Attachment theory proposes that children make significant and early attachments to main caregivers, and failure to secure these attachments has long-lasting and deleterious effects on the individual and his future relationships (Bowlby, 1969). Object-relations theory views an infant's first relationship with his mother as the prototypical relationship in a child's life (Freud and Burlingham, 1973). This prototype can be a positive or negative experience for the child depending upon the ensuing dynamic.

Bowlby describes this as an inner-working model in which the infant creates a representation of the primary caregiver and which is critical for the development of the self. When things go well in the relationship, the infant develops a sense of himself as lovable, of others as loving, and of the world as a safe place to explore. The opposite develops when the parent-child relationship doesn't go well. This inner representation, or schemata, occurs during what Siegel (2003) calls the "brain-to-brain" interactions of the parent and child. The child feels joined with the parent because he sees his mind as existing inside his parent's mind. Early communication occurs in the form of non-verbal language, paralanguage, and gestures, and is reflected to the child through emotional dialogue. It is through this process that the child is able to develop a "mind's eye," which is the ability to think and feel what goes on in the mind of his caregiver and leads to the development of pro-social skills such as empathy, awareness of others, and compromise (Siegel, 2003).

In healthy relationships a positive loop is created in which infant and parent establish a symbiotic relationship. Both parent and child are acutely attuned to the signals and responses of the other. Conversely, negative bonding between the mother and infant could be the result of a physical, emotional, or intellectual insult to the child or parent. If a parent is emotionally unavailable to the child due to previous life experiences, she may be unable to interpret the child's cues. Additionally, a mismatch between infant temperament and parenting style could negatively affect the parent-child attachment. A child who has a difficult temperament may be disengaged from a parent with a laissez-faire or authoritarian style of parenting. A negative bond interrupts the positive loop resulting in a breakdown in the relationship. Theraplay aims to improve this bond by providing the structure and nurturing the child lacked due to the breakdown during the early attachment process (Jernberg, 1979).

These theories are, in part, derived from the works of ethologist Konrad Lorenz and psychologist Harry Harlow. Lorenz's (1961) concept of imprinting provided support for the notion of "hard-wired" processes influencing survival behavior. Infant survival mechanism utilized attachment forming responses of signal (i.e., crying, smiling, babbling) and approach (i.e., clinging, following, reaching) in order to bring adults into close proximity (Bowlby, 1969). Similarly, Harlow's work (1958) with rhesus monkeys established the importance of touch in attachment. Harlow observed that monkeys chose the relative warmth and comfort of the terry cloth surrogate mothers over the cold, harsh metal of the wire-mesh surrogate mothers, even when the latter provided the only source of nutrition.

Research indicates that physical touch has positive outcomes in both biology and psychoneuroimmunology. Hugging and touching release hormones into the bloodstream to help suppress viruses and depression (Cousins, 1989). Infants of depressed mothers experience biochemical changes to brain matter after daily massage therapy (Jones and Field, 1998) and significantly increase their body weight when given daily body massage (Field, 1995). A primary outcome of touch is the fostering of positive attachments between parent and child. Touch, which is processed by the right hemisphere of the brain, may prime the regulatory system for learning because the neural circuitry of the stress system is located in the early developing right brain. Infants under the age of two demonstrate higher right-brained hemispheric volumes. Attachment experiences during the first 2 years of life directly influence the experience-dependent maturation of the right brain (Schore, 2001).

Theraplay strives to replicate the healthy attachments found in positive parent-child relationships. This is accomplished by alternating between fun, engaging activities and calm, soothing ones. The therapist establishes a bond with the child through the five dimensions of parenting identified by Jernberg (1979): structure, challenge, engagement, nurturing, and playfulness. In healthy relationships parents provide unconditional nurturing in order to create an atmosphere of caring and trust. Trust enables the child to see his world as safe and secure and to explore his environment with confidence. Engagement elicits responses from the infant, encourages curiosity, and enables the child to differentiate himself from others, as well as creating a sense of connection with another. Structure creates boundaries and sets external limits, which eventually allows the child to regulate his own behavior. Challenge provides the child with a sense of fulfillment, competence, pride, and the development of a positive self-image. Playfulness creates an inviting, exciting, and positive atmosphere, and signals to the child that he can simultaneously give and receive positive experiences.

Do mothers and fathers differ along these dimensions, in particular the dimension of playfulness? Mothers and fathers are generally more similar than different during parent-child interactions (Hughes, 1999). However, differences in play tendencies between mothers and fathers may exist. Fathers are more physical and active, use rough and tumble play, bouncing, tickling, chasing, and tossing-in-the-air games; whereas mothers are less abrupt, use more toys, and more verbal forms of interactions (Hughes, 1999). Mothers seem more closely attuned to their infants and are more likely to provide for their child's needs (Hughes, 1999).

It appears these differences may be more attributable to experience than to biology (Schaffer and Emerson, 1964). Field (1978) studied the parent-child interactions of three groups of parents: mothers as primary caregivers, fathers as primary caregivers, and fathers as secondary caregivers. Differences in the quality of the interaction were found mainly between the primary and secondary caretakers, regardless of gender. Similarly, fathers were noted as equally competent and confident as mothers during observations of feeding (Parke, 1981), and physiological measures assessing child responsiveness (Berman, 1980). This suggests that fathers may be equally capable as mothers at meeting their children's needs.

Schaffer investigated the concept of monotropism; that infants attach to one caregiver at a time. He studied the attachment levels of a group of sixty infants and noted that one-third had formed attachments to more than 1 person, and by 18 months of age all had formed several healthy attachments with varying degrees of intensity. At six months the most intense attachments were to the mother, and were significantly greater than to any other individual. At eighteen months the intensity of the attachment to the father was only slightly less than to the mother (Schaffer and Emerson, 1964). Mothers carry and feed their infants and therefore have more opportunity to develop highly intense relationships. Given time and opportunity fathers may also be able to develop equally intense relationships.

Fathers play an important role in the social and emotional development of their children. A growing body of evidence suggests that the father-son relationship, in particular, is greatly influenced by positive attachments.

Fathers of securely attached infants tend to be more extroverted and agreeable than fathers of insecurely attached infants (Belsky, 1996). Attachment to the father is generally a good predictor of social competence, which, in turn, significantly predicts emotional adjustment (Rice et al., 1997). A feeling of well-being in adolescent boys is associated with positive attachment to the father (Kenny et al., 1998). Additionally, the warmth of the father makes positive contributions to the preschool child's intellectual development (Liang and Sugawara, 1996).

What is responsible for the disconnection between fathers and sons who struggle with their relationship? Western culture is filled with father-son relationship archetypes. Literature and mythology promote the notion of the overbearing, emotionally absent father and the usurping son. In William Pollack's 1998 book *Real Boys,* he describes 20 years of research which he feels informs the myth of boyhood. Dr. Pollack identifies the "boy code" where feelings of vulnerability, powerlessness, and isolation lead to fear, uncertainty, and loneliness. These feelings turn to shame, whereby boys prefer to be alone with the pain of humiliation and embarrassment. They then suffer through the trauma of disconnectedness as they are ripped away from their homes and placed in a school environment.

Pollack puts forth the notion of the gender straightjacket, whereby male infants are initially more expressive than infant females as they tend to demonstrate greater startle behavior, are more excitable, and tend to fuss and cry more. However, parents use more vivid facial expressions and emotion-laden language with girls, which may be a factor in boys' developing a more limited emotional range. Dr. Pollack states that the emotional range of pre-latency boys is far greater prior to the premature separation of going to school. As a result, boys may develop an "outward mask" which acts as a barrier to communication and intimacy. This may contribute to problems in the classroom as boys are more likely to receive lower grades, be held back, transfer to special education, receive suspensions, and be identified as hyperactive. Another contributing factor may be that a greater percentage of boys' physiological development may require them to be more active and energetic, and in greater need of more gross motor movements and tension releasing activities. Most school systems do not accommodate students in this manner, and instead require them to sit quietly at their desks for long periods of time.

This chapter recounts the journey made by a Theraplay group of fathers and their troubled sons. The purpose of this group was to promote the development of responsiveness and attunement of the fathers toward their sons through the dimensions of Theraplay in an attempt to create deeper and stronger attachments. It was our belief that the fathers could adopt more playful and nurturing interactions with their sons, and their sons would, in turn, develop more positive relationships with their fathers.

Counseling sessions with the fathers also provided opportunities to discuss some of Dr. Pollack's strategies for getting behind the mask. In particular, strategies such as connecting through actions in an attempt to engage with the child, and sharing personal experiences as a way of reducing shame were included. Additionally, we wondered if the enhanced positive attachments would affect the children's social/emotional interactions at school.

This group was conducted at Blue Hills Child and Family Centre in Aurora, Ontario, under the supervision of Dr. Evangeline Munns. The group consisted of 6 father-son dyads and was lead by three male Theraplay therapists. All fathers joined the group voluntarily and provided a family history which included describing the reasons for referral and the parent-child relationship. They also completed, along with their child's mother, the Child Behaviour Checklist and individual parent rating forms before and after treatment (Achenbach and Edelbrock, 1983). Theraplay goals were identified based on family history and rating scales.

The boys ranged in ages from 6 to 9 years. Four of the dyads were from intact families, one included a new stepfather, and one father was separated, but held an equal and shared custody arrangement. The presenting problems for this group of children included aggression, non-compliance, Attention Deficit Hyperactivity Disorder (predominantly hyperactive-impulsive type), poor self-esteem, depression, low frustration tolerance, severe sibling rivalry, frequent temper tantrums and other negative attention seeking behaviors, learning challenges, and poor school performance. Three common characteristics emerged from the presenting issues: 1) poor self-regulation, 2) low self-esteem, and 3) anti-social behaviors.

The fathers experienced great difficulty in positively attaching to their children at home. They felt rejected by their sons, and were uncomfortable with nurturing and playful activities. During the initial intakes the fathers admitted to discipline styles that were either punitive and authoritarian or laissez-faire. Some fathers revealed traumatic experiences from their childhood, citing examples of abuse, neglect, and feelings of betrayal from their own parents. Some of the fathers were experiencing personal afflictions in the form of depression, substance abuse, and uncontrollable rage. The fathers hoped the group would enable them to feel closer to their sons, and would help their children to make friends, develop empathy, reduce violent tendencies, and become less defiant.

The group goals established by the therapeutic team were 1) To increase the fathers' comfort and competence in giving affection and thus to enhance father/son attachments, 2) For the children to show affection toward their fathers, 3) For the fathers to provide external structure for their children and for the children to cooperate with adult directions, 4) To increase the children's self-esteem by promoting feelings of self-worth and affirmation. The sessions took place one night per week over a ten-week period.

Each session lasted 45 minutes, and was followed by a brief counseling session with the fathers. Fathers were encouraged, as well, to practice Theraplay activities at home. Three independent observers rated each session using a numeric rating scale from 1 (low) to 5 (high). The characteristics observed were affection, eye contact, smiles/laughter, reciprocal attention, cooperation, and physical proximity. Additionally, the therapists discussed each dyad after every session and recorded anecdotal comments.

A menu of 12–14 activities was prepared prior to each session accentuating the various Theraplay dimensions. A typical session began with fathers, sons, and therapists huddled in the foyer for a grand entrance into the 200-square-foot room (for example, "follow the leader," "wall ball," or "choo-choo" train) (see appendix). This high energy activity released tension and started the session in a playful manner. The group then sat in a circle in the middle of the room and sang a welcome song to reacquaint with each other and to create an atmosphere of belongingness. This was followed by a group game that promoted enjoyment, relaxation, and connection (i.e., "zip, zap, zop"—see appendix). Children then sat down forming an inner circle facing outwards, while their fathers sat in front of them. Fathers performed a check-up on their sons by taking an inventory of physical features (i.e., counting freckles and teeth, noticing something positive such as shiny hair or sparkling eyes). They then looked for hurts on their son's hands and carefully applied lotion to them. These tender and nurturing moments were intentionally regressive to reflect the initial physical intimacy between infant and parent, because as a newborn child his predominant contact with the world was through the sense of touch. The "check-up" always ended with each father gazing into his child's eyes while identifying one positive attribute. An engaging dyadic activity designed to increase intimacy always followed the "check-up." All group members then participated in large group activities which alternated by dimension, physical proximity, and energy level. In this way, moments of direct intimacy between father and son, such as "nose cluck" (see appendix), were alternated with opportunities to develop a sense of community as all fathers provided nurturing to all children collectively through activities such as "cookie machine" (see appendix), where the children felt safe and protected despite the high level of physical interaction. (These moments replicated and were reminiscent of typical games of parents tossing their young child in the air whereby the child develops a deep sense of trust that, despite the physical discrepancy in size and playful risk taking, his parent would never harm him.) Each session ended with the therapists feeding chips to all participants, and sometimes fathers fed their sons. The final session ended with a party of the children's favorite activities and snacks prepared by the participants.

In order for any significant gains to be made in this group, the fathers needed permission to play with their children in engaging ways and to show them the efficacy of affection and nurturing. They required the experience of being with their children in qualitatively positive ways. The most effective strategy employed was for the therapists to model the activities for the group prior to asking the participants to engage in the activity. After all, once they witnessed a grown man being fed while sitting in the lap of another man, what could the fathers and sons possibly object to? The sight of the therapists engaging in the activities with each other was often met with uproarious laughter, but acted as an icebreaker. It allowed the fathers to interact with their children without fear of ridicule from their peers. The fathers were boys once as well and the group was surely revising their "old boy" code.

The fathers, whose many interactions with their sons were previously met with hostility and rejection, were now feeding their children by hand, gently caressing their faces with cotton, and enjoying engaging interactions. Indifference was replaced with warmth; rejection with connectedness; and hostility with playfulness. One prominent moment occurred during session 5 when the dyads engaged in a mirroring activity. The fathers and sons held their hands toward each other (but not touching), with the fathers leading the activity and the sons instructed to mirror their fathers. (This activity was an excellent one for increasing attunement between the dyads). The therapists allowed the activity to continue longer than anticipated, because the effect was mesmerizing. The children were completely engaged with their fathers, following their every move. The silence in the room betrayed the fact that it was filled with 15 bodies. It was hard to imagine that these 6 children were previously diagnosed with an overwhelming array of externalizing behaviors, because at that very moment they were one-hundred percent compliant, engaged, and regulated.

After the dyads (and the therapists to some degree) got past their discomfort during the early sessions, the therapists became group facilitators. Rather than providing direct instructions, or replacing the father for the purpose of demonstration, they guided the dyad through the process and then moved away. The therapists were cognizant of empowering the fathers to grow into their new roles with their children. This group became a very cohesive unit quite quickly. They all seemed to be craving what the group offered. The aspect of community played a large role in the success of this group as the fathers supported each other during difficult times, and offered praise and comfort. The fathers greatly enjoyed the opportunity to connect with one another and discussed their shared values and philosophy on parenting. During one session a parent posed the question, "My son gets very upset when he loses. How do I strike a balance between showing him its ok to lose, but also allow him to have success?" Each father had a similar story to share, and by the end of the session came to appreciate his shared experiences. The group offered all of its members an opportunity to participate in fun and engaging activities in a safe, caring, and supportive atmosphere. In addition, the group offered an opportunity for the children and their fathers to create a social network outside the Theraplay sessions. The children would often show up to group discussing their shared experiences with each other during play dates and birthday parties that occurred during the previous week. This encouraged the therapeutic team as all of the children experienced peer socialization difficulties prior to the onset of treatment.

Data for this group was collected and interpreted from several sources: the pre and post parent personality ratings, observer numeric ratings scales, therapist anecdotal reporting, and a post treatment counseling session with each father. The children's behavior was coded using internalized and externalized categories (Achenbach and Edelbrock, 1983). Examples of internalizing behaviors were depression, anxiety, and stress. Examples of externalizing behaviors were hyperactivity, aggression, and non-compliance.

Results from the pre and post reports indicted a significant decrease in externalizing behaviors as was expected, but also surprisingly, a slight increase in internalizing behaviors (Munns, Jensen, and Berger, 1997). Numeric scales, coded from observer's ratings, indicated high increases in reciprocal attention and physical attention, some increase in cooperation, eye contact and smiles/laughter, and no increase in affection. Raters indicated gains for all 6 dyads, with four noted as gaining sharply. The anecdotal reports of the therapists indicated that the fathers demonstrated uncertainty and were slow to react during the first few sessions, but by the end of treatment were noted as being more intimate and self-assured in their interactions. In contrast to the observer reports, the therapists noted that the children displayed more spontaneous affection toward their fathers and were more compliant. During follow-up interviews, all 6 fathers reported sharing a closer relationship with their own sons. They reported feeling more confident in their abilities to reach out to their children and were less fearful of having their demonstrations of affection rejected. Two comments in particular stand out. Regarding "lotioning hurts" one father said, "I never looked at my son for this long before." A second father reported that he understood how his own attitude affected his son's behavior. However, only one father reported a positive change in his son's school environment.

Attunement and responsiveness are vital components in the attachment process, and are reflected in the ability to provide undivided and sustained attention to one's partner. Reciprocal attention and physical proximity are reflective of this process and were perhaps rated higher because of the 5–7 minute inventory period. An increase in these interactions might also reflect an improvement in the attachment process, which is consistent with the therapists reports of more intimacy and more spontaneous affection from the sons to the fathers, as well as the parent's self reporting of a closer attachment to their sons.

Why didn't raters observe a change in affection? One possible explanation is that the characteristics of eye-contact, smiles, laughter, cooperation and physical proximity were easier to detect than signs of affection, because the latter involved tone of voice, facial expressions, and body language in addition to physical forms of hugs, kisses, and ruffling hair. The raters may have focused on the physical demonstrations of affection. Additionally, the observers sat behind a one-way mirror where the subtle cues may have been difficult to assess. A second explanation may be that observers were looking for signs of affection from the fathers to their sons exclusively, whereas the therapists reported increased affection on the part of the children. More affection from the sons to the fathers may have been indicative of enhanced attachment.

The decrease in externalizing behaviors may have reflected an increase in self-control on the part of the children due to more effective parenting strategies by the fathers. Why was self-control not generalized to the school setting? Perhaps the children were adjusting to the new dynamic created in their homes and not enough time had elapsed to incorporate this change in the school. Or, perhaps the teachers' behavior and attitude toward the children remained constant despite the change in the children's behavior. However, if a stronger attachment was observed between the fathers and sons, why were internalizing behaviors reported as increased? A plausible explanation is that the personality scales were subjective parent reports of their children's behavior, meaning parents were reporting on inferences of their children's behavior.

Additionally, a decrease in externalizing behaviors likely indicated a more trusting relationship due to more consistent expectations and stronger attachments. Strong attachments reflect increased responsiveness and attunement. Since the fathers were more sophisticated at reading their sons' emotions and non-verbal language, they more likely noticed internalized emotional states such as depression and anxiety. The fathers' awareness of the behaviors may have increased rather than the actual behaviors. Perhaps no change was observed at school, regarding these behaviors, because there was no actual change in the anxiety levels of the children. Awareness, however, is the first step to therapeutic change. Since the fathers were more aware they were better equipped to help their children cope in the future.

The therapeutic goals of increased affection from the children, an increase in the fathers' comfort and competence in providing affection (as observed by the therapists), and greater parental structure were observed. An increase in the children's self-esteem in the school setting was not indicated, although a greater attachment was observed between all father-son dyads. The Theraplay treatment was successful as it aided in the improvement of the attachment within the father-son relationship in both treatment and home settings. It was hoped that continued attunement and responsiveness would lead to greater feelings of well-being for the children both at home and at school. A subsequent father-son group was conducted with 6 new dyads of fathers and sons with similar outcomes to the original group.

Note: I wish to thank the therapeutic team with whom I worked. To Dr. Munns for your supervision, guidance, and patience. To my co-leaders Doug Loweth and Andrew Legatto. You are both dynamic colleagues, but more importantly you are incredibly attuned and responsive fathers.

AGENDAS

First Session (#1)

Entrance-walking in to circle
Welcome song
Hello whip/name whip
Hello/Thank you
Check in

- inventory
- powder hurts

Lap sit tag
Hum garden
Feeding
Goodbye song

Beginning Session (#2)

Entrance-wall ball
Welcome song
Create a new handshake
Hand tangle
Check in

- Inventory/measure body parts
- Lotion/powder hurts
- Hello . . . goodbye
- Say one nice thing

Piggy back red light, green light
Cotton ball fight
Cotton ball soothe
Feeding chips
Goodbye song

Middle Session (#5)

Entrance-elephant walk in
Welcome song
Silly bones
Check in

- Inventory
- Lotion/powder hurts
- Mirroring
- Say one nice thing

Cookie machine
Simon says
Row your boat
Feather blow
Feather touch
Feeding chips
Goodbye

Ending Session (#9)

Entrance-wheelbarrow
Welcome song
Pass a secret message
Check in

- Inventory
- Lotion hurts
- Cradle child and feed pudding
- Tell child one nice thing

Elbow tag
Ping pong ball blow
Barber shop
Feed chips
Goodbye

REFERENCES

Achenbach, T. E., and Edelbrock, C. (1983). Manual for the Child Behavior Checklist and Revised Behavior Profile. Burlington, VT: University of Vermont Department of Psychiatry.

Belsky, J. (1996). Parent, infant and social-contextual antecedents of father-son attachment security. *Developmental Psychology*, 32, 905–913.

Berman, P. W. (1980). Are women more responsive than men to the young? A review of developmental and situational variables. *Psychological Bulletin*, 88, 668–695.

Bowlby, J. (1969). *Attachment and Loss.* Volume I, *Attachment.* London: Hogarth Press.

Cousins, R. (1989). *Head First: The Biology of Hope and the Healing Power of the Human Spirit.* New York: Penguin Books.

Field, T. (1978). Interaction behaviors of primary versus secondary caretaker fathers. *Developmental Psychology, 14, 183–184.*

Field, T. (1995). *Touch in Early Development.* Hillsdale, NJ: Lawrence Erlbaum

Freud, A., and Burlingham, D. (1973). Infants without families: Reports on the Hampstead Nurseries. In A. Freud, *The Writings of Anna Freud.* Volume III. New York: International University Press.

Harlow, H. (1958). The nature of love. *American Psychologist,* 13, 573–685.

Hughes, F. (1999). *Children, Play, and Development.* Boston, Mass.: Allyn and Bacon.

Jernberg, A. (1979). *Theraplay: A New Treatment Using Structured Play for Problem Children and Their Families.* San Francisco: Jossey-Bass.

Jones, N., and Field, T. (1998). Newborns of mothers with depressive symptoms are physiologically less developed. *Infant Behaviour and Development,* vol. 21, 537–541.

Jones, N., Field, T., and Davalos, M. (1998). Massage therapy attenuates right frontal asymmetry in 1-month-old infants of depressed mothers. *Infant Behaviour and Development,* vol. 21, 527–530.

Kenny, M., Lomax, R., Brabeck, M., and Fife, J. (1998). Longitudinal pathways linking adolescent reports of maternal and paternal attachments to psychological well-being. *Journal of Early Adolescence,* 18, 221–243.

Liang, S., and Sugawara, A. (1996). Family size, birth order, socioeconomic status, ethnicity, parent-child relationship, and preschool children's intellectual development. *Early Child Development and Care,* 124, 69–79.

Lorenz, K. (1961) *King Solomon's Ring.* Translated by Marjorie Kerr Wilson. London: Methuen.

Munns, E., Jensen, D., and Berger, L. (1997). Theraplay and the reduction of aggression. Unpublished research, Blue Hills Child and Family Centre. Aurora, Ontario.

Parke, R. D. (1981). *Fathering.* London: Collins; Cambridge, Mass.: Harvard University Press.

Pollack, W. (1998). *Real Boys.* New York: Henry Holt and Company.

Rice, K., Cunningham, T., and Young, M. (1997). Attachment to parents, social competence, and emotional well-being: A comparison of black and white late adolescents. *Journal of Counselling Psychology,* 44, 89–101.

Schaffer, H. R., and Emerson, P. E. (1964). The development of social attachments in infancy. *Monographs of the Society for Research in Child Development,* 29, 3.

Schore, A. (2001). Effects of secure attachment relationship on right brain development, affect regulation, and infant mental health. *Infant Mental Health Journal,* 22(1–2), 7–66.

Siegel, D. (2003). An interpersonal neurobiology of psychotherapy: The developing mind and the resolution of trauma. pp. 1–56. In M. F. Solomon, and D. J. Siegel (Eds), *Healing Trauma: Attachment, Mind, Body, Brain.* New York: W. W. Norton & Co.

19

Working with Adolescents

Brijin Gardner and Mary Spickelmier

This chapter is a product of our work with troubled adolescents and juvenile offenders. After experiencing the benefits of using Theraplay® in elementary classrooms and with families and children in private practice, we took a chance and applied it to our most problematic and difficult population: adolescents. The trial of becoming a teenager is a rite of passage that bears numerous struggles ranging from seeking independence from parents, craving intimate relationships with peers (Kindlon and Thompson, 1999), creating a personal identity, grasping at self-acceptance and body image (Pipher, 1994), all the while coping with daily life stressors such as home and school.

Working with adolescents is often a challenge for many mental health professionals. Developmentally, adolescents are transitioning from childhood into adulthood (Garbarino, 1999). Adolescents need to feel their ideas are being heard. This can be accomplished by allowing them to make choices and have input in the therapeutic process. The therapist maintains control of the sessions by setting boundaries around suitable choices (Munns, 2000; Rubin and Tregay 1989); this requires a great deal of flexibility on the part of the therapist, as there is not a one-size-fits-all formula.

TIPS FOR WORKING WITH ADOLESCENTS

1. Keep it fresh, be a little daring and do not be afraid to mix things up. Use teen culture to enhance traditional techniques.

2. Use their terminology and lingo when possible. Take time to ask teens for "definitions" when you hear unfamiliar terms during conversation. Learning slang used by adolescents will help you to understand and relate to your clients better. It also empowers the client, as they know you are listening to them.
3. Have clear rules. Go over the rules at the beginning of each session; this can help with redirecting behaviors during group sessions. Therapists may go over the rules during the intake and have the client initial each rule individually.
4. Be conscious of heightened sexual awareness. You may want to consider having gender specific groups to lessen the effects of this. In addition, be prepared to address sexual innuendos that may come up. For example, in the Juvenile Offender Program, Mary once had a male client say, "Did you get all dressed up just for me"? She responded with humor and invited the group to feel free to wear ties, to "dress up for her." It became an inside joke and a few weeks later all of the boys wore ties to the group.
5. Let their ideas be heard and incorporate them into the group. Brijin encourages her groups to take turns making up creative welcomes or handshakes to start the group. Allow them to have choices and input, but do not let them take control of the group.
6. Establishing a solid relationship is imperative. Adolescents must trust and respect you before they will fully partake in the activities. There is no influence without a relationship, and meaningful connections can be established quickly when using Theraplay as a group modality.
7. Be honest and straightforward. In order for adolescents to trust, they must believe in the relationship; be genuine. They don't want to feel they are being judged, so it is important to keep an open mind and accept them for who they are as an individual.
8. Never let them see you sweat. You must stay confident and sell the product before they will buy into it. Often times they will reject activities up front, especially if they are new to treatment, however, if you stay upbeat and positive they will usually try the activity and enjoy it.
9. Be patient with yourself and the adolescent. Stick with an activity; don't give up on it just because they reject it. It is their job to be resistive and reject the things they may need the most. However, if they trust you and you give them a chance, they will participate.
10. Use humor. Groups with adolescents can be enjoyable and entertaining because they like to have fun. They love to laugh and have inside jokes.
11. Keep structure within sessions. Have a clear beginning, middle, and end to every session.

12. Be prepared to talk more. Developmentally, adolescents are abstract thinkers, at times processing therapeutic experiences in a more cognitive and verbal way.
13. Incorporate plenty of challenge activities into each session; providing a place for healthy competition is important.

CONSIDERATIONS AND EXPLANATIONS

Theraplay offers a different message and method than types of talk-therapies; as there is no need to muscle a point across or force conversation. Theraplay addresses problems without directly mentioning the cause for referral and does not threaten the feelings, beliefs, or opinions of the adolescent. Rather, Theraplay can help resuscitate a sense of hope and revive relationships with peers and adults in their lives.

There are several considerations when using Theraplay with adolescents. In our experience, this population tends to be very self-conscious about what their peers think, as well as being pre-occupied with creating their own identity. A therapist must have confidence and a good understanding of attachment theory and Theraplay techniques. Along with this, therapists must carefully plan activities that are catered toward the group dynamic and needs. Adolescents must believe that you know and trust what you are doing, as they will question most everything you do in the first few sessions.

Another factor to acknowledge is adolescent physical development; issues of sexuality heighten the therapist's awareness (Munns, 2000). Games must be modified to eliminate contact that could be construed as sexual. It is highly recommended to have another therapist or adult to assist with adolescent groups. Ideally, it is best to have both a male and a female present. However, if this is impossible consider videotaping the sessions.

Check-ins and addressing hurts may look different with teens; however, they maintain the same level of importance and need with this age group. Instead of counting freckles, we may specifically check out scars or body piercing (nose, ear, and tongue) as a check in or just make the observations throughout the group session. A serious clinical concern we have noticed more frequently with this population, is the infliction of self-harm or self-mutilation. It is important to take time to notice this when it might be hidden from other adults in their lives. We have become aware of the necessity to "sneak" in the nurturing piece, especially with adolescents. Teens are often more receptive to nurture when it is concealed within other activities. This may be the result of their striving to become adults; some nurturing activities may seem to be too regressive from their viewpoint, at least in the beginning of the group sessions.

Adapting and modifying the activities to fit the troubled adolescent and juvenile offender populations takes thought, creativity, and going out on an edge (that might not feel as safe as the tried-and-true techniques). We have found that tapping into teen culture can enhance traditional techniques and inspire the creation of new ones. Today's adolescent is very technologically advanced and highly influenced by media and the internet; determining what your client is listening, watching, and downloading, can give you hints as to where to go. Another common denominator for teens is music; regardless of the genre, they all like to download, listen to, and lose themselves in their favorite music. Most of our teens use music as a self-soothing mechanism and it can be a validating experience to have an adult listen and respond, by creating a game using their tune. Be aware that some of the adolescents are selecting explicit and graphic music; although we may not agree with what they are listening to, it is formative and speaks volumes in relation to the adolescent and their experiences or current situation.

Throughout our work with juvenile offenders and adolescents, we have noticed there are several differences when using Theraplay with teens as compared to younger children. One difference we have found is that there are more conversations throughout sessions. In some instances with the juvenile offender group, the processing is part of the activity. Another suggestion for working with teens is using language that maintains sensitivity to the adolescent (who is one part-child and one part-adult). We can be playful and nurturing to them, as long as we don't use language that seems too babyish or condescending. Finally, we have found the use of certain nonconventional props helpful in attracting and engaging the adolescent's interest. Many of the activities we draw on combine several Theraplay components at the same time.

Developmentally, adolescents are transitioning from childhood into adulthood, a time where they separate from their parents and seek to find their own identities. Taking this into consideration it is important for adolescents to feel their ideas are being heard. This can be accomplished by allowing them to make choices and have input into the therapeutic process, while the therapist maintains control of the sessions by setting boundaries around those choices. This requires a great deal of flexibility on the part of the therapist, because what works for one group, may not work for another.

It has become clear throughout our work with adolescents; keeping things contemporary and innovative helps maintain their interest and can enhance relationships within the groups. Keeping things fresh takes time and a personal investment in determining with what adolescents are filling their time: music, activities, television, etc. We have also discovered that the cleverly named activities are more marketable and enticing to the group. Some days, it is all in how you market the idea.

Below are two individual programs that utilize Theraplay groups with adolescents; both demonstrate ways to modify and adapt the technique to fit this difficult population.

The Theraplay groups in the schools use strictly Theraplay structure while the juvenile offender program uses Theraplay techniques infused with some cognitive behavioral components.

BRIJIN GARDNER'S ADOLESCENT THERAPLAY GROUPS IN SCHOOLS

Clients

Group size was typically between three and seven students from a public high school or middle school; age range 12–17 years old. Groups were all male at both levels. The high school students were referred via the behavior disorder classroom and a computer-based school completion program. Students referred to the middle school group had Individualized Education Plans (IEP) or received Special Education Services for learning or behavioral difficulties.

Presenting Problem and Treatment Goals

Overall, group members chronically struggled with peer and adult interactions. Most had a history of suspension or expulsion from school due to aggressive behavior toward peers, non-compliance and aggression toward authority figures, and involvement with the justice system. Each student had a DSM-IV TR Axis I and/or II diagnoses, along with a learning disability and speech or language concern. Individual goals varied based on the student's IEP, but overall the group focus was on increasing positive relationships with peers and adults in school, complying with adult directions, decreasing aggressive behaviors, enhancing self-esteem, and experiencing success while working with peers.

Setting

Theraplay groups were led by the school social worker, typically without a co-therapist: whenever possible paraprofessionals provided support in the group. Individuals received four sessions alone with the social worker before joining the closed 10-week group. During these 4 individual sessions, the social worker assessed the student for eligibility for the group, as well as establishing rapport and gaining insight into current issues in their lives. Sessions were weekly and lasted 45 minutes.

Considerations

Using Theraplay in the school required adaptations and implications that must be mentioned. First, in the adolescent groups, there was not a direct parent component. Parents or guardians were initially contacted and interviewed by the social worker for a family history and assessment, but were not a part of the group. Also, due to restrictions and school guidelines, the use of highly regressive techniques was omitted (such as using a bottle or holding the child).

Below are examples of activities used during various stages of group sessions employed with an adolescent boy's Theraplay group in the high school/middle school setting. Descriptions of original and modified games are included in the session models. Note that a feeding (nurturing activity) was always included within each session.

Beginning Session

1. Rules: *Zip it, Stick it, Give 'Em Props . . . Awww Snap*: A group of 14-year old-boys created this version of the group rules: "Zip it" implies being quiet, listening to the adult; "Stick it" means sitting together in the group, not leaving, following the rules, participating in the games; and "Give them props" suggests that only positive language is used and no put-downs are allowed. Loosely translated, they maintained the rules, but created their own spin and identity.
2. Welcome: *High Five with an H-to-the-ELLO*: Group members give a high-five to their neighbor and say "H-to-the-ELLO, Mrs. Gardner." This goes all around the group circle. The group session would conclude by passing "G-to-the-OOD-BYE" at the end.
3. Inventory: *Scab, Scar, and Piercing check*
4. *Measure hand-span with fruit roll-up*—then therapist feeds it to them
5. *Drop It like It's Hot* to music: This is the teen version of hot-potato. I use a song by the rapper, Snoop Dogg, called *Drop It Like It's Hot* (I edit and play the most appropriate parts of the song). The leader plays the music. Teens pass the hot-potato around the circle until the music stops. The person holding the object gets a high five or fist bump from their neighbors. Music is turned back on and play is resumed. Not all music and lyrics are conducive to all groups; be careful and plan ahead to have music that is fun, but appropriate for your setting.
6. *Shake and Stop*
7. *Building Blocks*: Using blocks or large Legos, group members get 6–8 pieces each. In silence, taking turns, and not touching a block set by another person, they build a structure together.

8. *Fist Stack*: This is a variation of the game hand-stack or ketchup/mustard. Teens pair up and build up a tower of fists. Although there is physical contact, it seems more "masculine" than a game of hand-stack to teenage boys.
9. *Cotton Ball Fight*
10. *M & M Balance*
11. *G-to-the-OOD-BYE*

Middle Session

1. Welcome: *Add It Up Handshake:* Teens make up a handshake to pass around the circle with a greeting; each student adds a "move" to the handshake. What begins as a high-five goes around the group, with each member adding to the sequence. It could be a high-five, thumb-wrestle, knuckle bump, and a snap by the time the handshake makes it completely around the circle.
2. *TAG, you're it*: This nurturing activity is named after a men's body spray (found at drug stores). The leader lets group members sniff each scent and select one. Then the leader sprays and pats the scent into place (neck or wrist).
3. *Mad Skills*: In this check-in activity, "mad" is not an emotion, rather it means cool, different, or unique. We go around the group demonstrating or telling about a "mad skill" that we have, for example, touching your tongue to your nose, moving one eyeball at a time, or finishing all your math homework would be considered "mad skills."
4. *K.C. Ink*: This nurturing technique taps the interests of teens. A few teen clients were interested in a genre of reality television shows called L.A. Ink and Miami Ink (both about tattoo parlors); many adolescents are intrigued by the taboo of body art and piercing. One can create fake tattoos using paint brushes or finger tips or one can purchase fake, but cool tattoos to apply to their skin. The students pick where they want the "tattoo" along with the design they want. This is a great way to give a mini massage on a back, arm, and neck.
5. *Chop Stick Stack*: Collect several dozen unused chopsticks for this game. Start by distributing the chop sticks to group members. Place a ceramic coffee cup in the center of the group/circle. The goal is to stack all the chopsticks on top without any sticks falling off. Talking during the game or touching another member's chop stick is not allowed. Once the group masters a large cup, you can reduce the size to in crease the challenge in future sessions. This technique can help assess where the group is in the therapeutic process based on the verbalizations and outcome.
6. *Loudest Crunch with chips*

7. *No Fear Challenge*: Group Twister with 6–12 colored foam squares. Give directions to each player individually, using one foot or hand at a time; eventually all players will have all 4 (hands/feet) on the floor. The leader acts as the "spinner," calling out directions to create the challenge. Once all members are in their spot with "4 on the floor," the leader counts 15 seconds without anyone falling over or losing their balance—in order to "win" the challenge.
8. *London Bridge*: This is one of those times the leader dances (literally) on the edge. Find some music your adolescents appreciate and have it ready to play. Group members stand up and pair off, raising their hands above their heads and connecting with their partners, they make a bridge. Each pair does a hand-dance with their neighbor while the leader scoots underneath the bridges facilitating the activity. For more resistant clients, the therapist can engage each client in a "hand-dance" (pushing palms of client and therapist together) separately rather than through pairing off group members.
9. *Balloon Bag Bop—Level I:* Fill a large trash bag with several blown-up balloons. Tie the bag off with rubber bands. If you have an aggressive group, use two trash bags, so the balloons do not burst out. Group members stand in a circle. The goal is for group members to only use their hands to keep the balloon bag up in the air without it touching the ground. The leader may sit in the center to assist. You can have the teens shout their name as they hit the bag for an added level of involvement.
10. *Psychic Skittles or M&Ms*: Leader presents group with the colors of candy held in hand. Group members must close their eyes and guess the color of candy the leader placed in their mouth. For added challenge, have the group members take turns feeding one another; guessing both the color of the candy and the person who fed them.
11. *Add It Up Handshake Goodbye*: Teens try to replicate the original welcome handshake as they pass the goodbye around the circle.

Final Session

1. Welcome: *Thumb Wrestling*
2. *Group Noodle Doodle*: Using *Magic Nuudles* (a brand name biodegradable building block), allow group members to take turns becoming the "doodle." Each member selects the location (face, arm, leg) of the group's noodle doodle. Members are given several *Magic Nuudles* and take turns making a design on the selected individual. Leaders may take a photograph of the final design.
3. *Taco-Schmaco or Burly Burrito*: This is an updated version of making a sandwich or rolling the child up in a blanket. Instead, the leader pre-

tends to order food from a Mexican fast-food chain and the client becomes the food. Have the adolescent stand in the center of the circle and select a taco or burrito from the "menu." The leader proceeds to "make" the main course by wrapping the adolescent up in a blanket; have the adolescent hold onto the corner of the blanket near their shoulder. The leader winds the blanket around the adolescent and then adds extras (lettuce, salsa, cheese) by playfully ruffling hair exposed. To "eat" the burrito, the individual spins or unrolls out of the blanket.

4. *Balloon Bag Bop—Level II:* Using the large trash bag filled with balloons, the group divides into two sections. One group lies on their backs with feet in the air; they try to push the balloon bag using only their feet back to the group that is standing; depending on the group size, this can be done in rows or a circle. The second group stands above the group on the ground, using only hands to push the balloon bag past the other group. Groups rotate standing and lying on the ground. (Rhonke and Butler, 1995)
5. *Can You Hear Me Now?*: This game is the enhanced version of telephone or secret message. In a circle, the leader sends a message by whispering in one person's ear; the message is passed around the circle. If you re-name it, teens will play it! You can also play this game using a cell phone (not turned on!) as a prop; having the teens say "It's for you," and then adding on who is calling them. The phone is passed around the circle and goes something like this, starting with the leader: "Tyler, it's for you. The President is calling." "Thanks, Mrs. Gardner," passing the phone to the next group member, "Actually, it's for you, Kevin. It's American Idol calling." Use this game with clients who are cognitively able to think quickly, it can be too much pressure for some people to create this on the spot. Ideally this is used later on in sessions as clients feel more comfortable and have shared some personal information.
6. *Loudest crunch or pretzel challenge*
7. *Walk the Plank*: This is a trust walk that meets an obstacle course. An obstacle course is created within the room or hallway using desks, pillows, people, etc. At the end of the obstacle course is a long, squishy "plank" made from a bathtub safety-liner. This activity takes some time as members take turns "walking the plank." One at a time, members take off their shoes/socks and are blind-folded. The leader gently spins them around and the individual is guided by the words and hands of other group members and the leader. Once the student reaches "the plank," group members spritz their feet with water in spray bottles. The obstacle course is changed multiple times to maintain challenge.

8. *Snowboard or Skateboard Face*: This is the cotton-ball-soothe with adolescent modifications. Using a cotton ball or blush brush, the leader sits in front of the teenager whose eyes are closed. The leader uses current terminology and/or names idols from the snowboarding/skateboarding sport. The leader narrates what the boarder or skater is doing as it coasts around the client's face.
9. *Magic 8 Ball*: This is a prop-based activity that can be used at any point in treatment. If used in the final session, the leader makes positive projections and predictions for each group member. Using a Magic 8 Ball (sold in toy departments) the leader has the adolescent hold the ball in their hands; the client asks a question about their life/future/etc. The leader places their hands on top of the client's hands; they shake the ball and turn it over to read the answer. This can be done several times until the "right" answer is received.
10. *Celebration Smorgasbord:* Therapist provides various snacks (chips, candies, fruit, etc.) used within the feeding activities of the group sessions. This acts as a final celebration of the group experience together.
11. *Thumb Wrestle Goodbye*

OUTCOMES AND RESULTS FROM THERAPLAY SESSIONS IN SCHOOL

The measurements utilized to assess outcomes for the Theraplay groups in school were: social worker observations, teacher report and grade card comments, behavioral goals from student Individual Education Plans, discipline referrals to the office, and self-report. The observations and reflections of the social worker and teacher over time indicated that the peers were interacting in a more positive way with one another. We also noticed an increase in student's trust level during group sessions with both the peers and the therapist. The initial group sessions were met with some resistance and mistrust from the group; however, over the sessions all the boys demonstrated a greater willingness to participate and engaged actively with each other.

The classroom teacher's data showed a large reduction in the account of verbal arguments and physical aggression between peers that participated in the group. Student grade cards also demonstrated that teachers noticed changes such as: an increase in positive student behaviors in class, fewer disruptions, getting along with peers, and enhanced self-esteem. Several teachers commented on increased participation in the class discussions and homework being turned in; thus increasing the several students' grades.

Discipline referrals were also tracked and there was a marked difference from the beginning of the school year to when the Theraplay group was completed. Administrative data was calculated over the course of eight months and found there was a 40 percent decrease in office referrals or out-of-school suspensions for the students participating in the Theraplay groups. Overall, the quantitative results demonstrate the positive impact that Theraplay groups can have with adolescent clients.

MARY SPICKELMIER'S JUVENILE OFFENDER PROGRAM

Clients

Approximately 4 to 8 adolescents participate in the Juvenile Offender Program at any given time. They range in ages from 13 to 19 years old. Referrals for the group come from local diversion and probation officers after clients have been charged with a variety of criminal acts ranging from theft to battery.

Setting

The group meets in a private practice office with a couch and several beanbag chairs that form a circle for participants to sit in. I divide the group by gender and we meet one hour weekly for 12 to 20 sessions based on the clients' needs. It is an open-ended group, so group members begin and end at different times. Sessions are led without a co-therapist.

Rationale for Theraplay

Theraplay focuses on positive relationships with others, increasing self-esteem, and building trust in others, all of which are important factors to address when working with juvenile offenders. The activities are fun and engaging, while the sessions are structured, with the therapist clearly being in charge.

Innovations

Adolescents are developmentally at a very cognitive stage. They like to talk and process things. Although typically Theraplay is a non-verbal form of treatment, my program incorporates Theraplay activities with cognitive behavioral strategies. Other modifications made are: rather than doing inventory at the beginning of group, it is done throughout the session. It was found that if the leader goes around the circle, noticing something special about each adolescent, they consider it "cheesy" and not sincere. Therefore, the leader notices things throughout the session so it appears more spontaneous and genuine.

Treatment Goals

The focus of the Juvenile Offender Program is to help juvenile offenders identify and cope with life challenges in healthy and positive ways. Sessions focus on: expressing feelings, anger management, stress management, social skills, self-control, problem-solving, improving relationships, improving communication, increasing self esteem, positive self-talk, and taking responsibility.

Beginning and Ending Sessions

The first session is always an intake session completed with the adolescent and at least one parent in which a typical assessment is completed. The adolescent is required to initial that they understand and agree to all program rules and expectations which include: 1) The number of sessions they will be required to attend, 2) What day and time they will start the program, 3) They are not allowed to miss more than two sessions without having to restart, 4) They may only restart the program one time, 5) They cannot be more than 10 minutes late to group or they will not be able to attend and it will count as an absent, 6) They cannot use alcohol or drugs while they are in the program, 7) They cannot be physically or verbally abusive or threaten violence. Final sessions are always done individually with the client, rather than in the group. Due to the group being an open one rather than closed, the sequence of sessions varies from client to client.

Examples of Group Sessions for Juvenile Offenders

Session on Anger Management

Welcome: Say our names

Rules: Go over rules: "nobody gets hurt, tell the truth, no smoking outside the building, what we talk about in group stays in group" (and so forth—it varies from group to group).

Inventory: Do throughout the session.

Highs and Lows: Clients tell about the best and worst thing that happened over the week.

Clay Splat: I like to compare this technique to the paper punch activity for younger kids. Each client takes a piece of clay and throws it as hard as they can at a table cloth that is spread out on the ground. While throwing the clay, clients identify things that make them angry.

Clay Soothe: Clients hold clay in their hands and close their eyes while feeling the clay in their hands. Many of the Juvenile Offenders struggle with closing their eyes because they have issues around trusting others.

Clay Creation: Clients are asked to make something out of the clay.

Nurture: After clients wash the clay off of their hands (or if time allows the therapist can wash the clay off of their hands), lotion their hands while you are discussing the activity. For hard-core kids, simply put the lotion from your hand onto the palm of their hand making a nurturing contact.

Discussion Points: 1) Feeling angry is a normal emotion, 2) Anger is energy and individuals can choose to use that energy in a positive or negative way, 3) Discuss positive ways people use energy such as writing music, motivation, writing poems or speeches, dancing, art, etc.

Goodbyes

Session on Stress Management for Girls

Welcome: Say our names

Rules: Go over group rules

Inventory: Notice a scar or tattoo on someone and compare it to others in the group. I may rub my hand or finger over it as we talk about it.

Highs and Lows: Clients tell about the best and worst thing that happened over the week.

Spa Day: Put girls in groups of two or three. Have teens put blindfolds or cucumber slices over their eyes and play soft music in the background. They rub lotion on each other's arms from the elbow down. The therapist massages the girl's head and or face. Everyone gets a turn.

Feeding Activity: If you use cucumber slices to cover the eyes, there is usually a chunk of cucumber left over. Slice the remainder of the cucumber and feed it to the group members.

Discussion Points: 1) Identify triggers for stress, 2) Identify physical and mental responses to stress, 3) Identify positive ways to manage stress

Goodbyes

Session on Stress Management for Boys

Welcome: Say our names

Rules: Go over group rules

Inventory: Notice the energy level of group members.

Highs and Lows: Clients tell about the best and worst thing that happened over the week.

Balloon Up

Cotton Ball Fight

Zoom Eek

Feed Chips off of Different Body Parts

Discussion Points: 1) Identify triggers for stress, 2) Identify physical and mental responses to stress, 3) Identify positive ways to manage stress

Goodbyes

Session on Making Change

Welcome: Say our names
Rules: Go over group rules
Inventory: Do throughout the group
Highs and Lows: Clients tell about the best and worst thing that happened over the week.

Tarp Challenge: Have clients write three problems they are working on onto three separate pieces of masking tape. Then have them write three goals they have for themselves on three separate pieces of masking tape. Put a tarp on the floor. Have participants put the pieces of tape with the problems on one side of the tarp and their goals on the other side of the tarp. Flip the tarp with the problem side up. Have everyone stand on the tarp and flip it over without anyone touching the floor or other objects in the room. They will usually start off on the tarp very far apart, but need to touch each other and work together to get the tarp flipped over. If someone steps off the tarp you start over (Lowenstein, 1999).

Discussion Points: 1) Turning over a new leaf and how difficult it is to make changes in our lives, 2) Who is on their team, as they try to accomplish their personal goals, 3) What would happen if someone on their team sabotaged their efforts?

Goodbyes

Session on Setting Goals

Welcome: Say our names
Rules: Go over group rules
Inventory: Throughout group
Highs and Lows: Clients tell about the best and worst thing that happened over the week.

Cup Stacking Challenge: Tie four 5- to 6-foot-long pieces of string onto a rubber band. You should have eight shorter strings when you are done. Each group member is given a string that is attached to the rubber band so they are all connected. Then you place 16 oz. paper cups around the room and tell the group they have to work together to stack the cups into each other to form one stack. They cannot touch the cups with anything but the strings or rubber band and they cannot touch anyone else's string besides their own.

Discussion Points: 1) Many steps toward one goal. The stack represents the overall goal and each cup represents a sub-goal that needs to be accomplished to reach their larger goal, 2) Identify personal goals and subgoals.

Goodbyes

OUTCOMES AND RESULTS OF JUVENILE OFFENDER PROGRAM

Most of the juvenile offenders that I work with have already been treated by a multitude of therapists, many of whom they feel are incompetent and worthless. This is definitely a strike against me. Then, strike two comes in the common consensus that they do not like being told what to do. So when the judge or probation officer informs them they have to participate in the program as a condition of their diversion or probation, they are extremely resistant to the idea that this program may actually help them. Strike three is the fact, that in their eyes, this is a total waste of their time. Time they could be spending with their friends or having fun. It is difficult to measure the effectiveness of treatment when it seems as though I have struck out before I even started.

Although I do not have any research based evidence to support the effectiveness of the Juvenile Offender Program, I do give the kids surveys to complete at the end of the program as a method to make improvements for future clients. On the survey clients are asked to rank several questions on a scale from one to ten, with one being not at all and ten being very helpful. Two questions on the survey are as follows: 1) When you first found out that you had to come to group how helpful did you think it would be? A majority of the juveniles responded with a 3 or 4. 2) Now that you have completed the program how helpful was it for you? A majority of the juveniles responded to this question with an 8, 9, or 10. The feedback from the kids I work with clearly shows that they feel the program has helped them.

After conducting the Juvenile Offender Program for almost three years, I realized while writing this chapter that I really had no idea how my program compared to other community programs in effectiveness. I asked a local probation officer for feedback and this is how she replied, "I wanted to tell you that I really appreciate the work you do with the juvenile offenders in our community. We have a few introductory programs that we offer for first-time offenders, but your program definitely offers more in the way of therapeutic help for offenders. I have had such positive feedback from the offenders (and their families) that have attended your Juvenile Offender Program. You have a special way of connecting with youth where they can grasp the concepts and learn the tools needed to be successful. You know you are doing a good job when offenders tell other youth about your program and suggest to their friends that they contact you. I have even had parents of youth who have completed your program call me years later to ask for your phone number, because they know someone who would benefit from your program. I am looking forward to many more years of working with you to help the youth in our community. Sincerely, Linda Huggins."

FINAL THOUGHTS ON THERAPLAY WITH ADOLESCENTS

Theraplay provides remarkable possibility for tough clients, especially for reluctant teens with complex and difficult backgrounds. Teens crave authenticity and connections; being "real" with them is a proficiency therapists must have, when working with adolescents. The adolescent's reluctance to engage can make for an arduous beginning for treatment. Our motto when working with teenagers is to "never let them see you sweat!" When the therapist approaches the adolescent with patience, humor, creativity, and confidence the outcomes can be inspiring.

REFERENCES

Garbarino, James. (1999). *Lost Boys: Why Our Sons Turn Violent and How We Can Save Them.* New York: The Free Press.

Jernberg, Ann, and Phyllis Booth. (1999). *Theraplay: Helping Parents and Children Build Better Relationships Through Attachment-Based Play,* 2nd ed. San Francisco: Jossey-Bass.

Kindlon, Dan, and Michael Thompson. (1999). *Raising Cain: Protecting the Emotional Life of Boys.* New York: Ballantine.

Lowenstein, Liana. (1999). *Creative Interventions for Troubled Children and Youth.* Toronto: Champion Press.

Munns, Evangeline, ed. (2000). *Theraplay: Innovations in Attachment-Enhancing Play Therapy.* Northvale, NJ: Jason Aronson Inc.

Pipher, Mary. (1994). *Reviving Ophelia: Saving the Selves of Adolescent Girls.* New York: Grosset Putnam.

Rhonke, Karl, and Steve Butler. (1995). *Quicksilver.* Dubuque, Iowa: Kendall Hunt Publishers.

Rubin, Phyllis, and Jeanine Tregay. (1989). *Play with Them: Theraplay Groups in the Classroom.* Spring field, Ill.: Charles C. Thomas.

Appendix

Theraplay Activities

TYPICAL STRUCTURE OF THERAPLAY® SESSION

Entrance—Opening Song or Handshake—Inventory/checkup—Lotioning/ Powdering of Hurts—Activities from the 4 dimensions: Structure, Challenge, Engagement, Nurturing—Feeding—Goodbye Song.

Entrance Ideas

Backwards Walk: Participants line up single file and enter the room backwards.

Piggy Back: Parent places child on his back and enters the room by walking or galloping. Child may direct parent.

Choo choo train: All participants single file with hands on shoulders of person in front. Stick together and move around the room as a locomotive, varying speed.

Follow the Leader: Therapist, parents, or children take turns leading the rest of the family into and about the room in fun and interesting ways, imitating the leader, one behind the other.

Leap Frog: Group lines up in single file with leader crouching down making himself small while next person leaps over him and crouches down so the next person can leap over, etc.

Over and Under: Therapist has participants get in a line behind him/her and initiates passing a ball over her head to the person behind and that person passes the ball under to next person. Continue to alternate until person at end of line has it and runs to the front to proceed with the same pattern of over/under. Different speeds increase the challenge.

Stepping Stones: Pieces of paper (stepping stones) are laid on the floor from door into the room leading to the pillow where child is to sit. M&Ms are hidden (on top of a Kleenex) under some of the stepping stones. The child steps on the stones after peeking under the paper to discover an M&M. If finding one then can eat it and proceeds to the next stepping stone.

Tunnel: First person on hands and knees as next person crawls underneath and becomes the next part of tunnel. Continue entering the room in this fashion.

Wall Ball: Group members form a circle and hold hands. They enter the room in circular fashion with everyone touching their backs to wall as they move around the perimeter of the room.

Opening Ideas

Song: "Hello Sally, hello mom, hello dad and Evangeline—we're glad you came to play."

Create a Handshake: Group members sit in circle. Group leader shakes hand of person sitting next to him and instructs person to shake hands with next person and to add an element. This continues until a group handshake is created.

Hello Secret Handshake: Therapist or parent initiates making up a secret handshake and have child make up his /her own as well. Handshakes are shared around the circle and can be part of the ritual of meeting each week.

Inventory or Checkup Ideas

Check-In: Therapist and parent notice specific physical characteristics of the child that make him/her unique. At the beginning of each session, the therapist enlists the parents help the make sure the child has brought all those special parts. For example, the therapist might count the freckles on the child's cheeks during the first session and then check to make sure all the freckles came back the second time.

Check to see what the child brought with them such as a smile, warm or cold fingers or toes, bright eyes, curly hair, number of fingers or toes, etc.

Measuring: Using a measuring tape measure the child's height, length of arms, legs, feet, hands, ears, etc. Also measure surprising things such as the child's smile, muscles, and how high he can jump. Write down the measurements and keep them for later comparisons. Note that paper streamers, yarn, ribbon, or fruit roll ups can all be used as measuring tools.

Measuring with Fruit Tape: Use "Fruit by the Foot" to measure parts of the child's body—(i.e., smile) and as you measure, tear off the fruit tape and feed it to the child.

Wiggly Parts/Stiff Parts: An inventory activity as parent or therapist finds which body parts are wiggly or stiff. "I wonder if your nose wiggles, what about your ears, your tongue," etc.

Caring of Hurts

Helping Hurts: Therapist and parent look over the child to see if there are any scratches, scrapes, bruises, hang nails, etc., that may need lotioning, powdering, or band-aids. The child may point out places where there is no noticeable "boo-boo." It is very important that we attend to those places just as if there were a visible hurt. In this way, we communicate the message that we understand that the child has hurts we can't see and that we will help to heal these too. If there are no visible hurts, then the therapist makes one up such as lotioning a freckle or a red spot. If the child resists lotioning or powdering then try a band-aid or simply blowing on the hurt.

DIMENSIONS

1. Structure

This dimension reflects the importance of rules and limits for the child's behavior in order to make his world safe, secure, and predictable. The activities are led by the therapist or parent in a clear, consistent, and firm way that the child can easily understand. This dimension is often needed with dysregulated, impulsive, acting out children or those who have become tyrants or those whose inner world is in chaos.

Beanbag Game: This is a great activity for augmenting structure and engagement in a fun way. The therapist places a beanbag on the child's head and then picks a cue word, for example, "wiggle" that is shared with the child. The therapist may say a couple of other words beginning with "w" while making eye contact with the child. When the therapist says the cue word, the child drops his head and the therapist catches the beanbag in her hands. The parent and child then play the game. The child's ability to wait, listen carefully, and drop the beanbag at exactly the right time is celebrated. Cues can move from verbal to non-verbal as the child's skills in reading caregivers improve.

Clap Patterns: Therapist or parent makes different clapping sounds with hands starting with a simple sequence of claps, and others copy it. The sequence can include touching safe body parts of neighbors in group. Everyone can take a turn leading the clap patterns.

Freeze and Thaw: Child is told a secret spot on body, above the waist. Child stands as a frozen statue, and thaws out when parent is able to touch the secret spot.

The Grand Ol' Duke of York: Hold hands standing in a circle: "The grand ol' Duke of York, He had ten thousand men (sing and walk in a circle) He marched them up to the top of the hill (move toward the center of the circle raising arms) and he marched them down again (step back while lowering arms). And when they were up, they were up (move toward center of circle raising arms). And when they were down, they were down (step back and lower arms). And when they were only half way up, they were neither up nor down (raise arms half way up, then fully up, then fully down). He marched them to the left (move to the left). He marched them to the right (move to the right). He marched them all around the town and he marched them out of sight" (Let go of hands, turn around and clap hands).

Hand Stacking: In circle formation facing inwards, on knees, leader puts his hand palm down near the floor. His neighbor places his hand on top of the leader's hand. The next person places his hand on top and this continues until all have stacked their hands on top of one another. Then the leader takes his bottom hand and puts it on top of the last person's hand and this continues with the stack of hands rising until everyone is on tiptoe. Then the reverse order of hands comes down to the floor again. For younger children call out each person's name to signal their turn—this also helps if attention is an issue.

Hand, Foot, or Body Outline: Child lies on back on large piece of paper, while therapist or parent outline his body with a felt pen. Later everyone fills out physical features while commenting positively—i.e., "black shiny hair, rosy cheeks, strong arms, etc."

Head and Shoulders, Knees and Toes: Sing this song while pointing to the body parts when they are named:

Head and shoulders, knees and toes
Knees and toes, knees and toes
Head and shoulders, knees and toes
Eyes, ears, mouth and nose.

Hokey Pokey: Sing and act out the motions:

You put your right hand in
You put your right hand out

You put your right hand in
And you shake it all about
You do the hokey pokey (wiggle body)
And you turn yourself about (turn around)
And that's what it's all about (clap hands)

Repeat with left hand and different body parts such as foot, head, butt, whole self.

Instrument Attunement: Child and parent are each given the same instrument. The parent is encouraged to create a simple rhythm and the child is encouraged to mirror this. Parent, child, and therapist can take turns leading and following.

Mirroring: Parent and child sit or stand facing each other, hands raised in front with palms facing, but not touching, each other. Parent begins to move hands slowly and child must shadow (mirror) movements.

Mother May I: Leader stands at one end of the room while all others stand in a row at the opposite end of the room facing the leader. First person asks the leader, "Mother may I take 2 giant steps forward?" (or something equivalent). Leader answers, "Yes you may" (or not). Each person makes a request starting with "Mother may I" and if they don't, they miss their turn. If anyone tries to sneak forward when it is not their turn, the leader can send them back to the starting point. First person to reach "Mother" is the leader of the next round.

Motor Boat: Group stands in circle holding hands. They move in circular fashion slowly in clockwise manner while singing "motor boat, motor boat go so slow." Group speeds up as they sing, "motor boat, motor boat go so fast." They speed up again as they sing, "motor boat, motor boat, step on the gas." Group slows down and speeds up again while singing appropriate phrase. On the final stanza, "motor boat, motor boat, out of gas," the group collapses to the ground.

Pass a Gentle Squeeze: Group sits in circle, holding hands. Leader gently squeezes hand of person beside him in Morse code fashion and tells him to send it on, until it returns to leader.

"Peanut Butter" . . . "Jelly": Leader says "peanut butter" and group responds "jelly," while copying vocal inflection (loud, soft, fast, slow, etc.).

Red Light, Green Light: Group lines up against wall facing leader, who is at opposite wall with back to group. Leader says "green light" and the group advances (holding hands with impulsive children). Leader says, "red light" and turns around as group stops. If leader catches anyone moving, he returns to wall and starts again. Objective is to reach and gently touch leader.

Row, Row, Row Your Boat: The parent sits cross-legged with the child on her lap facing her. The therapist sits behind the child, facing the mother. Together the therapist and parent sing "Row, Row, Row Your Boat" while the parent rocks the child. The therapist can help catch the child on the fall away from the parent if this provides additional safety for the child.

Simon Says: Played in traditional way where leader calls out "Simon says put your hand up" and the group does this. The group obeys leader's commands as long as they are prefaced with "Simon says." If this is not done then the group does not obey. If someone obeys a command not preceded with "Simon says" then that person is "it" and becomes the next leader. This can be varied with commands such as "Simon says give your neighbor a hug (or a handshake)," or "Simon says say one nice thing you like about your neighbor."

Soft and Floppy: Have the child lie on the floor and help him get "all soft and floppy like spaghetti." Gently jiggle each arm and let it flop to the floor—then each leg. If a child has difficulty getting floppy, have him get "stiff like a board" and then let it go and relax. Once the child is relaxed, ask him to wiggle just one part of his body, such as his tongue, big toe, baby finger, ears, and so forth.

The Dyadic Dance: The parent and child stand up facing each other holding hands. The parent uses facial gestures and body movements (a wink of the right eye, a nod of the head) to tell child to move one step to the right or to the left. Parent and child must make good eye contact for this game to be successful and the roles of leader and follower can switch throughout.

The Eyeball Toss: Therapist, parent, and child all sit on the floor in a wide triangle. Whoever has the ball (which looks like an eyeball) must make eye contact with the person that is going to get the ball next. The game can be played with simple eye contact, or with facial gestures.

Tracing Hands: The therapist provides paper and markers and helps the parent place the child's hand flat on the paper. As the parent traces the child's hand, the therapist can give a running commentary, "Now your mom is tracing right around your thumb . . . and down in the valley," etc.

Yarn Web: Group sits in a circle. Leader holds onto the end of a ball of yarn and passes it to another group member. That person holds the string as he passes it to someone else. Continue until everyone is holding a piece of string. Last person then reverses ball of yarn until it returns to leader.

2. Challenge

This dimension relates to a child's need to explore and to take age appropriate risks, which when mastered, gives him/her a feeling of mastery and self-confidence. Challenging activities are often done cooperatively with parent or therapist, or the child may compete with himself.

Balloon between Two Bodies: Hold a balloon between you and the child (such as between hips, legs, foreheads, elbows) and move across the room without dropping or popping the balloon. You can make this more challenging by returning to your start position by going backwards.

Balloon Tennis: Hit a balloon back and forth, trying to keep it in the air. You can make this more challenging by seeing if you can hit it back and forth a specified number of times, increasing the number on further trials if you are successful.

Blanket Hug: Group sits in a circle. Leader asks 1 child to sit in middle and covers him with blanket. Leader prompts everyone to stand and walk in circle around the child, stomping loudly. Leader designates one person to hug child as the group stomps around, and then signals everyone to sit down. Child under blanket then tries to guess who hugged him.

Bubble Catch: Have the child try and catch as many bubbles as they can before they reach the floor. For an added challenge they can use only one body part, or they need to be "linked" (holding hands, linked elbows) to another person to catch the bubbles.

Cotton Ball Hockey: Therapist/parent and child lie on tummies facing each other or sit at opposite sides of a large, preferably firm, pillow. Adult places a cotton ball in the middle of the pillow. On the cue of 1-2-3-Go, adult and child try to blow the cotton ball off the other person's side of the pillow. You can increase the complexity by saying how many blows can be used to get the ball across the pillow, or by both trying to blow at the same time to keep the ball in the middle. Let the child win!

Elbow Tag: Group is divided into sets of three, with one runner and one tagger. Sets form a circle with space to allow runners in between each set. Runner tries to escape tagger by moving in between sets, or locking elbows with person at either end of the set. The person on the opposite end of the set then becomes the runner.

Feather Blow: Child and therapist or parent each hold a piece of construction paper (or a pillow) in front of them. Blow a feather from adult's paper (pillow) to the child's. Child must catch the feather on her paper (pillow) and then blow it back. For more challenge for an older child more than one feather can be used.

Feather Blow: Group forms a circle. Each person holds a piece of construction paper. Group leader places a feather on his paper and blows it to the person beside him. Each person blows the feather to the next person.

Feather Guess/Cotton Ball Guess: Child closes eyes. Therapist or parent lightly touches different parts of child's body and child tells the therapist what part of body he is touching.

Finding Powder Shapes in Hands: The therapist puts powder on the palms of both parent and child. The therapist helps the child find shapes, lines and letters in his own hand that are also found in the parent's hand. The parent then gets to do the same.

Free Throw: Divide into two teams (the child and parent are always a team). Using masking tape, make a line on the floor and have each team facing each other across the line. Place small piles of cotton balls on each side of the line. When you give the "go" signal, each team throws the balls at the other team, trying to get rid of all the balls on their side. When you give the "stop" signal, direct players to freeze in position.

Lap Sit Tag: Group moves around room as leader sings. When singing stops 1 person must act as chair for second person. Whoever does not have a chair becomes leader.

Magic Carpet Ride: Child sits on a blanket on the floor while parent or therapist pulls him/her around the room at different speeds, alternating going in circles, zig zags, or straight.

Mountain of Bubbles: Use a large plastic bowl or basin. Fill the bowl about two-thirds full with water. Add several squirts of dish soap. Give each participant a straw. On a signal challenge them to make a "mountain of bubbles." They can also "blow the mountain down" after by gently blowing air at the suds.

Paper Punch and Basketball: The therapist or parent holds a newspaper sheet tautly so the child can break it easily in half as he/she punches through the paper with his/her fist. Then the child punches through the half sheet so it becomes two quarter sheets. For older, stronger children, the newspaper can be a double thickness (two sheets). The child punches through a number of newspapers and then tightly squeezes each piece into a ball that is used to toss into a basket holder made by the therapist's or parent's arms joined in a circle like a hoop.

Peanut Toss: Have child pick up a peanut (or pasta noodle) with his toes and see how far child can toss it across the room with his feet.

Ping Pong Ball Blow: Everyone gets down on the floor on their stomachs facing inwards in a circle or facing each other if only two people. A ping-pong ball is placed in the center and each person tries to blow it away from himself and toward the other person. Holding hands helps to form boundaries for the ping-pong ball.

Ping Pong Ball Blow: Group lay on stomach on floor, facing each other and holding hands. Leader blows ping pong ball to another person, who then does the same until everyone has a chance. Try adding several balls, or try to blow one ball completely around the circle.

Pop the Bubbles: Blow a bubble and have the child pop it with a particular body part, such as finger, elbow, toe, or by clapping.

Push Me over-Pull Me up: Therapist and child sit facing each other. Hands out in front of them, with their palms touching. When the therapist gives the cue word, the child gets to push the therapist over and pull her back up. After the therapist has modeled the intervention, the parent and child can take turns together.

Silly Bones/People to People: All group members pair up. Leader says, "silly, bones, silly bones, touch (body part)," and partners touch those parts to each other. After 2 or 3 attempts, leader calls "people to people" and members rush to the center to get a new partner. The last person without a partner, or the last couple to form a partnership, becomes the new "leader."

Slippery, Slippery, Slip: The therapist puts lots of lotion on the child's arm and hand and then invites the child to pull his arm away as the therapist tries to hold onto it. Of course, the arm is so slippery that the child wins every time. Therapist can delight in the child's strength, making statements like, "You're so strong, you keep getting away!" After the game is modeled, parent and child can play.

Sock and Shoe Race: This is a great activity for ending sessions. Therapist and parent each take one of child's shoes. Either the adults together or the child can give the cue (Ready, Set, Go), and the adults try to see who can get the shoe on the child's foot the fastest. Of course, the parent always wins. If both parents do the race, then they tie!

Straw Wars: Use milk shake straws and Q-tips. Give each participant one straw and several Q-tips. You "load the straw" by inserting the Q-tip in the end closest to the mouth. Give a signal for everyone to shoot the Q-tip across the room. You can make it more interesting by challenging them to hit a target, such as a door or mirror. (This activity was invented by Jennifer Curtis, Winnipeg MB, Canada.)

Stretchy Tube (plastic accordion-like tube): If the therapist felt as if the sound produced by the tube when stretched might be too adversive the therapist would demonstrate stretching the tube so that the child could acclimate to the sound and stretch of the tube. The tube was placed in both of the child's hands. If it appeared as if the child's hands might slip or not grip strongly enough at first the therapist had one hand over the child's and one hand to stretch the tube. The stretching out of the tube was exaggerated by the therapist by leaning back as far as possible. While the tube was stretched the therapist commented with an animated tone of voice about the length of the tube and the child's strength and skill. This is an engaging activity that had variations. The variations included pulling the tube between the therapist and child when eye contact was established, and signaling the child (either with words or facial signals such as blinking) when the tube should be stretched. The child and therapist also pushed the tube together as a joint activity so that it was small. The tube was also made into a circle so that the therapist and child played peek-a-boo with each other. The tube in the circle shape could be made into a "hat."

Toilet Paper Bust-Out: The therapist and parent wrap toilet paper around the child's arms and body several times and then delight in the child's strength as he busts free from the wrapping, when a cue word is given.

Tube (poster board thickness paper rolled and taped into a tube) with four to five beanbags: The therapist holds the paper tube and puts the child's hands on the bottom of the tube to receive the bean bags inserted one by one. The therapist holds the beanbags at eye level and when eye contact is established with the child the beanbag is put in the tube. The element is often one of surprise as the beanbag is felt by the child as it is dropped in his/her hands. Some children have said that this activity is like a magic trick.

Wheelbarrow: Parent or therapist lifts and holds up child's legs while child braces herself on her arms with head up. Child moves forward by "walking" with her hands.

3. Engagement

This dimension relates to connecting with the child in a playful, positive, joyful way that entices the child to interact with the adult. The therapist will often use activities that include surprise, novelty, and warmth that get the child's attention and create a sense of delight. Engagement is emphasized with withdrawn children such as those that are depressed or autistic.

Ball with Holes: uses approximately five multi-colored chiffon scarves- Balls with holes are designed to be caught easily and become a unique and fun activity when scarves are used. The ball should be held by both the child and the therapist so that this becomes an engaging activity that affords eye contact between the child and therapist or parent. Scarves are presented to the child one by one with the therapist showing the child how the scarf could be inserted in the holes in the ball. Each time the scarf is presented to the child the therapist is playful in the presentation of the scarf. Options include playing peek-a-boo with the scarf, putting the scarf on the therapist's head so that it can be taken off while maintaining eye contact or bringing the scarf up to the therapist's face. These placements on the part of the therapist ensure that the child doesn't simply take the scarf from the therapist, but plays an engaging game with another person. The scarves are put in the holes by the child or therapist together. The therapist comments on the beauty of the child's hands and fingers while doing this activity and also on the beauty of the ball with the scarves clearly visible inside. The action of pulling the scarves out of the ball becomes a fun activity as well.

Beep Honk: Adult takes child's hand and gently guides child to touch adult's nose. Adult says, "Beep!" when child touches. Do this a few times. Then have child touch adult's ear (or chin) and say, "Honk!" (with a lower voice). You can go between noses, ears, and chins for fun. Then adult gently touches child's nose, then ears and chin. If child makes the noise, that's great. If not, the adult makes the sound for him so he gets the idea of how to do it.

Cotton Ball Fight: Sitting in circle, every member is given a pile of cotton balls. Instructed to throw 1 cotton ball at someone when code word announced, and then stop. Process repeated for handful of balls. Then told to throw cotton balls continuously at everybody until instructed to stop.

Cookie Machine: Adults form two lines facing each other, sitting on knees. Child is hoisted in air and body surfed along the machine, adding pieces to cookie.

Dancing In: Have child stand on adult's feet while adult supports child there with one arm around her back and holding her other hand in dancing form, singing a song, i.e., "The more we dance together, together, together, the more we dance together, the happier we'll be, dance this way and that way, now this way and that way, the more we dance together the happier we'll be." Or make up a song with the child's name in it.

Foil prints: Using aluminum foil, shape a piece of foil around the child's elbow, hand, foot, face, ear, and so forth. It helps to place a pillow under the foil and have the child press her hand or foot into the soft surface to get impressions of the fingers and toes.

Hand Tangle: Group members stand in a circle. Group leader reaches out to shake hands with person opposite him while introducing himself and tells that person to do the same with someone else. Continue in this manner until everyone is holding hands and the group is entangled. Then, work collaboratively to untangle arms without letting go of hands.

Hello . . . Goodbye: Child sits in parent's lap, facing each other. Parent places hands behind child to support him. Parent says 'hello', and then dips child backwards and says "goodbye." Parent brings child back up and says "hello."

Hello . . . Thank you: Group stands in circle. Leader says "hello . . . " to someone calling out his/her name and tosses beanbag to him. Receiver says "thank you . . . " using thrower's name and tosses beanbag to another person and says "hello. . . . " Continue until everyone has said hello and thank you only once. Leader starts again and continues to toss several more beanbags, repeating the exact same pattern only going faster.

Hello Whip/Name: Group stands in circle. Leader turns his head and says "hello" to person beside him. Continue until hello returns to leader. Repeat process several times, speeding up each time. Repeat by substituting own name for "hello."

Hide Notes: Write questions about the child on small pieces of paper. Examples of questions are: "What is your child's favorite color," "What is your child's favorite food," "What is your child's favorite movie/TV show/book." Lay the child down on his back on pillows. Ask the parent to hide his or her eyes. Hide the notes on the child and direct the parent to find them and answer the questions as they find the notes.

Hiding with Deep Pressure (using a deep pressure, playful squeeze): A variation on the Theraplay activity of hiding the child consisted of hiding the child behind or between two couch sized cushions or medium to large size pillows. Care was taken to have a cushion or pillow be placed not higher than the child's collarbone so that the child's face is carefully observed for an indication of discomfort as well as establishment of eye contact. The child is "hidden" between the two pillows which can be placed on the floor or propped up on the wall. Firm, even pressure is applied when the child is between the pillows. The therapist often says: "squeeze!" to accompany each application of pressure. The child can also be "hidden" for a parent to happily discover or made into a pizza, sandwich, or hot dog. The therapist and parent can put imaginary toppings such as cheese, mustard, ketchup, tomato sauce, etc. on the cushion. Different speeds and amounts of pressure are applied as the imaginary toppings are applied.

Mirror, Mirror on the Wall: Child and parent stand facing each other. The parent moves her arms slowly and the child copies this movement as if they are mirror images of each other. This is an especially fun activity to do with facial gestures.

Musical Pillows: Have each participant sit on a pillow or a piece of paper in a circle. As the music plays (or you sing a song) everyone stands up and walks around the circle. When the music stops, everyone stands on a pillow. Remove one pillow each time you stop. Inform participants that there can be more than one person on a pillow. At the end there is one pillow and everyone must try to stand on it for a group hug.

Nose Cluck: Parent and child sit facing each other with child's eyes closed. Parent makes clucking noise with tongue as child attempts to gently touch his nose to parents nose while keeping his eyes closed.

One Potato, Two Potato: Group sits in circle, making fists. Turn fists sideways, thumbs facing up and hold them out in front. Leader touches fists as he moves around circle saying, "one potato, two potato, three potato, four. Five potato, six potato, seven potato, more." Whoever is touched at "more" receives a hug from the people on either side of him.

Pass a Silly Face: Everyone sits in a circle. The first person makes a funny face and "passes" it to the person sitting next to them, who passes it to the next person and so on until it comes back to the first person. Participants can take turns starting off and passing the funny face.

Peekaboo: Therapist or parent sits in front of the child, puts their hands over their eyes, and then peeks out, saying, "Peekaboo!" The first time, parent can hold child's hands over hers while she hides her eyes and peeks out. Gently, the parent can hide child's eyes and then move her hands for child to peek out. The child can also hide his own eyes.

Play-Doh Trophies: Child sits facing adult. Adult uses Play-Doh as mold, and takes an imprint of child's body part (i.e, ear, chin, thumb), and shows it to child as they investigate the Play-Doh.

Popcorn Blanket: Place a small blanket on the floor and tell the child it is a pan to make popcorn. Then add several "popcorns" (pom-poms or cotton balls) to the pan. Have the child hold onto two corners of the blanket while you hold onto the other corners. As the pan "heats up," using the blanket, make the popcorn "pop."

Popcorn Toes: After taking off socks, parent holds up child's foot and checks between each toe, blowing between toes to blow out the sock fluff.

Push Me over, Pull Me up: Sit on the floor in front of the child. Place the child's palms against yours. On a signal, such as a word or eye blink, have the child push you over. Fall back in an exaggerated way. Stretch out your hands so that the child can pull you back up.

Row Your Boat: Two people sit facing each other, and holding hands. Rest of group each take up a position directly behind one of them, placing hands on shoulders of person in front, until there are two equal lines. Lines then move in unison singing song "Row your boat." Vary speed and movements.

Scarves on Head Became a Hat: Scarves are placed on the child's head. The children often comment that this is a hat. They enjoy feeling the scarves on their head as they are placed there by the therapist. The child also likes the feeling of the scarf on the face while the therapist directs a peek-a-boo game. The scarves are placed one by one or together on the head. A variation includes the therapist assisting the child with placing the scarves on the therapist and parent's head. A group activity develops as each person feels the scarf on their head and face and looks at and comments on the other person's scarf.

Silly Bones: Two people face each other or can be done by a whole group. Therapist calls out "Silly Bones says touch our hands." Child and therapist then touch hands. Leader calls another body part, and so on.

Smooth Ride: Have the child sit on your lap, bounce the child gently while saying "It's a smooth road, a smooth road, a smooth road." Bounce with a little more vigor and say "It's a bumpy road, a bumpy road, a bumpy road." After the "bumpy road," while holding the child, say "It's a hole" and have the child drop through your legs.

Somersaults: Child stands with therapist across the mat or rug from the parent. Parent gives the cue for child to somersault to parent. On cue, child (with help from therapist if needed) somersaults, and parent takes hold and pulls child close to welcome him/her. Then child stands near parent and therapist cues the child to somersault back. This can also be done with two parents.

Special Delivery: For child who is small enough to be picked up, parent sits in a designated comfortable place (couch, seat on floor supported by pillows), and therapist scoops up child in cradle hold and rocks child back and forth toward parent while singing "I've got a little Janie, and she's going to her mommy, a one, and a two, and a threeeeeee!" On three, place child in parent's lap.

The Twizzler Test: This is a game in which the parent, child, and therapist all explore physical boundaries using Twizzlers as a unit of measurement. Therapist gives the parent and child several Twizzlers and they decide how many Twizzler lengths they like to have between them. Parent and therapist can take the role of teachers, students, or friends of the child and play around with appropriate distances and physical proximity issues for different kinds of relationships.

Toe Touch under Blanket: Sit in a circle with feet under a blanket. Each person takes a turn touching another's feet with their feet and tries to guess whose foot they are touching by looking at their facial expressions.

Wiggly Parts/Stiff Parts: An inventory activity as parent or therapist find which body parts are wiggly and which parts are stiff—"I wonder if your nose wiggles, what about your ears, your tongue . . . ."

"Yes" . . . "No": Whenever child says "yes," parent says "no," and vice versa.

Zip, Zap, Zop: Participants form an inward facing circle. The leader rubs her hands each time as she says, "zip, zap, zop." On "zop," she points her hand at another group member who then repeats the phrase and action to another member of the group.

Zoom-erk: Sitting in a circle, the word "zoom" is passed around the circle quickly. When one person stops the action by saying "erk," the "zoom" reverses and is sent back the way it came.

4. Nurture

This is the most important dimension of all and is needed by every human being, but particularly children who have been neglected or abused. All children need loving care, affection, warm appropriate touch, a feeling of unconditional acceptance, and a feeling that they are valued and loved.

Barber Shop: Child sits in chair in front of mirror. Parent acts as barber and pretends to cut hair, applies shaving cream and removes it with popsicle stick, and applies after shave lotion.

Blanket Swing: Spread a blanket on the floor and have the child lie down in the middle. The adults gather up the corners and gently swing the child while singing a song with his/her name in it (ie "Rock-a-bye Sally in the tree top" . . . . Position the parents so they can see the child's face. At the end, bring him down gently. (We then direct the parent to sit down so they are comfortable. The therapists wrap the child in the blanket and swing the child into his mother's arms.)

Butterfly/Elephant/Eskimo Kisses: Do a combination of different kinds of kisses—butterfly is with adult's eye lashes fluttering against child's cheek; elephant is putting one fist on top of the other and put against mouth and make sucking noises and circular motions with the fists held together as adult moves toward the child and touches top fist to child's cheek to give an elephant kiss; Eskimo—touching noses with child and rubbing back and forth.

Caring for Hurts: At the start of sessions, caring for hurts is often part of Check-ups. But caring for hurts can occur at any time. When the adult sees a hurt occur or sees or learns about a past one, she explicitly cares for it by: (1) rubbing lotion *around* (so as not to sting) the hurt; (2) blowing on the hurt; (3) or stroking it with a cotton ball or feather.

Cotton Ball Soothe: Have child lie down with head on pillow or on adult's lap, closing his eyes while therapist or parent gently but firmly touches child with cotton ball around facial features. Adult can do this quietly or verbalize process while emphasizing uniqueness —"round little face, soft rosy cheeks, rosebud lips, curvy ears, gently sloped nose," etc.

Cradle in Arms and Feed Pudding: Child cradles in parent's lap and is fed pudding by spoon.

Feather Touch: Child closes eyes. Parent touches part of face with feather and asks child to guess where he was touched, or, child rolls up sleeve and closes eyes. Parent tells child to say "stop" when feather reaches crook of arm, and then proceeds to slowly move feather along child's arm.

Feeding: Have a small snack and drink available. Have the child sitting comfortably against pillows, facing you, or take the child on your lap. Feed the child, listening for crunches, noticing whether the child likes the snack and when the child is ready for more. Encourage eye contact.

Feeding Hide and Seek: The therapist hides special treats on the child (like M&Ms) and the parent has to find them. When the parent finds a treat, he or she feeds it to the child.

Helping Hurts: Therapist and parent look over the child to see if there are any scratches, scrapes, bruises, hang nails, etc. that may need lotioning, powdering, or band-aids. The child may point out places where there is no noticeable "boo-boo." It is very important that we attend to those places just as if there were a visible hurt. In this way, we communicate the message that we understand that the child has hurts we can't see and that we will help to heal these too.

Hum Garden: Sitting in circle on knees holding hands. Everyone touches forehead to the ground and very quietly begins to hum. Humming crescendos as the group members begin to rise, until everyone is on tiptoes, hands raised yelling full voice. Then reverse by returning slowly to original position in decrescendo. Repeat, but replace humming with phrase 'we are great'.

Lotioning Hurts: Therapist or parent find "hurts" (scratches, bruises, old scars, etc.) on child's hands, arms, feet or legs, face/neck and gently applies lotion or powder around the "hurt."

Lotion-Powder Handprints: Have ready lotion, powder, dark construction paper, an extra sheet of paper (newspaper is fine), and optional hair spray. Therapist/parent puts lotion generously on child's hand (feet are OK, too) and helps child press hands, one at a time, onto the construction paper. Then shake powder over the handprints. On cue, therapist shakes powder off the handprints and onto the extra paper, and all can delight over the handprint. Hair spray fixes the prints.

Lotion with Dots: The lotion bottle is held by the adult and the lotion put on the child. One of the most successful activities can be lotioning. Often lotion is the activity that seems to become central in the treatment and becomes the "ice breaker" when the child maintains some eye contact and is delighted, and relaxed. Smiles and laughter are elicited. The lotion is often tolerated and the activity can be sustained because of the deep, firm pressure applied. For some children the lotion is enjoyed if it is dotted on the hands, arms, and legs. The dots can be counted as each dot of lotion is applied. The routine and familiarity of counting is pleasing to the child. Younger children or those who appear more sensitive to big movement have relished having the lotion applied in dots on each finger while the therapist expressed delight in the child's fingers, arms, toes, and legs. Older children or children of a higher developmental level also enjoy the application of stripes or their names written in lotion. Once trust is established with the child dotting lotion on the face with gentle circles can be very nurturing.

Plant a Garden: Child lies on the floor or across adult's lap face down while the adult uses her hands to prepare the ground (child's back) for planting seeds. Adult gently massages child's back as she works the soil; then adult makes furrows on child's back for the seeds; adult puts pretend seeds into the furrows so child can feel adult's finger as each one (seed) is being placed. Adult smoothes her hands over the child's back as if pushing soil into the furrows and smoothing the soil. Adult gently taps all fingers onto child's back as she waters the seeds. Adult puts hands on child's back to warm it saying, "The sun is shining down to make the seeds grow." Adult puts words to the motions as she goes along.

Ring Pop and Lullaby: Parent feeds the child a ring pop (candy sucker shaped like an infant's soother) or a lollipop or a baby bottle with juice or pop, while singing a lullaby.

Rock in a Blanket: Child lies quietly on the floor in the center of a sturdy blanket. Therapist and parents hold corners and sides of the blanket, raise it gently off the floor and softly swing it back and forth while singing a song about the child, such as "Rock a Bye (child's name)." At the end of the song sing, "When the bough breaks the cradle won't fall and up will come (child's name), cradle and all" as the group swings the child into the parent's arms. For older child can sing, "(Child's name) lies over the ocean, (child's name) lies over the sea, (child's name) lies over the ocean, oh bring back (child's name) to me. Bring back, bring back, oh bring back (child's name) to me," as child is swung up into parent's arms.

Say One Nice Thing: Parent looks directly into child's eyes and states one positive attribute about child.

Shaving: Sit the child on a stool or chair facing a mirror. Pretend you are a barber and are giving the child his first shave. Place a towel around the child's shoulders. Apply shaving cream to the child's cheeks and chin and pretend to shave it off with a popsicle stick. At the end, admire the smoothness of the child's face.

Special Features in Mirror: Parent and child look in mirror as parent points out child's special features to him.

Story/ Lullaby and Juice: While parent holds child in his arms and gives child juice box or bottle, he sings a favorite lullaby or makes up a story about the child.

Taco Roll (or Hotdog Roll): While child lies on a blanket on his/her back the therapist or parent puts the child's favorite things on her as if she is a taco (hotdog); can also include therapist or parent's favorite things. Wrap the blanket around the child and have parent or therapist gather the child into their arms and pretend to eat up their favorite taco (hotdog).

The Doughnut/Pretzel Challenge: The therapist places a mini-doughnut or a pretzel on the parent's finger. The child is then challenged to see how many bites they can take before the doughnut falls apart. The therapist and parent count out loud with each bite. The game can be played multiple times over several sessions, while the child works to increase the number of bites he can take before the doughnut crumbles.

The "I Remember When" Story: This usually accompanies a feeding activity and allows the child to listen while eating. The parent tells a story about the child. The content can be funny or poignant, but is often most effective if it describes a time when the child accomplished some new developmental milestone, or a time when the parent helped the child or met a need in the child. The therapist can encourage close physical proximity between parent and child during the telling of this story.

Zip: After lotion is applied the therapist (or parent after learning the activity) holds one hand on the top of the child's arm and one hand on the underside of the child's arm. With firm pressure the therapist's hands glides over the child's arm while counting, "1-2-3 zip!" The "1-2-3" is only done after eye contact is established and "zip" is said while the therapist's hands quickly glide over the child's arm. This activity can also be done on a child's leg in the same way.

Index

About the Contributors

ABOUT THE EDITOR

Evangeline Munns PhD, CPsych, RPT/S, CTT/S, is a certified clinical psychologist who recently retired as the director of Blue Hills Play Therapy Services, which she founded and which now has the largest training school in Theraplay in Canada. She is a certified Theraplay® trainer/supervisor with the Theraplay Institute in Chicago, the Association for Play Therapy in the United States (APT), and the Canadian Association for Child and Play Therapy (CACPT). (On the latter she serves as a consultant on the education committee.) She is a popular presenter and has given numerous workshops on play therapy across Canada, the United States, and internationally. In recent years, much of her time has been spent in training and supervising therapists in Theraplay and /or non-directive play therapy including teaching as a guest lecturer at Western University in London, Ontario, and Sir Wilfred Laurier University in Kitchener, Ontario. She has served as a consultant to many agencies. Dr. Munns has written numerous chapters in other books on Theraplay and has edited a book entitled *Theraplay: Innovations in Attachment-Enhancing Play Therapy*. In the past, she received the Monica Herbert award from the Canadian Association for Child and Play Therapy (CACPT) for "an outstanding contribution to the field of play therapy in Canada." Recently she was the first therapist described in a list by CACPT of the 5 top play therapists in Canada.

CONTRIBUTORS

Nancy Atkinson, MA, MFCC, RP, has been the CEO Clinical Supervisor for the YWCA of Contra Costa/Sacramento for over five years. She supervises interns who are responsible for providing individual and family therapy for many children and families who are part of the Child Protective Service system. Theraplay is used for reunification of children with their parents and 75 percent of all clients are introduced to Theraplay. Nancy is a registered play therapist and an attachment specialist. She has an MA in Agency/School Counseling Psychology from Michigan State University and an MA in Counseling Psychology from National University. She is a licensed MFCC in the State of California.

Maria Boada, BS, has worked in the adult mental health field for over 16 years, but has found a new passion in working with children and their families in Theraplay. She graduated with her Bachelors of Social Work in the summer of 2008 and at that time looked forward to continuing her work in Theraplay. Each and every family she has worked with inspires her about the possibilities and resiliency of the human spirit.

Carol R. Bettendorf, PT, MS, PCS, has a master's degree in pediatric physical therapy. She is a Partner in Birth to Three & Beyond Pediatric Therapies, LLC. She is a certified Theraplay therapist who has studied and worked for over twenty years with children on the Autism Spectrum as a subspecialty of her pediatric practice. She has taught pediatric physical therapy at what is now Rosalyn Franklin University. She is a Feldenkrais Method® practitioner, is certified in the Sensory Integration and Praxis Test (SIPT), and has extensive experience using craniosacral therapy.

Terra Bovingdon, BSW, MSW, RSW, completed her Masters of Social Work in 1999 from the University of Calgary and is presently employed at Calgary Family Services since 1999 in the Adoptions Counselling Program. Terra is the clinical supervisor for the adoption program and the In Sync program. Terra's clinical practice focuses on stabilizing children in foster families, addressing attachment and adoption issues, and enhancing family cohesion. Clinical work in the program has expanded to include relinquishment visits and therapeutic supervised visits with birth families.

Karen Doyle Buckwalter, MSW, LCSW, is Director of Treatment Services at Chaddock, an innovative residential program for adolescents, ages 8–16, with Reactive Attachment Disorder and Complex Trauma. Karen is a Certified Theraplay® therapist, trainer, and supervisor, and her energetic and interactive style make her a sought-after speaker and trainer, having presented at numerous national and international conferences. Karen has published in the *Journal of Child and Adolescent Social Work* and is a contributor to *Creating Capacity for Attachment*. Karen received her MSW from Temple University and trained at the Menninger Clinic in their Family Therapy Training Program.

Lisbeth DiPasquale, Dip. CS, C. Psych. Assoc., CTT, is a psychological associate registered with the College of Psychologists of Ontario. She worked for the Psychology Department of the York Region District School Board, Ontario, Canada, for fourteen years and now has a private practice in psychological assessment and counseling for children, adolescents, and families. She is a certified Theraplay therapist on staff at Blue Hills Child and Family Centre, Aurora, Ontario, where she has been doing Theraplay with individual families and groups for over twelve years. She is also a published author with a chapter entitled "The Marschak Interaction Method" in the book *Theraplay Innovations in Attachment-Enhancing Play Therapy*, edited by Evangeline Munns.

Shirley Eyles, RN, BA, CTT, has a private practice in Aurora, Ontario, and also works as a mental health nurse in a hospital setting. She is a certified Theraplay therapist and is in process of becoming a certified supervisor. She became passionately interested in the emotional well-being of children and families in the midst of her own journey as a mother of three children. She believes that the primary motivating force in human behavior is a drive toward connectedness and strives to facilitate this process through Theraplay.

Karen Fabian, BA, BSc, MS Ed, has worked in supporting children and families for over a decade and has two undergraduate degrees from the University of Victoria (BSc in Psychology, BA in Child and Youth Care). Karen has her master's degree in applied psychology from the University of Calgary with a specialization in parent-child attachment theory, early child development, narrative therapy, and cultural competency. Her clinical focus is on attachment-disruption, anxiety, and grief, and her primary interventions are Theraplay and Dyadic Developmental Psychotherapy. Karen presently works in the Adoption Counselling Program, in Calgary, Alberta, specifically addressing the attachment-related issues of children and supporting parents as a therapeutic influence in their child's life.

Anita Finlay, MS Ed, is associate director of Family Services at Chaddock, a multi-service agency providing a range of residential, educational, and community-based services for youth, birth through age 21, and their families. She has worked in direct care in the residential program, supervised case management in the foster care/adoption programs, and played a key role in developing the parent liaison role in the agency's innovative residential program for youth with attachment and complex trauma issues, including development of a parent education curriculum to further involve parents in their child's treatment.

Ulrike Franke, SLP, CTT/S, was born in 1946 in a little German village. After kindergarten and school, Gymnasium, she had eight years at home raising children, worked in a rehabilitation hospital, then trained as a speech- and language pathologist at the University of Mainz. Later she had additional training as a teacher for SLP at the universities of Frankfurt/M. and Osnabrück. She conducted therapy, assessments, and teaching in a phoniatric-logopedic Department of the Heidelberg Rehabilitation Center for many years. Since then (2006) she has worked in her private practice. Ulrike is a certified therapist, supervisor, and trainer in Theraplay and an editor of a Theraplay journal.

Brijin Johnson Gardner, LSCSW, LCSW, RPT/S, has worked with children and adolescents for over twelve years in public schools, private practice, and youth ministry. Ms. Gardner provides play therapy training and supervision; she has also presented at the Theraplay International Conference and the Association for Play Therapy regarding her work with adolescents. Brijin has written and received several grants to fund her Theraplay work in the school setting. She received her BA from Bethany College in Lindsborg, KS, and her MSW from the University of Kansas.

Paris Goodyear-Brown, MSW, RPT/S, is a licensed clinical social worker and registered play therapist-supervisor specializing in clinical work with children and families. She currently serves as guest lecturer and adjunct faculty for several universities in middle Tennessee while maintaining a private practice. She has recently won the Association for Play Therapy's award for Public Education and Promotion and has an international reputation as an innovative speaker and author. In addition to conducting research with Vanderbilt University and contributing several chapters to play therapy texts, her publications include *Digging for Buried Treasure* (volumes 1 & 2), *Gabby the Gecko*, and a training DVD entitled *Peas in a Pod.*

Minna Laakso, MA, CTT, is a psychologist and Theraplay therapist. She is also a qualified teacher of psychology. She has been working at a child psychiatric out-patient department for 15 years. Currently she is participating in a Theraplay Supervisor practicum organized by the Finnish Theraplay Association. She is also a postgraduate student in Helsinki University studying to be an integrative psychotherapist.

Dafna Lender, MSW, is a licensed clinical social worker and is a certified Theraplay therapist and trainer. She is the training director for the Theraplay Institute in Chicago. She worked as a policy analyst in the Illinois State Senate and earned her MSW from Yeshiva University in New York. In the past Dafna was a foster care case worker for specialized children and a therapist for Fetal Alcohol Syndrome and orphanage neglect. She wrote the chapter, "Therapeutic Use of Self in Dyadic Developmental Psychotherapy" in the book *Creating Capacity for Attachment.*

Sandra Lindaman, MA, CCC-SLP, MSW, LCSW, is a licensed speech-language pathologist and clinical social worker. She is a certified Theraplay® therapist, supervisor, and trainer and training advisor at The Theraplay Institute in Wilmette, Illinois, USA. Sandra joined The Theraplay Institute in1990. She wrote the chapter, "Theraplay for Children Who Are Adopted or in Foster Care" in the second edition of *Theraplay: Helping Parents and Children Build Better Relationships Through Attachment-Based Play*. Sandra has been involved in the training and supervision of professionals in the Theraplay® model internationally. She is the 2004 recipient of the Ann M. Jernberg award for outstanding contributions to Theraplay.

Anita Johanson Maddox, MA, LCPC, RPT, CTT, is a licensed clinical professional counselor in Illinois and a licensed counselor in Wisconsin. Anita has over twenty years experience in pediatrics. She is a certified Theraplay therapist who has a private practice and is also a therapist at the Theraplay Institute. Anita has worked individually and in groups with children who have characteristics of autism as well as with a variety of parent-child difficulties. Anita is grateful to her family for their influence, support, and encouragement.

Linda Meyer, PhD, is a certified Theraplay therapist in private practice in Champaign, Illinois. She is the author of numerous articles, book chapters, and three books. She is also trained in Dyadic Developmental Psychotherapy (DDP) as well as play therapy.

Jessica Mroz Miller, MSW, CTT/S, is a licensed clinical social worker. She is a certified Theraplay therapist and trainer with The Theraplay Institute. Jessica provides treatment to families and children at The Theraplay Institute in Wilmette, Illinois, and at Personal Solutions Counseling in Frankfort, Illinois. Jessica trained for six years in Dyadic Developmental Psychotherapy (DDP) with Dan Hughes and co-authored a chapter about DDP in *Creating Capacity for Attachment* by Becker-Weidman and Shell. She has presented on Theraplay, attachment and trauma, and the integration of Theraplay and DDP at national and international conferences.

Catherine Munns, MA, DPsych grad student, is at present pursuing her doctoral studies at James Madison University. She has had extensive experience working with troubled children including autistic children and their parents using a variety of treatment methods such as Theraplay, non-directive playtherapy, intensive behavioral analysis, etc. Catherine is working on completing her certification in Theraplay and formerly was an extern in the play therapy training program at Blue Hills Child and Family Centre in Aurora, Ontario. She has made presentations at a number of international conferences.

Linda Perry, MA, MSW, CPT/S, is employed at the Elizabeth Hill Counselling Centre, University of Manitoba, as the program manager of the Strengthening Families Program. In partnership with a residential center for Aboriginal women and their children, she was lead clinician of a Child Therapy Program where Theraplay was one of the primary interventions. Her role includes training of students from the Faculty of Social Work, University of Manitoba, and staff of Aboriginal agencies, in child therapy and attachment-based interventions.

Phyllis Rubin, CCC, SLP, PsyD,CTT/S, is a licensed clinical psychologist and speech and language pathologist with a private practice in Oak Park, IL. She is a certified Theraplay® therapist and trainer with The Theraplay Institute and trained for six years in Dyadic Developmental Psychotherapy (DDP) with Dan Hughes. Phyllis is co-author of *Play with Them: Theraplay Groups in the Classroom*, wrote the "Group Theraplay" chapter in *Theraplay* by Jernberg and Booth, a chapter in *Theraplay: Innovations in Attachment Therapy* by Munns, and co-authored, with Jess Mroz Miller, a chapter on DDP in *Creating Capacity for Attachment* by Becker-Weidman and Shell. She has presented on Theraplay and Group Theraplay nationally and internationally and has also presented on integrating Theraplay and DDP.

Jamie Sherman, MS Ed, CTT/S, is a special education teacher and certified Theraplay therapist and supervisor. He has extensive experience working with children with special needs, including autism spectrum disorder. He works in the York Region District School Board and is the Theraplay clinical supervisor at Blue Hills Child and Family Centre. Jamie lives in Toronto, Canada, with his wife, Karen, their three boys, Jonah, Elijah, and Ezra, and their pug, Gomez.

Gail Smillie, MA, has a masters degree in counseling psychology and has worked in the field of children's mental health for over 30 years. As a registered clinical counsellor, certified Canadian counselor, and board certified expert in traumatic stress, Gail is currently a manager with Calgary Family

Services, where she specializes in the area of trauma and attachment doing program development, training, supervision, and clinical work with families.

Mary Spickelmier, MSW, LSCSW, RPT/S, Theraplay Practitioner Level, is a licensed specialist clinical social worker and registered play therapist-supervisor with 12 years of experience. She specializes in helping children and adolescents and their families deal with such issues as domestic violence, grief and trauma, anxiety disorders, divorce, behavioral problems, attachment disorders, and pervasive developmental disorders. Mary has provided trainings at the local and international level: for both the Theraplay Institute and Association for Play Therapy. She currently is a board member for the Kansas Association for Play Therapy. Mary received her BSW and MSW from the University of Missouri.

Angela Siu, PhD, CTT, is a certified Theraplay therapist. She is also a registered clinical psychologist who has experience working with children and families in Hong Kong and in Canada. Currently, she is an assistant professor in the Department of Educational Psychology of the Chinese University of Hong Kong.

Patti Sutherland, MSW, CPT, is employed at the Elizabeth Hill Counselling Centre, University of Manitoba, as a therapist in the Strengthening Families Program. Patti's job includes training and supervision of students from the Faculty of Social Work, University of Manitoba, and staff of Aboriginal agencies. She has worked in Aboriginal agencies, particularly with children exposed to family violence, and has adapted Theraplay for use in multi-family groups, the school system, and traditional parent-child sessions.

Jim Wardrop, PhD, after receiving his PhD in psychology from Washington University in St Louis, spent a year as a postdoctoral fellow at the Research and Developmental Center for Cognitive Learning, University of Wisconsin at Madison. In 1967, he joined the faculty of the Educational Psychology Department at the University of Illinois, Urbana, where he served in a variety of roles: research professor, department chairperson, and teaching faculty. His research and teaching activities have spanned the areas of research methods, educational program evaluation, statistical analysis, and measurement and assessment. He retired in 2003, but continues to be active in both teaching and research.

Deborah Weiss, BMusEd, has combined her passion for working outdoors, with her love of working with children, and with horses. She has attained certifications as an Epona approved instructor, Irwin EAPD facilitator, and

EAGALA (Equine Assisted Growth and Learning Association) level one instructor. She is a member of the Ontario Therapeutic Riding Association, the North American Riding for the Handicapped Association, and The Theraplay Institute. Deborah is currently completing her master's degree in counseling psychology.